Called to Happiness
~ *Guiding Ethical Principles*

Third Edition

Sister Terese Auer, O.P.
Dominican Sisters of St. Cecilia Congregation
Nashville, Tennessee

Nihil obstat: Reverend John Rock, S.J.
Diocese of Nashville
August 1, 2009

Imprimatur: Most Reverend David R. Choby, S.T.B., J.C.L.
Bishop, Diocese of Nashville
August 1, 2009

Copyright © 2009, 2011, 2018 by St. Cecilia Congregation, LBP Communications. All rights reserved.

Published by St. Cecilia Congregation
801 Dominican Drive, Nashville, TN, 37228
615-256-5486
615-726-1333 (fax)
www.nashvilledominican.org

Cover design: Sister Mary Justin Haltom, O.P.

Printed in the United States of America

ISBN 978-0-615-30852-4

ACKNOWLEDGEMENTS

Special thanks to:

- Mrs. Therese Polakovic and ENDOW *[Educating in the Nature and Dignity of Women]* for their support and encouragement in this project;

- Sister Marian Sartain, O.P., and Sister Margaret Mary Sallwasser, O.P., for their reading and invaluable critiquing of the text.

- Mr. Kevin Keiser for his insights regarding the human act.

- Bill O'Connor and the art students at Pope John Paul the Great Catholic High School, Dumfries, VA, for illustrating the text;

- Reverend John Rock, S.J., for his careful reading of the text and for his constructive comments;

- Mother Ann Marie Karlovic, O.P., and my Dominican Sisters for their love and prayerful support.

O Mary, Mother of Mercy,

watch over all people,

that the Cross of Christ may not be emptied of its power,

that man may not stray from the path of the good or become blind to sin,

but may put his hope ever more fully in God who is 'rich in mercy' (Eph. 2:4).

May he carry out the good works prepared by God beforehand

and so live completely 'for the praise of his glory' (Eph. 1:12).

Saint John Paul the Great

Dedicated to

Mary,

the one to whom Saint John Paul the Great entrusted himself completely.

May she who *"lived and exercised her freedom*

precisely by giving herself to God

and accepting God's gift within herself"

be for us *"the radiant sign and inviting model*

of the moral life."[1]

May we allow her to teach us how to enter fully

into the plan of God

Who longs to make us truly happy.

---

[1] Saint John Paul II, *The Splendor of Truth*, 120.

CONTENTS

Prologue 1

Chapter I: Why Do We Do What We Do?... 5

Chapter II: Happiness: What Is It?... 15

Chapter III: Moral Law and Freedom 39

Chapter IV: Conscience and Truth 73

Chapter V: The Human Act 95

Chapter VI: The Moral Act 111

Chapter VII: Virtue and Vice 145

Conclusion 183

Appendices:

    A. *The Virtue of Tolerance* 185

    B. *Ethical Principles Used in Medicine* 189

Glossary... 193

Resources Cited 201

Called to Happiness ~ Guiding Ethical Principles

Prologue

"What must I do in order to be happy?" No one can escape wrestling with this question because we all want to be happy. Happiness is our most basic desire, "programmed" into our very nature. It is because of this desire that we make the choices and the decisions we do -- about relationships and jobs; about where and how to spend our time, money, and energy; even about what we will call "good" and "evil."

Now some people might argue that there is nothing here to "study." "After all," they might say, "don't we each determine for ourselves what we want to make us happy?" Such people assume that no matter what we choose, we will all find the fulfillment, the happiness, we seek. It does not take much experience in living, however, to realize that they are mistaken. We all know people who, though they pursue it feverishly, are not finding the happiness they seek. Because this is so, we would do well to look very closely and carefully into this question of **happiness** and how to achieve it. If it is true that not everyone achieves the happiness they seek, and if happiness is, in fact, the ultimate goal of us all, then we surely do not want to be included among those who "miss the whole point," and find themselves *forever* **un**happy.

This is why our present study of Ethics is so vitally important. The science of Ethics studies man's pursuit of happiness. It delves into both the ultimate or final end which the human person seeks, as well as the free acts he does in pursuing that end. As a science, Ethics is based on universal principles which -- as true -- apply to *all* human beings, not just to a few.

As we did in our study of the Human Person, we will take St. Thomas Aquinas, the great Dominican teacher and lover of truth, as our guide in this study. St. Thomas, following the ancient Greek philosopher Aristotle and the early Christian philosopher Augustine, held that achieving happiness is not a sure thing. It takes consistent, life-long effort on our part. Unlike those who think that *whatever we choose* will make us happy, Aquinas understood that happiness depends on our choosing *only what is truly good for us.* For in desiring and choosing the true good, we actually make ourselves to be *good* people. Acquiring this *personal goodness,* through our ways of thinking, choosing, and acting is what will lead us to the happiness we desire. Thus, for St. Thomas as well as for Aristotle and Augustine

NOTES

"What must I do? *'What must I do to inherit eternal life?'* What must I do *so that my life* may have full *value* and full *meaning*?"
Saint John Paul, *Apostolic Letter to the Youth of the World*, 1985, #3

"Dear young people, do not let the culture of possessions and pleasure lull your consciences! Be vigilant and alert 'sentinels,' in order to be genuine protagonists of a new humanity."
Saint John Paul,
Angelus Address, July 7, 2002

Called to Happiness ~ Guiding Ethical Principles

NOTES

who preceded him, the study of Ethics is simply training in how to be happy.

Only what is *truly* good will lead us to happiness!

In addition to taking St. Thomas as our guide, we want to invoke Saint John Paul the Great as our intercessor before the Father as we begin our present study. Saint John Paul had a special love for young people. He understood that a person's youth is a critical time of intense discovery about himself. During this time, the young person comes to know his unique and unrepeatable potential as a human being. Within this awareness of his potential, he discovers the plan for his whole life, a plan whose value for leading him to happiness will depend completely on his response to *moral good* and *evil*.

"In the moral conscience of a ... young person who is forming the plan for his or her whole life, there is hidden *an aspiration to 'something more'*."
Saint John Paul, *Apostolic Letter to the Youth of the World*, 1985, #8

The "treasure of youth," according to Saint John Paul, is both the treasure of discovering his life's goal as well as the *organizing*, the *choosing*, the *foreseeing*, and the *making of his first personal decisions*.[1] These first decisions have great importance both for the young person himself and for society in general. For in and through these first decisions a person begins to develop the character and personal integrity that will enable him to move beyond himself toward "something more."[2]

*History is written not only by the events which
in a certain sense happen 'from outside';
it is written first of all 'from within';
it is the history of human consciences,
of moral victories and defeats.
Here too the essential greatness of man
finds its foundation:
his authentically human dignity.
This is that interior treasure whereby man continually goes beyond
himself in the direction of eternity.*[3]

"Truth is the light of the human intellect. If the intellect seeks, from youth onwards, to know reality in its different dimensions, it does so in order to possess the truth: in order to live the truth. Such is the structure of the human spirit. Hunger for truth is its fundamental aspiration and expression."
Saint John Paul, *Apostolic Letter to the Youth of the World*, 1985, #12

The ability of the human person freely to choose and to make decisions in light of an "interior truth" known by conscience enables him to be held responsible for the direction he goes in life. If he chooses to act in light of moral values, then he moves himself "in the direction of eternity." Not only that but he also "imprints the most expressive seal" upon others in his generation and the next, upon societies, nations and humanity in general.[4]

---

[1] Saint John Paul, *Apostolic Letter to the Youth of the World*, 1985, #3.
[2] Ibid., #8.
[3] Ibid., #3.
[4] Ibid.

Today, as in every age, there is need for young people who are sensitive to moral good and evil, who make decisions which will lead them toward *true* happiness. At the beginning of the 21st Century, however, this need is perhaps even more keenly felt. Loud and powerful voices cry out today telling us that happiness consists in pleasure-seeking (hedonism) and that we ourselves personally determine what will make us happy and thus what good and evil are (subjectivism).

Our study here is designed to help young people in this process of discerning moral truth. Building on what we learned in the course on the Human Person, we will investigate the purpose of human life and the nature of human action. We will search out the criteria for determining the moral quality of our acts, noting especially the role of moral law, conscience and virtue in our pursuit of genuine human happiness.

"Truth enlightens man's intelligence and shapes his freedom, leading him to know and love the Lord."
Saint John Paul,
The Splendor of Truth, Prologue

Saint John Paul expresses well the hope which is ours at the outset of our study:

Indeed, it is my hope that your youth will provide you
with a sturdy basis of sound principles,
that your conscience will attain in these years of your youth that
mature clear-sightedness that during your whole lives will enable each
one of you to remain always
a 'person of conscience',
a 'person of principles',
a 'person <u>who inspires trust</u>',
in other words, a person who is credible.[5]

"Do not forget that 'the future of humanity is in the hands of those men who are capable of providing the generations to come with reasons for life and optimism.'"
Saint John Paul,
Message for XI World Youth Day,
#8

With these challenging words of Saint John Paul fresh in our minds, let us resolve to make the most of our present study -- for our own personal good, for the good of the society in which we live, and for the good of all people, in every time and place.

---
[5] Ibid., #7.

Chapter I

Why Do We Do What We Do?

Have you ever noticed that when you set about doing anything at all, you always have a purpose or a reason for doing it? Think about it: There is nothing that we do, not even just for fun, which is not directed toward some goal or **end**. We do not take a step forward or backward unless we intend to move ourselves somewhere, towards some point. We do not stand up or lie down without a purpose in mind, even if it is simply to get into a more comfortable position so that we can think about what we want to do next. Human persons are **goal-oriented** creatures; we do not act haphazardly. We act for a reason -- all the time!

You might disagree with this, saying, "I do lots of things without deliberately thinking about why I am doing them." Perhaps at times you do act without being *conscious* of a specific goal, but that does not mean you do not really have one. Your lack of deliberate awareness of a goal simply shows that the acting for an end is so *second nature* to us human creatures, that we often do it without even being conscious of the fact. Walking along the street, for example, a person does not need to be thinking of his destination at every step.

Vocabulary

ethics	*first principle*	*formal object*
intention	*normative*	*material object*

Realizing this basic truth about us human persons will not only introduce to us the science of Ethics which we are now beginning to study, but it will also tell us something about *ourselves*. We can actually know ourselves better through the things we choose to do because with each of our free acts we have in mind some goal, some end that we want. We are "after something," seeking something we consider to be "**good**."

This good that we seek can be either relative or absolute. The good is *relative* if we seek it as a way of achieving some goal we have in mind. For example, the farmer will call the rain good because it

---

NOTES

End - from the Latin *finis* (end), an intended result of an action; an aim, purpose.

"Every agent, of necessity, acts for an end."
St. Thomas,
Summa Theologiae, I-II, 1, 2

"Every act has a mission to accomplish."
Paul Wadell, C.P.,
The Primacy of Love, p. 32

"...[E]very act begins from the end it seeks. We act because we want to gain some good. Before we act we focus on that good, we consider what it is and then we consider what we must do to attain it."
Paul Wadell, C.P.,
The Primacy of Love, p. 32-33

Good - (relative) conducive to well-being, to happiness; (absolute) the reality of completeness according to the nature or design of a thing.

5.

NOTES

Intention - the action of directing the mind or attention to something.

"Although the end be last in the order of execution, yet it is first in the order of the agent's intention."
St. Thomas,
Summa Theologiae, I-II, 1, 1

"According as their end is worthy of blame or praise so are our deeds worthy of blame or praise."
St. Augustine,
De Mor. Eccl. Et Manich. ii. 13

"One's character takes the shape of the choice one has made."
John Finnis,
Fundamentals of Ethics, p. 140

waters his fields. The good is *absolute* when it refers to certain objects in themselves, without reference to something else. That which is good in itself has achieved its full potential; it experiences a certain completeness according to its nature. Thus, we speak of a fruitful apple tree as being a good tree.[1]

Any person who acts always has the good in mind. This is what we mean when we speak of a person's **intention** in acting. The intention is what the person hopes his act will accomplish. The intention sets into motion all of our activity. It is true to say that we begin to act only once we have the intention of an end which we hope to gain.

Those goals that we are constantly seeking in choice after choice tell us something important about ourselves. They tell us who we are and what we are trying to achieve. In a very real sense, we can say that we shape or form ourselves to be the people we are becoming through the free choices that we make, through the voluntary acts we do. For example, the person who repeatedly chooses to do kind acts, to think first about the needs of others, actually becomes a kind and self-giving person. On the other hand, the person who chooses to cheat and steal time after time makes himself to be a person who is cut off from others and centered on himself.

From our study of the dignity of the human person we recall that plants and brute animals are unable to make free choices. They lack an intellect and a free will. Yes, they act always toward a goal (drawing in nutrients from the soil for nourishment, turning toward the sun for photosynthesis, or mating for the survival of the species); but they lack an awareness of themselves. They are not conscious of themselves. They act toward some end which is good for them *only* because they are predetermined to do so by their natures. They do automatically and necessarily what the One who designed them wants them to do. They cannot deviate from that plan.

Human persons are different. With our intellect and free will we are aware of ourselves and of the variety of "goods" we can choose to pursue or not. So, when we freely choose to act one way and not another, to do this rather than that, we are in a sense "creating" ourselves to be a certain kind of person -- one who loves this "good" rather than that one. Over a period of time, we bear the mark of these consistent choices. We actually become what we love!

---

[1] Andrew C. Varga, *On Being Human*, pp. 5-7.

Our intentions not only shape our actions, they also shape ourselves. Our purposes characterize us. Each of us carries the mark of what we most consistently will. It is not only our acts that are at stake in our intentions; we are as well. To intend to act a certain way is likewise to intend to be a certain way, the two are inseparable. …What we choose as our purposes makes all the difference because invariably we become what we love. Our primary intention in life expresses what we most love. … [A]nd because we tend to it eventually we become like it, not in any superficial sense, but in the radical sense that ultimately our self is nothing more than our most perduring intentions.[2]

Because intentions shape our acts, and our acts determine who we become, it is vitally important that we line ourselves up with an end which is really worthy of us. Determining this end is the first ethical decision any person makes. It is the choice of what we most love, the end of all ends, the final goal of our lives. It is the reason why we do all that we do. It is the good that we seek above all other goods. All of the other ethical decisions with which we are faced in our lives concern the **means** to this final or **ultimate end**. Regarding these decisions, we must ask the question, "Does this particular act I am considering doing really get me closer to the end I most love?" If it does, then I judge it to be an *ethically good act*, and I should do it. If it does not, then I judge it to be an *ethically evil act*, and I should avoid it.

The Science of Ethics

The investigation of worthy ends and the human acts which lead us to them is what the science of Ethics is all about. Ethics studies human acts in order to determine whether they will lead us to the ultimate end that we seek. The ethicist is the one who wants to know *why we do the acts that we do.* What he finds out is that we do the acts that we do because we are all seeking a good that we love above all else, a good that we consider to be the most perfect good. We consider it to be the most perfect good because we think that it will bring us ultimate fulfillment, complete satisfaction -- unending happiness. We all do what we do, then, because we want to be completely happy with all of our desires satisfied.

Since this search for happiness is the quest of our lives, it is strange that so many people seem unable to find real happiness in their lives. Why is this so? Why are so few of us able to rest in the abiding peacefulness of a supremely satisfied life? Why is it that we find it

---
[2] Paul Wadell, C.P. *The Primacy of Love*, p. 33.

NOTES

"[S]ince everything desires its own perfection, a man desires for his ultimate end, that which he desires as his perfect and crowning good. It is therefore necessary for the last end so to fill man's appetite that nothing is left besides it for man to desire."
St. Thomas, *Summa Theologiae*, I-II, 1, 5

Means - an action or thing that is used to achieve something else.

Ultimate End - from Latin *ultimus* (last, final); the end that lies beyond all others.

NOTES

apparently so difficult to fulfill this very basic desire of our being? What is it that will truly satisfy our seemingly insatiable desires and quiet our restless hearts?

Answering these questions is the concern of the science of Ethics. Yes, Ethics has other concerns such as moral laws, rights, obligations, and principles; and yes, Ethics also deals with particular issues and dilemmas that we run into in our lives. These, however, are not the *primary* concern of the science of Ethics. Ethics cares about moral laws, rights, and obligations because these things will in some way help to secure our happiness. Ethics wrestles with particular issues and dilemmas in an attempt not to be led "off course." That is, we do not want to make a mistake by choosing to act in a way that will ultimately make us unhappy.

Ethics, then, is a **science** which studies how human persons can be happy. That word "science" comes from the Latin *scientia,* meaning "knowledge." A science is *an organized body of knowledge.* Its organization stems from the fact that it reaches conclusions that can be traced back to certain *first principles* from which the conclusions are derived. A first principle is a *self-evident truth* that serves as a starting point for our reasoning. To say that a first principle is self-evident is to say that we do not need to prove it. In fact, we cannot prove it; it precedes a reasoning process. A first principle is *obviously* true. Anyone who merely thinks seriously about it and understands the meaning of its words will know it to be true. Let's see if this is so.

Science - from Latin *scientia* (knowledge); an organized body of knowledge.

First Principle - from Latin *principium* (origin, source); the ultimate basis upon which our reasoning depends; a self-evident truth that serves as a starting point for our reasoning.

Do Good and Avoid Evil

The *first principle of Ethics* is "Do good and avoid evil." Everyone who thinks seriously about this statement and understands the meaning of its terms will recognize its truth. Let us, then, take a closer look.

Is it self-evidently true that we should do good and avoid evil? What do the words "good" and "evil" mean? People disagree about this, don't they? Not really. We might disagree about *what actually is* good or evil, but we do not disagree about *the meaning of the words* "good" and "evil." We know, if we think about it, that when we say something is "good" we do so because we think that it will in some way make us happy.

Thus the alcoholic thinks it is "good" for him to drink another bottle of whiskey because he thinks it will lead to his happiness. If someone disagrees and claims that drinking the bottle of whiskey is a "bad" choice for the alcoholic, the two people are nevertheless agreeing on the meaning of the terms *good* and *bad*. Their disagreement arises from the fact that they have different views of what happiness really is. Because they do not agree on what will fully satisfy the human person, that is, on what is the greatest good, they will have different judgments regarding which acts are good and which are evil.

To claim, then, that we should "Do good and avoid evil" is simply another way of saying that we should do what we were created to do: move ourselves toward what we understand to be the most perfect good we can possess. Simply put: "Do good and avoid evil" means the same thing as "Pursue happiness." Once we understand the meaning of the words in the first principle of Ethics, we immediately realize that the principle rings true. We all must pursue happiness. It is "programmed" into us to do so because we are creatures designed to act towards an end which will bring us complete fulfillment.

The science of Ethics, then, starts with this self-evident truth that we should do what we are designed to do: pursue happiness. From this first principle, the science of Ethics proceeds to draw conclusions about what specific acts we should and should not do if we are going to achieve the happiness we so naturally desire.

The Form and Matter of Ethics

Because a science is an organized body of knowledge, it qualifies *in philosophy* as a "physical thing." As such, every science will have both a *formal* and a *material* component because, as we learned from Aristotle in our study of the human person, every physical thing is a composition of form and matter. The material component of a science is referred to as its ***material object***. The material object of a science is the same thing as its subject matter; it is *what the science studies*. The material object of Ethics is

Material Object of Ethics:

voluntary human acts

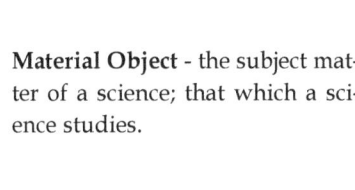

Material Object - the subject matter of a science; that which a science studies.

Called to Happiness ~ Guiding Ethical Principles

NOTES

Formal Object - the angle or point-of-view from which the subject matter of a science is studied.

any act of a human being which is a free or voluntary act. The science of Ethics studies *voluntary human acts.*

The formal component of a science is referred to as its ***formal object***. The formal object is *the angle or point-of-view from which the subject matter of the science is studied.* Because many sciences study the same subject matter, it is actually the formal object of a science that distinguishes one science from another. The formal object is what makes a science to be the kind of science that it is. The formal object of Ethics is *determining whether voluntary human acts lead to happiness.*

This is what we mean by the *ethical evaluation* of an act. The science of Ethics wants to figure out whether or not a person's free acts will actually lead him to happiness or not. If we determine that the act will lead

Formal Object of Ethics:

determining whether voluntary human acts lead to happiness

to happiness, then we judge that act to be ethically "good." If it will not lead to happiness, then we judge the act to be ethically "bad" or "evil."

A Normative Science

From what we have said so far, one can easily see that Ethics is not exactly like the science of biology or chemistry. These latter are **descriptive sciences**, that is, sciences which describe their subject but do not pass judgment on it. They seek to acquire knowledge about their subject simply for the sake of better understanding of objective reality.

Descriptive science - a science which describes objects and phenomena but does not pass judgment on their subject matter.

Normative science - a science which deals with the norms or criteria by which the objects of its study are judged.

Ethics is a little different. It is a **normative science**. Like the descriptive sciences, Ethics wants to understand some aspect of objective reality better: it seeks to understand *voluntary human acts.* The difference lies in the fact that Ethics is concerned with the norms or criteria by which we judge those acts to be good or evil.

The goal of the science of Ethics, then, is not simply to describe human acts; the goal is to judge those human acts so that we can determine which ones will, in fact, lead us to the happiness we desire and to avoid those acts that will not.

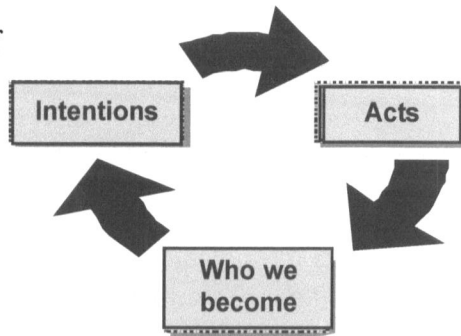

10.

Remember what we discussed at the beginning of this chapter: our intentions shape our acts, and our acts determine who we become -- the type of persons or characters we make ourselves to be. Studying Ethics is all about *character-building!* We do not want *simply* to do good *acts*; we want to become *good people*. Being good ourselves will make it possible for us to take great delight in our possession of the greatest good.

What's in a Name?

Once we understand this about the science of Ethics, we can better appreciate why this science has the name that it does. The word "Ethics" comes from the Greek word *ethos*, meaning "character." Unlike a person's temperament or personality which is God-given and stable, a person's character is something for which *he* is ultimately responsible. A person develops his character from the kinds of acts he consistently chooses to do or not do. For example, a person might be a "lazy character" because he normally chooses to do the bare minimum in whatever he does. If this person were greatly to exert himself on one occasion, thus departing from his usual way of acting, we would say that he is acting "out of character."

The science of Ethics is also called "Moral Philosophy." The term "moral" comes from the Latin word *mos*, which means "custom or manners." Ethics studies how human persons *should behave* if we are to be true to our nature as rational creatures. This means that Ethics figures out what is "customary" behavior for the human person who is gifted with an intellect. Because it is a branch of philosophy, Ethics uses only human reason and human experience in its investigation of human acts. The use of Faith and Revelation is reserved to those who study Moral *Theology*.

Conclusion

With this introduction to the science of Ethics, a question naturally arises: Shouldn't a *science* be able to give us knowledge which holds true for everyone? Unless it gives us such knowledge, we cannot accurately call it a science, can we? Right! If Ethics offers us only one person's subjective view of things, or the way things might objectively be for this one person only, then it is not a science. If that is the case, then there is nothing here for us to study. We can each simply decide for ourselves which acts we want to call "good" and which ones we want to call "evil."

NOTES

To call Ethics a science, then, is to claim that its conclusions are true for every person and not just for a few. In other words, to say that an act is ethically good or evil must be true for every person who does this same act, with the same intention, and under the same circumstances. Anyone doing an ethically good act will move himself closer to happiness, and conversely, anyone doing an ethically evil act will not. This indeed is what the science of Ethics offers us: A judgment about the ethical quality of our acts which holds true *for everyone!* Precisely <u>why</u> we can make this claim will be the subject of discussion in our next chapter.

Study Guide Questions:

1. *Why do you think a course on Ethics would be a very popular course to take?*

2. *Why are we going to be held responsible for the kind of people we become?*

3. *The first principle of the science of Ethics is self-evident. Do you agree? Explain.*

4. *What do we mean by the terms "formal object" and "material object" of a science? What are the formal and material objects of the science of Ethics?*

5. *Why do we say that Ethics is a normative science?*

6. *What do the names "Ethics" and "Moral Philosophy" tell us about the subject we are beginning to study?*

CASE IN POINT

St. Thomas Aquinas says the following: "That in which a man rests as in his last end is master of his affections, since he takes from it his entire rule of life."

St. Thomas, *Summa Theologiae*, I-II, 1, 5, *Sed contra*.

* *What does St. Thomas mean by "master of his affections"? By "entire rule of life"? State St. Thomas' point in your own words.*

* *In view of St. Thomas' statement, what might St. Paul mean when he writes the following about gluttons: "Their god is their belly; their glory is in their 'shame.' Their minds are occupied with earthly things." (Phil. 3:19)*

* *In light of the importance of the final end, why does Jesus make the following claim: "No man can serve two masters"? (Mt. 6:24) Why is this statement true?*

* *Larry is determined to make the football team next semester, but he hasn't eaten right or exercised regularly in a long time and has put on some weight. How does St. Thomas' statement above apply to Larry's situation as he faces some choices this semester?*

Point to Consider:

"My dear young people,
... If to live as a follower of the Lord becomes the highest value,
then all other values are given their rightful rank and importance.
Whoever depends solely on worldly goods will end up by losing,
even though there might seem to be an appearance of success.
Death will find that person with an abundance of possessions
but having lived a wasted life.
Therefore, the choice is between being and having,
between a full life and an empty existence,
between truth and falsehood."

Pope Saint John Paul the Great,
Message to the Youth of the World, February, 2001

Chapter II

Happiness: What Is It?

If you were to meet someone who said he <u>didn't</u> want to be happy, and who had no interest whatsoever in the subject, you would probably suspect something was wrong. For centuries such great philosophers as Aristotle, St. Augustine and our own St. Thomas Aquinas have taught that happiness is a desire all of us have in common: We all want to be happy! Many people, however, would not think of Ethics as a course in which the issue of **happiness** takes center stage. The truth is that the question of human happiness is very much at the heart of the study of Ethics.

In this chapter, we will see that there is much more to this question of happiness than our culture suggests or promises. This question is central to our fulfillment as human persons. Let us see why.

NOTES

Happiness - man's complete flourishing wherein there is nothing more he desires.

> **Vocabulary**
>
> *good*   *human nature*   *hierarchy of goods*
> *ultimate end*   *happiness*   *Beatific Vision*

I. What is Happiness?

We have seen that the science of Ethics judges whether our voluntary human acts are good or evil. These judgments are based on its first principle: Do good and avoid evil. A *good* act is one which will lead to our happiness and an *evil* act is one which will not, St. Thomas tells us.

It is obvious, then, that determining what human happiness entails is going to be all-important. It will determine which acts are good and which ones are evil.

Some might be tempted to think that the judgment about which acts are good or evil is a *subjective* one; that is, they think it differs from person to person. This, in fact, is something we experience in our modern culture. For example, some people say that sexual activity outside of marriage is good, while others say it is bad -- mortally sinful, in fact. Some say the direct killing of the innocent person in the womb of his mother is good; others say it is murder. Is it all just a subjective matter of personal opinion, or are there judgments of right and wrong that truly apply to everyone? If it is all simply a matter of personal opinion, then we are wrong to call Ethics a science. A science gives us knowledge that is *universal*. If Ethics is a science, then its knowledge must hold true for everyone who finds himself in the same situation.

Ethics *is* indeed a science. The knowledge it gives us applies to every human person. Another way of saying this is that Ethics is *objective*, at least the Ethical system of St. Thomas Aquinas is. According to him, ethical judgments concerning right and wrong are not based on a person's mere subjective opinion. They are based on our human nature which is the same for all human beings. Just as it is not good *for any one of us* to be hit by a moving car because our bodies are not made to withstand the impact, so too it is not good *for any one of us* intentionally to kill an innocent person who poses no threat to our lives. These judgments hold true for us all because we all share the same human nature.

As we pointed out in the previous chapter, all human persons want to be happy. We also all understand that whatever <u>truly</u> makes us happy will be <u>truly good</u> for us. Because happiness plays such a key role in determining what is good and evil, St. Thomas considered it to be a person's first and most important ethical concern. This is why before going any further in our study of ethics, we must first discover what happiness entails. Until we "get happiness right," we will never be able to "get it right" about which acts are good and evil.

Objective vs. Subjective Happiness

No doubt, some people will find it quite strange to think that it is possible to "get happiness wrong." They think that we determine *for ourselves* what will make us happy. If one person is hungry, his happiness might be a juicy hamburger. Another might decide that it is a chocolate milk shake. If a person has had a few sleepless nights, an undisturbed night's rest will make him happy; or perhaps he would prefer some drug to keep him *awake*. "People's individual needs and desires differ, so will what fulfills them differ." At least, so goes the argument. But is that really the case?

Even with regard to goods that do not fulfill some natural need, it seems clear to many people that what makes us happy is going to differ from person to person. An alcoholic, for example, finds his happiness in drinking, a gambler in winning the jackpot, and a religious person in praying. Such examples may *seem* to be adequate evidence for claiming that happiness is a *subjective* matter, that is, for asserting that what will make one person happy might not be what makes another person happy.

Before too quickly accepting this line of reasoning (which claims that we can determine for ourselves whatever we want happiness to be), we would do well to consider the *opposite* point-of-view.

Suppose there is a person who likes to eat dirt and drink gasoline. If you were to ask him what makes him happy, he would tell you that he is happy when he is eating dirt and drinking gasoline. We all know that even though he *subjectively* thinks this makes him happy, it *objectively* cannot make him happy. He is going to get sick and die if he does not stop doing it.

Peter Kreeft explains further:

> Some would say ... that happiness is totally subjective and relative to your desires: no matter what you desire, if only your desire is satisfied, that's all happiness is. But we all know this is not true. We all commonsensically distinguish between real and apparent happiness, true and false happiness. A temporary 'high' caused by a mind-destroying drug is not true happiness but false, pseudo-happiness. Satisfaction of the desire for personal revenge is not true happiness on a par with satisfaction of the desire for objective justice.[1]

What is it that leads some people, like Peter Kreeft and St. Thomas Aquinas, to think that true happiness is fundamentally an *objective* matter? The evidence is rather simple yet actually overwhelming. Good evidence always needs to be examined:

First, our <u>*feelings*</u> of happiness can be mistaken:

"You can feel quite healthy but really be dying. Or you can feel terribly sick but really be quite healthy. Similarly, you can feel very happy and yet be dying inside, dying in your soul, dying to your humanity....

---

[1] Peter Kreeft, *Making Choices*, p. 179.

Called to Happiness ~ Guiding Ethical Principles

NOTES

"... Or you could feel like a failure when in fact you are really a spiritual success and a hero, like Job."²

The fact that we can be wrong about happiness implies that there must be something to be wrong about -- some *objectively right* state of happiness.

Secondly, if everyone seeking happiness were able to choose whatever he wants happiness to be, then we all should be happy. There would be no excuse for being unhappy. Yet, we see many unhappy people in our world. Why is this?

Look at the story of the Prodigal Son, for example.³ Here is a young man who seems to have everything going for him as he sets out in pursuit of happiness from his father's house -- with inheritance and freedom in hand. Yet, by the end of the story, as a result of the choices he has made, we find him destitute and disillusioned, longing to eat even the scraps of food the pigs leave behind. Why was he unable to make his choices bring him happiness?

"OK," you might say, "but that is just a parable. It is not real life." True, Jesus' parable *is* just a story, but doesn't it reflect the lives of many people we all know? For some reason human beings are unable to make just *anything* we choose bring us happiness.

I'm going to have to get this happiness thing figured out!

Take St. Augustine (354-430 A.D.) as another classic example of someone who goes in all sorts of wrong directions in his search for happiness. In his *Confessions,* Augustine recounts in vivid detail his 33-year search for what would satisfy his restless heart. Augustine was a real person, and the story of his life is every person's story. It is one of increasing disillusionment and disappointment as he follows after and clings to goods which do not really satisfy him at all. The highly intelligent and talented Augustine first tries sexual pleasure in relationships outside of marriage. Next he hopes that his fame and reputation as a teacher and speaker will satisfy his hungering heart. Then he

18.

² Ibid.
³ Luke 15:11-31

gives himself over fully to the study of philosophy, trying to find supreme satisfaction in natural wisdom and in his high social standing. So desperate does Augustine become that he even consults astrologers in his pursuit of happiness. None of these experiences brings him the happiness he seeks. In the end he admits, "[I]n these days of my youth, ... I became in my own eyes a barren land,"[4] an "unhappy beast."[5]

The older Augustine becomes, the more he knows he is not happy, even though he is trying all the harder to achieve the happiness he seeks so desperately. From Augustine's life, we begin to grasp the fact that happiness is not acquired simply by personal choice or achievement. It is not something we can "get" for ourselves by simply exerting our own efforts or by exercising our wills, choosing just any good whatsoever. There must be something more involved.

In other words, there must be something *objective* about the happiness that we seek. Only this can explain why so many of us are unable to find that for which we are all searching so desperately. If we could actually "figure out" what happiness is, *objectively* speaking, then perhaps we could *subjectively* choose to move ourselves toward it. That is, we could choose to do those acts that will lead us to happiness, and reject those acts which do not.

Fulfilling our Human Nature

If your neighbor were to go on a two week vacation and asked you to take care of his dog while he was gone, you would know basically what to do in order to keep his dog "happy." You would keep the animal in a safe environment, give him nutritious food and plenty of water, and allow him enough room to run around for exercise. You would not think of feeding the dog <u>only</u> ice cream, or leaving him alone for a few hours in your deep pool to swim, or keeping him closed up in a small closet for days at a time. No, once you understand the **nature** of a dog, you would be able to figure out what would be **good** for him, that is, what would fulfill his nature. Thus, you would be able to make your neighbor's dog happy -- and any dog for that matter -- because all dogs share the same nature.

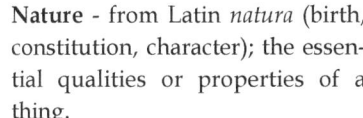

The same thing holds true with regard to a fish in its tank. If a person wants to keep the fish "happy," he can figure out what would be good for it

NOTES

Nature - from Latin *natura* (birth, constitution, character); the essential qualities or properties of a thing.

Good - conducive to well-being, to happiness; desirable; fitting to one's nature.

---
[4] St. Augustine, *The Confessions*, Book II.
[5] Ibid., Book III.

simply by correctly understanding the nature of the fish. The fish will not be happy if the water in its tank completely evaporates, freezes solid, or is mixed with a large amount of chlorine. Notice that this does not differ from fish to fish, as if it were a *subjective* matter. Rather, because all fish share the same fish nature, what satisfies or fulfills that nature will be the same for them all.

Consider one last example: If a person were to leave his car in your care for a week, and he asked you to take good care of it, would you know what to do in order to treat it well? Could you figure out what to do for the car that would make it "happy?" Perhaps, because you like chocolate shakes you think that it would be good for the car to have a shake poured down its gas tank. If you did that, you would find out rather soon that shakes do not make cars "happy." Just a little knowledge of the nature of a car would let you know that in order to make a car "happy," you should fill its tank with gas, give it an oil change and a tune-up, fill its tires with air, and wash down its exterior. These *goods* form a "recipe" for happiness which works for all cars because it is based on a correct understanding of what a car is and how it functions. Electric cars, of course, would have a different "recipe."

Human Nature - from Latin *natura* (birth, constitution, character); the general inherent character or disposition of mankind.

If we are able to use this kind of reasoning to determine what will make animals and cars "happy," then why can we not do the same thing for human beings? Why don't we try to understand **human nature** correctly, and *then* figure out what will be *good* for that nature? Doing it this way should enable us to come up with an answer that will apply to every human being because we all have the same human nature. Let's try doing just that.

Goods of the Body

We all have bodies. What will it take to make these bodies of ours "happy"? What will be *good* for them? *Objectively* speaking, we know that nutritious food, plenty of water, exercise, adequate rest, cleanliness, and appropriate temperatures are *good* for our bodies. Even though someone might object saying, "No, exercise does not make me happy," or "A constant diet of junk food makes me happy," we know that they are only speaking *subjectively* and that their subjective opinion is wrong. It is a fact that a human person is better off when his body is well-exercised: he can move himself around more freely, think more clearly, and function better as a living organism if his body is well exercised. The same is true regarding our eating habits. A constant diet of junk food affects a person's level of energy and performance as well as his overall bodily health. A person might "rest content" at the present moment and think of his "contentment" as "happiness," but the contentment will be short-lived. The happiness he thinks he is experiencing is a *false* happiness. If one's bodily needs are not being met, then the person himself cannot *truly* be happy in the long-run.

Goods of the Soul

We human beings are more than our bodies, though, and so our happiness must entail something more than just taking care of our bodies. We also need to care for our souls. The soul has a variety of powers or faculties. These powers are designed to "go for" certain objects, and they will be fulfilled only when they function the way they were designed and get their objects.

<u>Goods for the senses</u> -- Our five senses were designed to be able to "pick up" the exterior world so that we can be in touch with objective reality.

The senses are easily satisfied because they achieve their objects readily if the senses are working properly. Our sight is "fulfilled" when it perceives color. Our hearing is satisfied when it picks up the sounds around us -- and so on with each of the senses.

<u>Goods for the Sense appetites</u> -- The sense appetites are also easily satisfied insofar as their objects (particular goods which are sensed) are readily available to them. These lower appetites in man are satisfied simply when they do what they were made to do: respond to sensed goods. Thus, we are drawn to the beauty of a lovely sunset, or repelled by the sound of a musical instrument that is out of tune, etc. Because they are lower powers in the rational soul, the sense appetites are perfectly "content" when the intellect and will lead and direct them. The sense appetites in rational beings were not designed to be in charge.

Goods for the Intellect and Will -- The two highest powers of the human soul are those which are unique to human beings: the intellect and free will. Enabling these two rational powers to function as they were designed and to achieve what they seek will be the key to human happiness.

The intellect is designed to line itself up with objective reality. Knowing reality is a *good* for the intellect; it is what fulfills it. This is why we say that the object of the intellect is truth, for truth exists when the intellect's thinking corresponds to objective reality. It is because of the intellect's desire to know the truth about reality that we say that human beings are curious creatures. It seems that we always want to know more about whatever there is to know. The intellect is only truly satisfied when it understands a thing *fully*.

Understanding this about the intellect, we quickly realize an important dimension of human happiness: it must involve the intellect's being actively involved in knowing reality. This explains why human beings find joy in meeting new people, in learning about life in foreign lands, in discovering what causes things to work, in seeking cures for diseases, or in finding out more about any aspect of reality. The intellect is a seemingly insatiable power: it never tires of questioning and of learning more. If the intellect could come to know the First Cause of all of reality, however, then it would be completely satisfied. All of its questions would be answered by the One who is the Cause of it all.

The other power of the rational soul, the will, is designed "to go for" (to love) the good. Like the intellect, the will is seemingly insatiable. For example, if you are enjoying one delicious piece of pie, you begin to desire another one. If you receive a $200 bonus, you start to hope that you will receive one valued at $400. If you get a nice house, you want an even nicer one. The will never seems satisfied, but keeps going for a *better* good -- in fact, it seeks an object which is *completely* or *absolutely* good. This movement of the will toward the infinite good is what we mean when we say the will *loves* the good. Because the will does not find an object which is absolutely good among the finite goods of this earth, however, it is never really satisfied. The will always wants *more good* than it finds. If the will were able to find a being that is infinitely good, however, then the restlessness of the will would come to an end. The will would be completely fulfilled.

One other point about satisfying the intellect and the will: A person's happiness will be greater to the degree that the object he knows and loves is *higher in being*. For example, someone knowing about rocks (inanimate being) will not find as much satisfaction in this knowledge as would the person who knows about living beings (plants or animals). Likewise, someone who knows and loves human persons will experience much more satisfaction than if he merely knows and loves cats, dogs, or canaries. Following his reasoning, we realize that knowing and loving the highest being in reality would be the most satisfying for us.

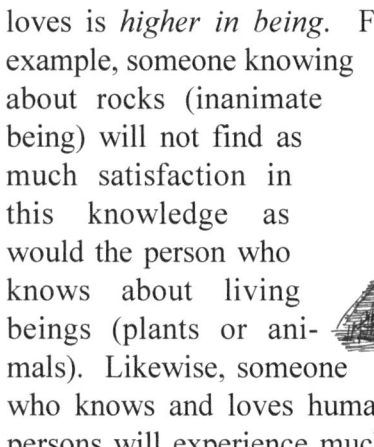

Since we know by reason and by faith that a Supreme Being does in fact exist, we can reasonably conclude that knowing and loving this Being will be essential to our happiness. In fact, once we become aware that such a Being is the Uncaused Cause of all that is, we realize that in knowing Him we will understand *fully* all of created reality. This First Cause -- a Being most fully in act -- is thus most perfect in goodness.[6] Upon beholding such a Being, the human will will have attained its long-desired object.

Study Guide Questions:

1. *What is the relationship between human happiness and the true good? What is the difference between happiness and contentment?*

2. *How can we be so sure that eating dirt and drinking gasoline can not make any human being truly happy?*

3. *What is meant by the phrase "objective happiness"? How does it differ from "subjective happiness"?*

4. *Explain how understanding our human nature can help us to figure out what will make us truly happy?*

5. *Do you agree that if the object we know and love is higher in being, then we will experience more happiness? Explain.*

6. *What will fully satisfy the human intellect and will?*

---

[6] St. Thomas Aquinas, *Summa Theologiae*, I, 4, 2.

Called to Happiness ~ Guiding Ethical Principles

NOTES

CASE IN POINT

A 25-year-old homeless man lives down by the creek in your neighborhood. You see him regularly because you walk by that area on the way to school. He has made a small little covering to protect himself from the rain, and it seems that he spends most of his time making mud pies from the dirt of the creek and letting them harden in the sun. If you were to ask him what makes him happy, he would tell you, "Making mud pies makes me happy. I know all about mud pies. I make them in different sizes and shapes. I love my mud pies."

- *Is this man truly happy? Explain.*
- *What would you suggest would make him genuinely happy? How can you know without even asking him for his opinion?*
- *Are we like this man in any way with regard to what makes us happy? Explain.*

II. Two Dimensions of Happiness

It is becoming clear that human happiness has two dimensions:

First, we recall from our study of the human person that left to himself, the human person is incomplete and unfulfilled - and therefore, unhappy. Happiness, then, is a question of human fulfillment: a quest for something outside ourselves that will "complete" and fulfill us. This must be a question involving something that is *tremendously good* for us -- so good that, once we attain it, we will be fully satisfied and want for nothing else. Once we possess this great good, there will be nothing left for us to desire! The restlessness of our hearts will be stilled. This first dimension of happiness, then, involves something *external to the person* -- some overwhelming good that will fully satisfy the human person, both in body and in soul.

Secondly, happiness *necessarily involves* a certain *transformation of the person* himself who possesses this great good. Such a transformation of the person is necessary in order for him to be able to take *supreme delight* in the great good which he possesses. It is not enough simply to *possess* the great good. Unless the person has the same *degree of goodness* himself, he will not truly be able to enjoy the good he possesses -- that is, really appreciate and take genuine delight in it. Selfish people, for example, cannot appreciate fully the happiness of possessing genuine friendship -- not until they change and learn to give of them-

"In order to be truly happy we must become the kind of person who loves the good where happiness is to be found. We must learn to desire this good and seek it more than we seek anything else."
Paul Wadell, C.P.
The Primacy of Love, p. 48

24.

selves to others. In the same way, evil people cannot enjoy being in Heaven, even if they could somehow get there. Although they would *possess* the great good of Heaven, they could not take delight in the total self-giving love which life in Heaven is all about.

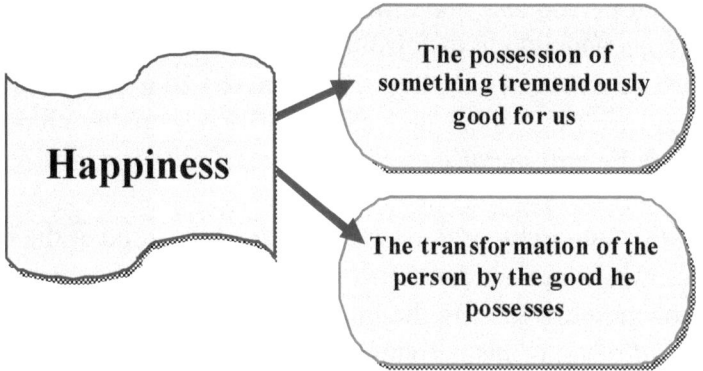

The point of all this is that in order for the person to delight in the great good, all the powers of his soul must act according to their "design": that is, all of the lower powers must follow the lead of the intellect, which is the highest power. We call this transformed condition of man the state of *virtue*. Because of this transformation, the happy person is not simply the one who possesses the great good; he is also the one *who has actually been changed* by the good he possesses. He is changed in such a way that he himself becomes good. Paul Wadell, a contemporary theologian, explains:

> Aquinas held that real happiness and real peace come from possessing whatever good can bring us to our fullest and most perfect development. We will be happy, Thomas thought, when we not only possess, but are also transformed by, whatever good is capable of bringing us to our utmost possible excellence as human beings - the good or goods that enable us to be who we are created to be.[7]

"...[I]n order to be happy we must be conformed to the good that offers it, we must be remade, redirected, internally transformed until we practice the love that brings true joy. Happiness hinges on becoming good."
Paul Wadell, C.P.,
The Primacy of Love, p. 48

The Greatest Good

As we have seen, human happiness involves many goods which help to fulfill the needs and desires of the body and soul. While it is true that we should never act *against* any of these goods, it is also true that we do not need to pursue them all at the same time. In fact, there are times when we *cannot* pursue them because the goods actually conflict with each other. For example, a mother in need of sleep

"To be happy ... is ultimately to possess the greatest possible good. If good things make us happy, then that which is best will bring us grandest joy."
Paul Wadell, C.P.,
The Primacy of Love, p. 50

---
[7] Paul J. Wadell, *Happiness and the Christian Moral Life*, p. 13.

NOTES

Hierarchy - a body of persons or things ranked in grades, orders, or classes, one above another.

Hierarchy of goods - a body of goods ranked in order one above another.

Ultimate End - from Latin *ultimus* (last, final); the end that lies beyond all others.

"Happiness is being related to whatever is best for us; it is a lovelife with whatever good enables our most noble possibility; put differently, happiness is lifelong friendship with our most promising good."
Paul Wadell, C.P.
The Primacy of Love, p. 46

"That is why all misplaced loves are idolatrous, and why all idolatrous loves are deadly. In expending ourselves on lesser goods, we are destroyed."
Paul Wadell, C.P.
The Primacy of Love, p. 50

will forgo the sleep she needs in order to care for her sick child. She does this because she judges that her loving care for her child is a *greater good* than is sleep. Or a person might choose to pass up a meal so that someone in greater need can eat it. He does this because he more highly values that person as a *good* than he does the food. Clearly, then, the various goods which help to fulfill our nature are not all of equal value. There must be a certain ordering or a **hierarchy of goods** which enables a person to prioritize them and so to make reasonable choices about which goods he will pursue.

In this hierarchy of goods, there must be a good at the top of the list, a good which ranks highest in value among all the goods. This most valuable or greatest good is the goal or purpose of a person's life, the **ultimate end** of all of his activity. It is what a person sets his heart on achieving with his life. Everything he does in his life he does in order to achieve this end. Pursuing this greatest good gives meaning to his life. Such a good is sought *for its own sake* and not for the sake of some other good. That's why we say that it is an *ultimate* end: we seek all other goods as a *means* to this good, but this greatest good we seek just for itself. Possessing this greatest good and being transformed by it constitute the *objective* state of *true* happiness for every human person.

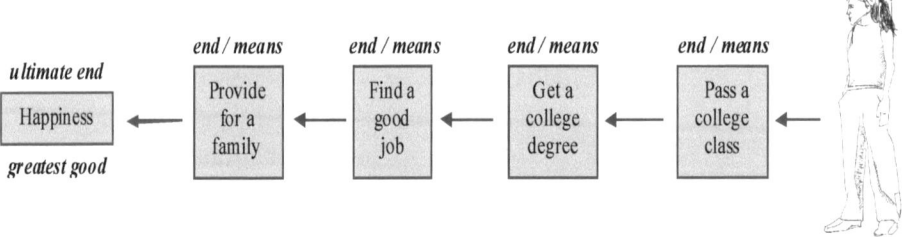

What is this greatest good? People do not agree on the answer to this question. That's why there are different ethical systems. That's also why we disagree on what we judge to be good or evil acts. Some people say the greatest good is money; others say it is pleasure; still others, fame, power, or health. St. Thomas investigated these popular candidates for the greatest good, and he came to the conclusion that none of them can *truly* satisfy the human person. In fact, if a person mistakenly pursues any of them as *his ultimate end*, they will lead not to his happiness and human flourishing but to his sadness and diminishment.

1. *Money*

Take money as an example. Many people live as if money is our greatest good. Money is surely a good, but it cannot be our greatest good, our ultimate end. Money is a *means* of exchange for acquiring other goods; it is not itself an *end*. Its value lies only in that it can be used for acquiring something other, something more valuable to us. Even though many people live as if it were their ultimate end, money is actually less than we are. Thus, living as if it were our ultimate end would only diminish us, make us less than we are meant to be. Happiness is the opposite: it entails the "full and most perfect development of ourselves."[8] St. Thomas explains:

> Man's happiness clearly cannot consist in natural riches. For they are sought for the sake of something else, namely the support of human life, and so are subordinate to its ultimate end, not the end itself. They are made for man, not man for them.[9]

Whatever will bring us happiness must be greater than we are, for by loving it we become fully what we were made to be. This "greater good" will perfect us and thus cause us to experience a lasting joy.

Money is a good, but it is not perfectly good, for in no way does it have the excellence necessary for lasting joy. It has tremendous power to entice, but absolutely no power to redeem. It can lure us, entangle us, seduce us, but it cannot complete us, which is why if we love it most of all we are morally disfigured.[10]

2. *Pleasure*

What about pleasure as a possible candidate for the greatest good? Pleasure is an emotional response to a good experienced by the body. It is a "bodily delight," to use St. Thomas' words.[11] For example, delicious food delights taste buds; brilliant colors excite the eyes; and soft, velvet pleases the touch. Pleasures are caused by material stimuli. They are localized in a particular part of the body, are limited in duration, and tend to focus our attention on the material world. Both brute animals and human beings are capable of pleasure.

Because they concern primarily the good of the body, St. Thomas argues, pleasures cannot constitute the happiness of a person. For example, a person who has enjoyed a delicious meal may still be terribly unhappy, or someone who is on the beach at spring

---

NOTES

"Whatever will bring us joy has to be capable of making us so much more than we already are. Money cannot do this."
Paul Wadell, C.P.
The Primacy of Love, p. 51

---

[8] St. Thomas Aquinas, *Summa Theologiae*, I-II, 2, 4.
[9] Ibid., 2, 1.
[10] Paul J. Wadell, C.P., *The Primacy of Love*, p. 51.
[11] St. Thomas Aquinas, *Summa Theologiae*, I-II, 2, 6.

break on a beautiful day may still find himself unsatisfied, wanting more. Pleasure may accompany happiness, but happiness is more than pleasure. St. Thomas says this because he understands that a person is more than a body; he is a body/soul unity. In fact, it is the soul that gives life to the body and that makes it to be a *human* body. The body, then, exists for the soul, and its goods are for the sake of the soul.

Man's happiness, St. Thomas claims, must entail a good of the soul. It must primarily involve that part of man which makes him distinctly human. Unlike pleasure, man's happiness cannot be restricted to a bodily area. It must entail the well-being of the person as a person. Human happiness is more than what a dog or a cat is capable of experiencing. It opens the person up to going beyond himself and the material world. Such happiness will last forever.[12]

3. *Health*

Just as pleasure cannot be the greatest good of man because it does not satisfy the whole of man, so too bodily health cannot be man's greatest good. Health concerns only the body. Someone may be in the best of health, the picture of physical fitness, a Gold Medalist in the Olympics -- but still not be fulfilled as a person. The goods of the rational soul rank higher in the hierarchy of goods than those of the body. These higher goods of the soul are not addressed by the health of the body.

4. *Honor, Fame, Glory*

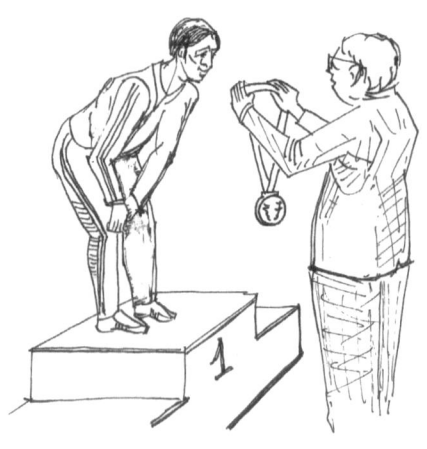

Honor, fame, or glory might appear at first to be more likely candidates for the greatest good because they concern more than the body. These are more spiritual goods. St. Thomas, though, does not think any of them can be the greatest good. He says this because honor, fame, and glory are possible *effects* of happiness but never its *cause*. In fact, a person might even attain fame or honor as a result of doing something wrong! People give genuine honor to someone because of some excellence he has achieved. The perfect excellence of a human being would be happiness. Honor, then, would *follow from* happiness.[13]

---
[12] Ibid., I-II, 2, 5.
[13] Ibid., I-II, 2, 2.

Fame and glory -- having people think well of us -- cannot make us happy. Remember what we learned about truth: In order to possess the truth, we must line up our thinking with objective reality. Man's thinking cannot change reality. Only God's thinking can do that. People thinking well of us, then, cannot *cause* our happiness. They might think well of us *because* we are happy, but even then their thinking could be in error.[14] As a matter of fact, it is sometimes the case that public opinion might actually be *against* someone who actually is *happy* -- for example, because they have done or said what is true, although it is unpopular.

5. *Power*

Power has at times been thought to be the cause of human happiness. St. Thomas, though, does not think that human happiness consists in power. Power is similar to money in that it is a *means* and not an end. With power, a person is able to get things, to destroy them, to change them, or to control them. Obviously, power can be used both for good and for evil. We can see examples of this in our world and throughout history. Since happiness is the ultimate end and the greatest good, power cannot be happiness.

6. *Virtue*

Surely virtue stands a good chance of being the greatest good because virtue is the health of the soul, the strength of a person's character! Right? After all, virtue is the beauty or excellence of the soul itself, isn't it? Virtue, we could say, is the person as a "work of art." All of this is certainly true, but it still does not follow that virtue is the greatest good. "Works of art" are not necessarily only *ends*. They can be produced for some other end, and it might not even be a good one. For that reason, they cannot be the ultimate end in themselves.

The excellence of the human soul entails its powers of thinking, choosing, and desiring all working as they were designed to work, but that by itself does not automatically mean that these powers have actually obtained their objects. Virtue is not really "its own reward." A person who is trying everyday to act virtuously is really seeking to reach a *higher* Good than his own goodness. He is really seeking an *infinite* good, one that leaves nothing else to be desired! Peter Kreeft explains:

> "To call virtue the end is to confuse the seeking with the thing sought. Virtue is like the clear quality of a telescope mirror: it exists to see the stars. We have not yet found the stars."[15]

---
[14] Ibid., I-II, 2, 3.
[15] Peter Kreeft, *Making Choices*, p. 88.

Called to Happiness ~ Guiding Ethical Principles

NOTES

"As the soul is the life of the body, so God is man's life of happiness...."
St. Augustine
The City of God, XIX, 26.

"God alone satisfies."
St. Thomas Aquinas

"What else does being happy mean, if not this: knowingly to possess something eternal?"
St. Augustine

Beatific Vision - from Latin *beatificus* (making blessed); imparting supreme happiness; the sight of the glories of Heaven.

Happiness in God

St. Thomas understood that no created, finite good is able to satisfy the human will, which longs for the infinite good. Health, honor, pleasure, power, money and virtue are truly goods for the human person, and we can pursue these goods legitimately so long as we do not sacrifice higher goods for them. None of these goods, however, can *objectively* be man's ultimate end, his greatest good. They simply are not *good enough* to fulfill us. None of them can bring us to the state of excellence for which we were created. St. Thomas knew that only a good which surpasses us in goodness will be able to fulfill us. In loving and possessing this greatest good, we will be perfected as human beings; our desires will all be fulfilled. Such unlimited goodness is found only in God, according to St. Thomas.[16] Nothing but God will completely satisfy our natural desire for the absolute good. Anything less will leave us dissatisfied and unfulfilled.

The highest power of the rational soul is the intellect. Not until this power achieves its proper object, can the human soul be at rest. The object of the intellect is the essences of created things. The intellect will not know fully *what a thing is*, however, unless it knows the essence of its cause. According to St. Thomas, then, the human intellect cannot be fully satisfied until it beholds the essence of the First Cause.[17] This beholding of the essence of the Uncaused Cause is what we mean when we speak of the **Beatific Vision**.

Study Guide Questions:

1. Name and explain the two "dimensions" of human happiness. Why is each of them necessary for true happiness?

2. If you arrange five human goods (of various kinds) in a hierarchy according to their value to you, what do you notice about the hierarchy? What type of goods are more valuable for fulfilling human beings?

3. Name each of the "candidates" often associated with happiness. Explain why each of them is not adequate.

4. What would you say is the difference between "happiness" and "contentment"? Why is the distinction between the two important to our discussion in this chapter?

5. The human person is the kind of creature that can only be completely satisfied by being united with God. Why is this true?

---

[16] St. Thomas Aquinas, *Summa Theologiae*, I-II, 2, **8**.
[17] Ibid., 3, **8**.

CASES IN POINT

#1 -- "Most people have a rather vague understanding of what the central purpose in their lives may be, and they often act impulsively and inconsistently, obscuring the direction and unity of their lives…."

* *What important point is this author making regarding human behavior?*
* *Do you agree that "most people" act this way? Can you give examples?*
* *How would you describe the way people ought to act, if this situation in our culture is to change?*

"…Yet, actually in every person's life, a commitment to some goal that has priority over all others is evident, shaping every important decision. Thus it is often said of a nurse or physician, 'She is someone who really cares about people, and it shows in everything she does, in both private and professional life,' or 'He may be an expert professional, but he is a selfish person who is always acting for personal advancement or money.' … Morality is thus first a matter of fundamental commitment or intention of the ultimate end, that is, the general intention that gives unity and pattern to one's whole life."

* *Why is the commitment of every person to "some goal that has priority over all others" important in their decisions and actions?*
* *This selection gives the example of nurses and physicians. How could the same principle be used to describe parents? Teachers? High school students?*

(Both quotations taken from *Health Care Ethics*, by Ashley and O'Rourke, p. 187.)

* * * * *

#2 -- In January, 2010, Grant Desme announced that he was leaving baseball to enter the priesthood. The 23-year-old outfielder was a top prospect for the Oakland Athletics, after completing a breakout season in which he became Most Valuable Player of the Arizona Fall League. Desme was the only minor league player with 30 home runs and 30 stolen bases in his last season.

A lifelong Catholic, Desme said, "I was doing well at ball. But I really had to get down to the bottom of things. I wasn't at peace with where I was at. ... I love the game, but I aspire to higher things." Desme intends to enter the seminary. "It's about a 10-year process," he said. "I desire and hope I become a priest."

During his first two years in the minors, Desme was beset by shoulder and wrist problems. He said that his days off the field at this time gave him a chance to think about what was most important to him, to read and study the Bible and to talk to teammates about his faith. Looking back, he considers those injuries to be "the biggest blessings God ever gave me."

(See the Associated Press article, "Top Baseball Prospect Retires to Enter Priesthood," 1/23/10)

* *Do you find Desme's dramatic change in his life's goal to be surprising? Why?*
* *How does Desme's decision to change his goal relate to our study about the Greatest Good?*
* *Why do you think Desme considers his past injuries to have been such wonderful blessings?*

Called to Happiness ~ Guiding Ethical Principles

NOTES

III. Purifying our Desires

Having seen what it will take to fulfill our human nature and having figured out which is the greatest good in objective reality, we are ready to talk about achieving human happiness. St. Augustine, the expert on seeking happiness, tells us that we will not be happy in any of the three following circumstances:

a) If we lack what we love,
b) If we possess what we love but it is harmful,
c) If we have not learned to love what is best.[18]

Simply *knowing* what is objectively good for us is not enough. There is a *subjective* dimension to happiness as well. We must learn to love what is truly good for us. For example, if a person's heart is still set on eating junk food all the time, then knowing that a well-balanced diet is good for him is not enough. Somehow he needs to *purify* his desires so that he actually learns to love the kinds of food that are part of a well-balanced diet. In other words, he must learn to line up his subjective happiness with what will objectively make him happy. He must learn to love the good that will truly bring him happiness. This means that he needs to get to the point where he actually *enjoys* nutritious foods!

Apparent Good - a good which attracts but which will not truly lead to our happiness.

"The Beatitudes confront us with decisive choices concerning earthly goods; they purify our hearts in order to teach us to love God above all things."
Catechism of the Catholic Church, #1728

In like manner, unless a person is correct about what his ultimate end is, he will make mistakes in his choice of human goods. Because he does not have the goods prioritized correctly, he will substitute lesser goods for higher ones. For example, if a man values his son's affection more highly than he values God, he might choose to ignore the truths of his faith in order to safeguard good relations with his son who is living with his girlfriend. Instead of lovingly challenging his son to abide by God's law, the man will ignore God's will in order to keep peace with his son. In doing so, he fails both God and his son.

Incomplete and Complete Happiness

If we do purify our desires and learn to love what is truly good for us, then is it possible to be happy on this earth? This question is worth looking into. What would a person's life look like who learned to love what is truly good for him and who prioritized the goods correctly?

---

[18] Paul J. Wadell, *Happiness and the Christian Moral Life*, p. 10.

First, he would be a person who loved the kinds and the amounts of food and drink that would bring him good health. He would love keeping his body physically fit with regular exercise of some sort, with adequate sleep, cleanliness, and recreation. All of these goods, however, would be the lowest in his hierarchy of goods.

More important than these goods to the person would be his ability to be in relation to the world around him. He would delight in the beauty, the fragrance, and the sounds which surround him. His sense appetites (emotions) would be active, but always guided by right reason. He would delight in knowing things: how to fix the engine of his car when it's not working; how to communicate with the immigrants in his neighborhood who don't speak English; how to best form and guide his children as they struggle through their teenage years. Of all the goods he would enjoy on this earth, though, he would most cherish the human persons in his life: his loving wife, his children, his parents, brothers and sisters, co-workers, neighbors, fellow parishioners. It would not be surprising to see him outside playing catch with his sons or sitting on the porch enjoying a conversation with his wife. In fact, he would even take great delight in helping out strangers. As a member of the St. Vincent de Paul Society, he would respond frequently to the needs of the homeless and poor. He would go to bed plenty tired at night, having spent himself selflessly in looking after the needs of others.

All of these "goods" which he enjoys, however, would hold a secondary place in his heart. First place would go to his Creator. This person would understand his complete dependence upon God for absolutely everything he has, even for his very life. He would consider all of his life, then, as his loving response back to the God whom he knows loves him profoundly. This loving relationship with his God he would consider to be his most precious treasure.

Would a person such as we have just described stand a good chance of being happy in this life here on earth? Would he be *completely* happy? We would have good reason to think that such a person would indeed be very happy, for he enjoys all of the human goods that fulfill his nature. His happiness, though, cannot ever be complete while he is living on this earth. Nor can anyone else's. Why is this so?

Limits of Earthly Happiness

Human happiness on earth is necessarily limited, for two very basic reasons: <u>First</u>, possessing all of the goods we need for happiness is beyond our control. In this life we all must deal with evil. Take for example the simple fact that we cannot guarantee that our bodies will remain disease-free. Nor can we guarantee what our neighbor will do in his free act.

A <u>second</u> reason why earthly happiness is limited is that we all still have unfulfilled desires. We do not yet possess the Ultimate End. An example of one very obvious unfulfilled desire that we all have is our desire for *unending* happiness. The very fact that we know that we and those we love will die someday makes our happiness on this earth incomplete.

Complete happiness is only possible after we die when -- if we merit Heaven by God's saving grace -- we will behold the essence of our God. In this union of ourselves with God, we will possess Him who is All-Good. No desire will be left unfulfilled. At this peak of human achievement, we will experience the actualization of the greatest human excellence possible.

Incomplete but genuine happiness, however, can begin right here and now to the degree that we learn to love what is truly good for us and to rightly prioritize those goods. Such happiness will involve experiencing *daily* -- to the extent that we are able in this life -- the good for which we were made, a good which totally satisfies us, completes us, and stills our restless hearts. Happiness involves living the good life; it entails "being good" at being human!

Is It Even Really Possible?

One remaining question concerning happiness waits to be addressed: Is complete happiness *really* possible considering our finite and limited condition as human beings? That is, how can we ever hope to be lovingly united with our all-good and all-loving Creator?

To answer this question, let us turn back to St. Augustine. Remember when we pointed out earlier how his repeated personal efforts at achieving happiness had failed? We noted then that *something more* was needed besides personal effort or willpower in order to achieve happiness.

That *something more* is not just a correct understanding of the objective dimension of happiness. If we turn again to the *Confessions*, Augustine shows us what this "something more" is. When he is nearly exhausted by the struggle within his soul and close to an emotional and psychological breakdown, Augustine escapes alone to a garden, throws himself on the ground and weeps. Unwilling to continue his life as it is and despairing of finding the happiness he seeks, Augustine allows his tears to flow like rivers.[19] It is at this point that he hears the voice of a child from a nearby house sing out to him, "Pick it up and read." Taking this to be a sign from God, Augustine takes up the Bible that he had set aside and begins reading the line he sees first:

> "Not in riotousness and drunkenness, not in lewdness and wantonness, not in strife and rivalry; but put on the Lord Jesus Christ, and make no provision for the flesh and its lusts."[20]

After thirty-three years of searching for happiness, Augustine "stumbles upon it" when he accepts God's invitation and opens his heart to His grace. Complete happiness is indeed possible for us human creatures, but it is made possible *as a gift of God's grace* and not merely as the result of our own efforts. In fact, St. Thomas says that left to ourselves complete happiness is not possible. It is primarily a gift of God's grace that we must freely accept and allow to transform us. Paul Wadell explains Augustine's situation:

> "Trying to arrange his life so that everything contributed to what he thought best for him left him famished. He kept missing happiness and remained a stranger to peace because he failed to understand that happiness begins in the gift of God's love -- happiness is born from grace -- and that he would be happy when he accepted, grew into, and conformed his life to the love from which he had been created."[21]

Surrendering himself to the gift of God's love, Augustine finally experienced the peace and joy for which he had so long searched. What began as a natural desire for unending happiness finds its complete fulfillment only by means of God's gift of grace, which is supernatural, that is, above our natural capacity to attain on our own. This indeed is exactly what our faith tells us:

---

[19] St. Augustine, *Confessions*, Book VIII.
[20] Romans 13:13-14.
[21] Paul Wadell, *Happiness and the Christian Moral Life*, p. 9.

NOTES

"Perfect and true happiness is simply not to be had in this life."
St. Thomas Aquinas,
Summa Theologiae, I-II, 5, 3

"To arrive at the vision of God in His essence is not only beyond the natural abilities of man, but beyond those of any created being."
St. Thomas Aquinas,
Summa Theologiae, I-II, 5, 5

"The beatitude of eternal life is a gratuitous gift of God. It is supernatural, as is the grace that leads us there."[22]

Conclusion

We now have a clearer understanding of the nature of human happiness: It ultimately will entail our complete fulfillment, our perfection as human beings. In such a state, all of our natural human desires will be wholly satisfied. This condition of happiness begins in this life here on earth to the extent that we learn to surrender to the gift of God's love. With the help of His grace, we can then work to purify our desires in order to prioritize them correctly, recognizing God Himself as our Ultimate End.

Having taken this first major step in our study of the science of Ethics by identifying the Ultimate End, we are ready now to proceed in our investigation. In the next chapter we will examine the nature of Moral Law and its relationship to genuine human freedom. At first glance, we might think that law has little to do with happiness; in fact, many people view the two concepts as being in opposition to each other. What we will soon see, however, is that the two are intimately connected -- along with genuine human freedom.

Study Guide Questions:

1. *Why isn't it enough simply to possess what is objectively good for us? What more is needed?*

2. *How does an incorrect understanding of what the ultimate end is affect a person's view of the hierarchy of goods?*

3. *Why is it impossible for a person to be completely happy while living on this earth?*

4. *What ultimately makes complete human happiness possible?*

---

[22] *The Catechism of the Catholic Church*, #1727.

Chapter II
Happiness: What Is It?

CASES IN POINT

#1 -- "'Happiness' is, in fact, an extremely difficult concept, psychologically and philosophically, too. It seems clear enough, no doubt, when we suffer from particular deprivations. When hungry, you can think of happiness as a big meal; when poor, you can think of it as a fat check.

"But while 'the affluent society' provides meals and checks in abundance -- for many people if not all -- it rather notoriously fails to provide happiness. It eases bodily troubles and replaces them with psychological ones.

"Consider the young people of today. In terms of possessions and personal freedoms, many of them are just about the most fortunate kids who have ever lived. But too often -- as we all know -- they behave as though drowning in despair. They can do exactly what they want; but they don't know what they want. That's what terrifies them…."

Christopher Derrick, "Pursuing Happiness, Finding Despair,"
Catholic Twin Circle

- *In your opinion, is Mr. Derrick correct in his analysis of our current human situation? Explain your reasoning, based on our discussions in this chapter.*
- *Why do you think finding happiness is such a struggle for us?*

* * * * *

#2 -- Professional basketball player and member of the NBA All-Star team in each of his first seven seasons in the league, Isiah Thomas earned reportedly $16 million over eight years. When interviewed, he said the following: "You know, the money and everything else does not necessarily make you a happy person. But if you're comfortable in your spiritual life and also in your family life, then you are going to be pretty happy and pretty successful as a person."

- *Isiah Thomas considered himself to have been blessed spiritually with a strong Catholic faith as well as with a large and loving family. Is there any reason to think that his opinion regarding what will make a person happy might actually line up with objective reality?*

* * * * *

#3 -- "Anyone who chooses to reflect on past excesses will appreciate how pleasures have sad endings."

St. Thomas Aquinas, *Summa Theologiae*, I-II, 2, 6

- *From your own experience, can you offer any examples of what St. Thomas is talking about?*

NOTES

"Happiness is a way of life characterized by loving, possessing, and enjoying what is supremely good for us as human beings."

Paul Wadell,
Happiness and the Christian Moral Life, p. 10

Point to Consider:

"Dear Young Friends! ... I have heard your festive voices, your cries, your songs, and I have felt the deep longing that beats within your hearts: you want to be happy! ... [M]any and enticing are the voices that call out to you from all sides: many of these voices speak to you of a joy that can be had with money, with success, with power. Mostly they propose a joy that comes from the superficial and fleeting pleasure of the senses.

"Dear friends, the aged Pope, full of years but still young at heart, answers your youthful desire for happiness with words that are not his own. They are words that rang out two thousand years ago. Words that we have heard again tonight: 'Blessed are they....' The key word in Jesus' teaching is a proclamation of joy: 'Blessed are they....'

"People are made for happiness. Rightly, then, you thirst for happiness. Christ has the answer to this desire of yours. But he asks you to trust him. True joy is a victory, something which cannot be obtained without a long and difficult struggle. Christ holds the secret of this victory."

Saint John Paul, *Address to the Youth in Toronto*, July, 2002, #1-2

Chapter III

Moral Law and Freedom

In a science that is concerned about human *acts*, it is not enough simply to know the meaning of the "Ultimate End" of the human person. Knowing the meaning of that term is just the first step. The all-important question remains: How do we most surely reach the Ultimate End? What must we *do*, how must we *act*, in order to ensure that we are, in fact, going in the direction of the Ultimate End of human life?

The **moral law** is going to play a key role in our "journey," as we will soon see. Just as knowledge of highway or airway laws aids us in travelling from Miami to New York, so too knowledge of the moral law will help us reach successfully the Ultimate End of our lives. Why this is the case will become clear to us once we understand the nature of law.

NOTES

Moral Law - law which governs the voluntary acts of human persons.

> **Vocabulary**
>
> law   *moral law*   *natural law*   *positive law*
> *freedom*   *necessity*   *promulgate*   *precept*

I. What is Law?

Do you remember what we said in Chapter One about Ethics being called "Moral Philosophy"? We explained that the term "moral" comes from a Latin word for customs or manners. In Moral Philosophy we study what is "customary behavior" for human beings. In other words, we are trying to determine the *norm* or *standard* for the behavior of rational creatures like ourselves. Once we realize this norm, another question might logically arise: Are we under any *obligation* to follow the norms once we know them?

It is true that the norms, in and of themselves, do not imply any obligation. A ruler is a *standard* we can use for determining the size of a piece of paper, but the ruler itself does not imply an obligation for us to make the paper any particular size. The ruler indicates a standard of measurement, but the ruler itself does not oblige us

Called to Happiness ~ Guiding Ethical Principles

NOTES

Law - a rule or measure of acts directing them to their proper ends.

Necessity - the quality of following inevitably from logical, physical, or moral laws.

to cut the paper a certain size. In a much more important way, a moral norm tells us *how* to act morally, but the norm itself is not a command to do so. If a person does not *want* to act morally, then he is certainly free to ignore the norm.

Any obligation to follow a norm must come from something beyond the norm itself. This is where **law** comes in. Law imposes an *"ought"* on us, an obligation to act in accord with the norm. The *ought* of law comes from the fact that it is the nature of law to direct acts to their proper ends. Law imposes a kind of ***necessity*** on whatever it directs. This necessity will be one of two kinds:

(a) *Physical law*, which imposes physical necessity, or

(b) *Moral law*, which imposes moral necessity.

Physical Law

Physical law directs all unthinking, non-free creatures to their ends. The necessity of physical law comes from the very nature of the creatures themselves and from the structure of the universe. For example, the various planets in our solar system *necessarily* do what they do because of the physical laws which govern them, laws such as the law of gravity and the law of inertia. Bears *necessarily* hibernate in the winter because their very nature directs them to do so in order to survive freezing temperatures. Even the human person, because he is *both* a physical and a spiritual being, is subject to the necessity of certain physical laws. If a person freely chooses to eat poison, then his body will *necessarily* react in very predictable ways; or if he chooses to walk off a cliff unprotected, then he will *necessarily* be pulled to the ground by the force of gravity -- with results which will *obviously* be bad for him! The necessity imposed by physical law is absolute. In other words, it is not possible to rebel against them or refuse to obey them.

Moral Law

"Happy those who observe God's decrees, who seek the Lord with all their heart. ... May my ways be firm in the observance of your laws!"
Psalm 119: 2, 5

Moral law directs to their proper ends *rational* creatures who are able to think and free to choose. Moral law, in other words, governs the free acts of human beings. It does so by imposing an obligation on our free wills, directing them to act in certain ways so as to achieve the end for which we were made. Moral necessity, then, is precisely this *ought* imposed on the free will of rational creatures. Because it is imposed on *free* creatures, moral law does not *physically* force its subjects to obey.

We can rebel and choose to disobey it. Nevertheless, moral laws are just as demanding of obedience as are physical laws, because if we choose to disobey them, we will not reach the end for which we were made.

Only the moral law is law in the strictest meaning of the term "law." St. Thomas Aquinas provides us with this strict meaning of law in his classic definition:

> **Law is nothing else than an ordinance of reason for the common good, promulgated by him who has the care of the community.**[1]

Let us take this definition apart in order to understand its terms:

(a) *An ordinance* -- This word means an order or a command given by someone who is in a position of authority. In other words, law is not a mere suggestion or kindly advice offered by a peer. Rather, it imposes an obligation and has binding force. When the principal says that all students must be in class by 7:45, she is not "suggesting" that everyone be in first period class on time!

(b) *Of reason* -- Law expresses the *mind* of the one in authority regarding how those subject to the law are to reach their ends. Law, therefore, must be reasonable. In order to be reasonable, law must be just. It cannot contradict higher laws. Law must be observable, enforceable, and useful for achieving the ends that are designated.[2] It would not be reasonable for the school handbook to impose a law that all students must make all A's at all times in order to graduate.

(c) *For the common good* -- Law is not given to an individual person; it is given to a community as a whole. It seeks not the good of a single person, but the benefit of an entire group of people. Law is relatively permanent insofar as it is not made to govern simply a single act; it is a rule of action. Law usually binds within certain regions, and it is always from a public authority. If one student has permission to be late for class because of a doctor's appointment, this does not mean that the law regarding the time class begins must change.

(d) *Promulgated* -- To promulgate means to make known. Law must be made known to those whom it binds. Once it is promulgated, law binds objectively, even though some people might not be aware of the law. If it is not promulgated, law does not bind; it is not law. If the school changes the time of the first class to 8:15, but does not publish this for the students, then the students cannot be expected to obey the new regulation.

---

[1] St. Thomas Aquinas, *Summa Theologiae*, I-II, q. 90, a. 4.
[2] See Austin Fagothey, S.J., *Right and Reason*, p. 163.

Called to Happiness ~ Guiding Ethical Principles

NOTES

(e) ***By him who has the care of the community*** -- The one who gives the law must have the authority to do so. He must be a legitimate superior with the jurisdiction to make the law. The senior class president cannot make a law that seniors do not have to be on time for their first period class!

With all of these important elements of St. Thomas' explanation of law in mind, we are able to draw the following conclusions:

> If a law is (a) not mandatory, (b) unreasonable, (c) harmful to the common good, (d) not promulgated, or (e) not authoritative, it is not real law; it is not binding.

Kinds of Law

Law can be categorized in a variety of ways. We will only look at those categories of law which will help us in our study of Ethics.[3]

1. Law can be categorized according to the *duration* of the law: how long is the law to be in effect? Within this category of law, there are two kinds: **eternal** or **temporal**. **Eternal law** refers to the unchanging order of things as it exists in the mind of God. In other words, the eternal law is the way God's intellect and will have determined that things in the entire universe will be, in keeping with the kind of universe He has chosen to create. This is the law by which He governs all that is. Because God is eternal -- without beginning or end -- His thinking about the universe which He governs will also be eternal. This is why we call it the eternal law. All other laws are **temporal** laws because they have a beginning and an end. They are made in time.

Eternal - infinite in past and future duration; without beginning or end.

Eternal law - the unchanging order of things as it exists in the mind of God.

Temporal - from Latin *temporale* (a point in time); lasting or existing only for a time; passing, temporary.

```
        According to
          Duration
         /        \
  Eternal Law   Temporal Law
```

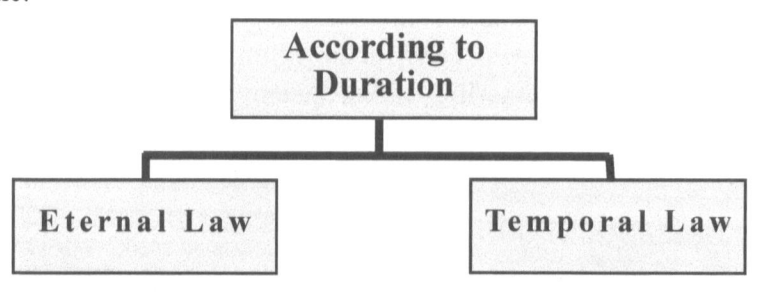

2. Law can be categorized according to way it is *promulgated*. Within this category of law, there again are two kinds: **natural** or **positive**. When law is made known by the very nature of the creature it governs, then it is called **natural law**. For example, we know about the law of gravity from seeing its effects on the things it governs *(natu-*

Natural law - moral law which is made known by man's very nature.

---
[3] See Austin Fagothey, S.J., *Right and Reason*, pp. 167-168.

ral physical law). We also know about how we ought to act sexually simply by understanding the functioning of our own bodies *(natural moral law)*.

Clearly, then, physical laws as well as moral laws can be included under this category of natural law. Usually we refer to physical laws known naturally as the *laws of nature*, and we refer to moral laws which are known naturally as the **natural law**.

The other way law can be promulgated is by means of an external sign of some sort by which the law is "laid down" or "posited." For example, road signs make known the law of the road regarding the speed limit. Our nation made known its own laws when it ratified its *Constitutions*. The Catholic Church made known its law when it approved what is called the *Code of Canon Law*. Even God Himself can spell out His law by means of an external sign, as He did when He gave Moses the Ten Commandments. Each of these is an example of law which has been "posited" or laid down, and so it is called **positive law**.

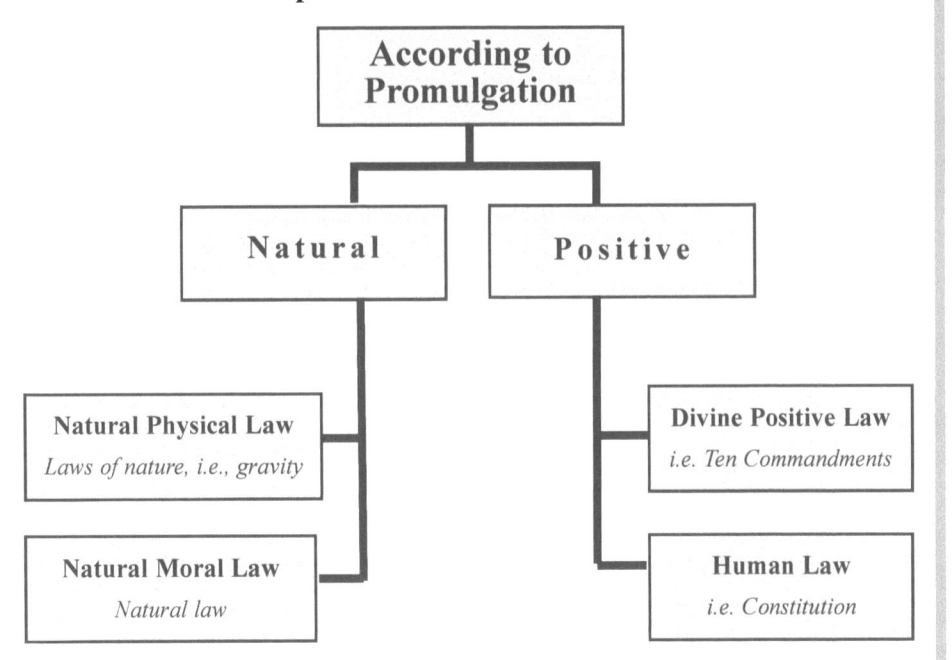

Positive law - from Latin *ponere* (to place, put, lay down); law which has been formally laid down or imposed; law made known to us by an external sign.

```
                According to
                Promulgation
                /          \
           Natural        Positive

Natural Physical Law         Divine Positive Law
Laws of nature, i.e., gravity   i.e. Ten Commandments

Natural Moral Law            Human Law
Natural law                  i.e. Constitution
```

3. Law can be categorized according to its *origin*. Within this category of law, there again are two kinds: **divine law** or **human law**. If God is the origin, then the law is divine. If human beings are the origin, then the law is human. Both the eternal and the natural law (physical and moral) are divine law. There is also such a thing as divine positive law: that is, law "laid down" whenever God intervenes in human history and reveals His law by means of an external sign. The Ten Commandments would be an example of divine positive law. Because these are divine, they are unchanging, just as

Divine law - law of which God is the origin.

Human law - law of which human persons are the origin.

Called to Happiness ~ Guiding Ethical Principles

NOTES

God Himself is unchanging. Human law, on the other hand, will always be both temporal and positive. There are two kinds of human law: ecclesiastical or civil, depending on whether it is the law of the Church or of the state.

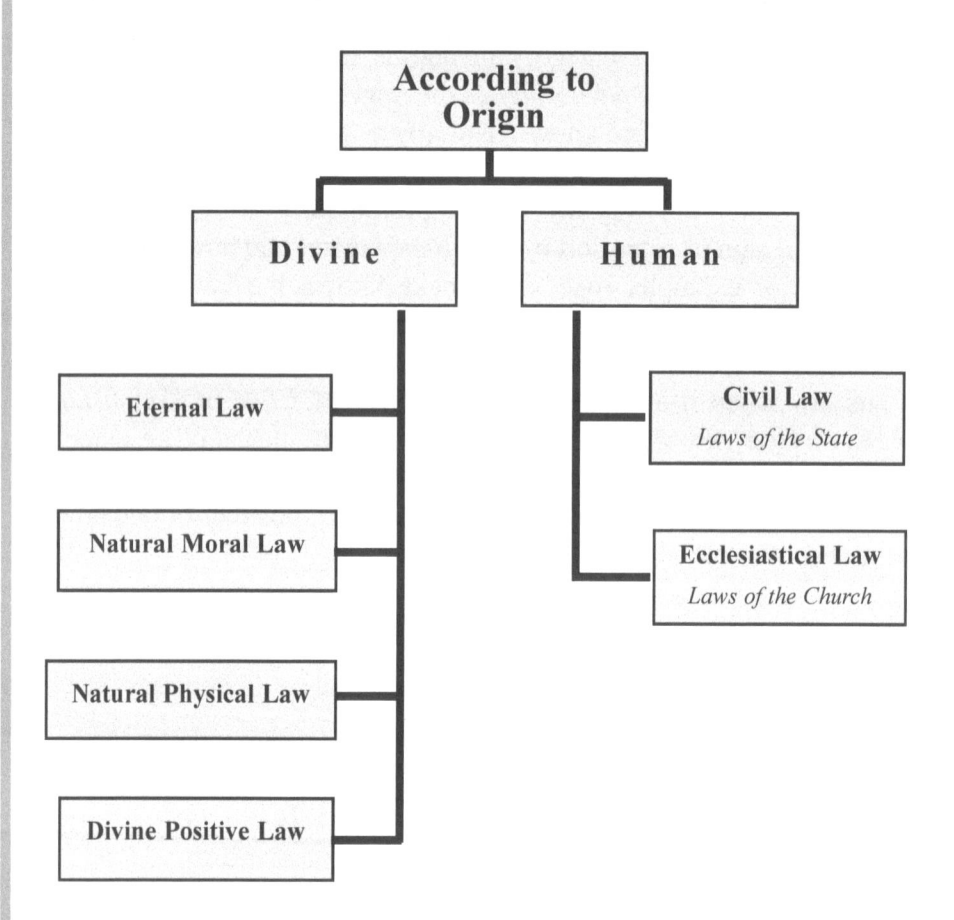

```
                    According to
                       Origin
                   ┌──────┴──────┐
                Divine         Human
           ┌──────┤              ├──────┐
       Eternal Law               Civil Law
                                 Laws of the State

       Natural Moral Law         Ecclesiastical Law
                                 Laws of the Church

       Natural Physical Law

       Divine Positive Law
```

Perhaps at this point it might be helpful to view all the kinds of laws we have been discussing as they relate to each other. Notice in the diagram below that the eternal law is the most all-encompassing. This is because it expresses the order of everything that exists as the mind of the Creator knows it and wants it to be. Every other kind of law is subordinate to the eternal law.

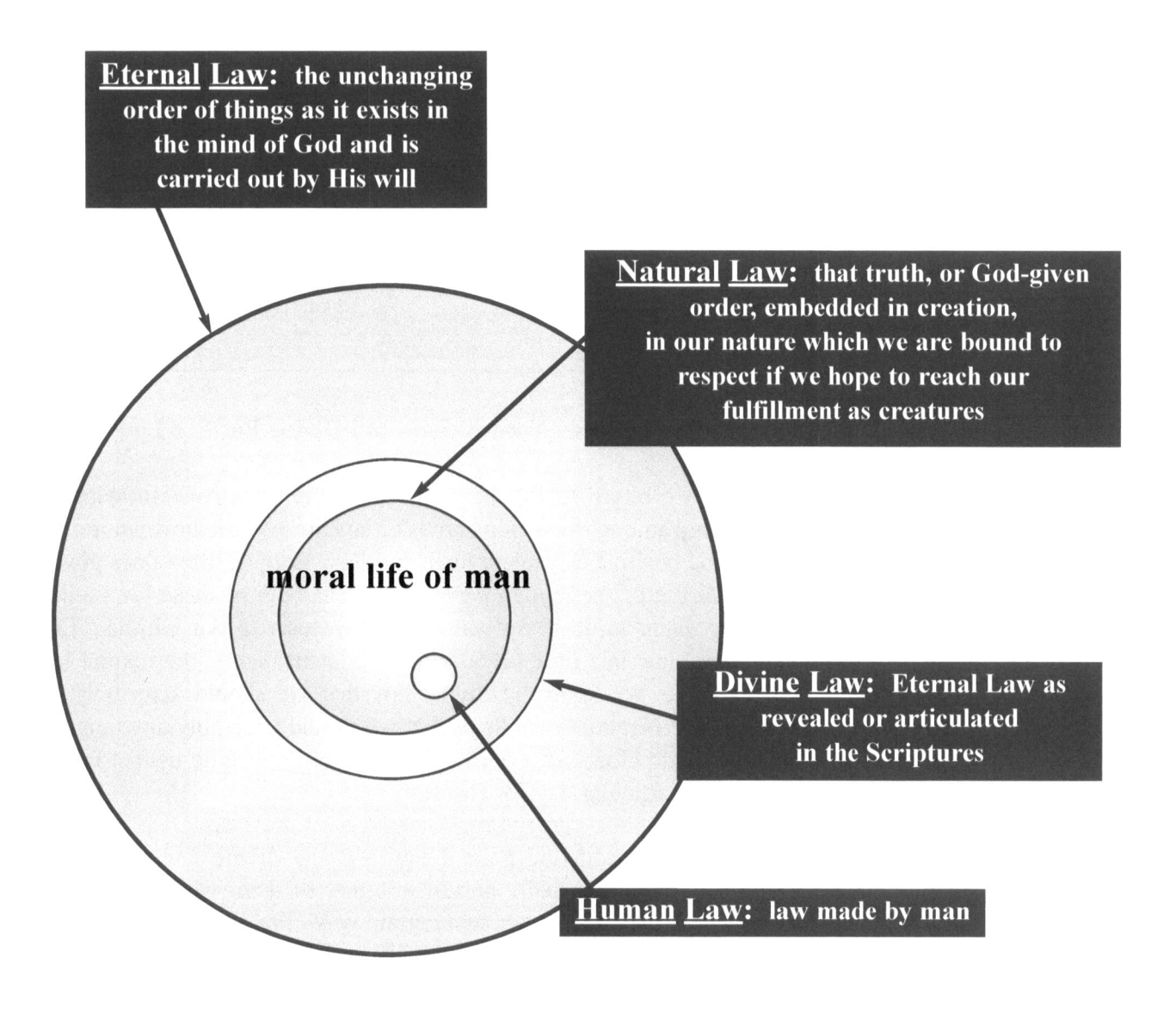

Eternal Law: the unchanging order of things as it exists in the mind of God and is carried out by His will

Natural Law: that truth, or God-given order, embedded in creation, in our nature which we are bound to respect if we hope to reach our fulfillment as creatures

moral life of man

Divine Law: Eternal Law as revealed or articulated in the Scriptures

Human Law: law made by man

The Moral Life of Man

Within the jurisdiction of the eternal law, we find the moral life of man. Just as the human body is subject to the physical laws of nature, so too is man's moral life subject to the moral law. In other words, just as the Creator has arranged the physical world so that everything moves as it should in order to reach their ends, so too has the Creator arranged the moral realm. Thus, the moral law to which we are bound reflects the Creator's plan for how we human beings are to achieve our Ultimate End.

We have seen that everything is subject to the eternal law. Human persons differ, however, in that we are able to *know* this law to some extent and to move ourselves *freely* to our End. All other earthly beings move towards their ends blindly and automatically. Of

"Happy those who do not follow the counsel of the wicked, ... Rather, the law of the Lord is their joy; God's law they study day and night."

Psalm 1:1-2

course, unlike everything else, we humans are also able to choose freely to act *contrary* to the law and thus are able not to attain our End.

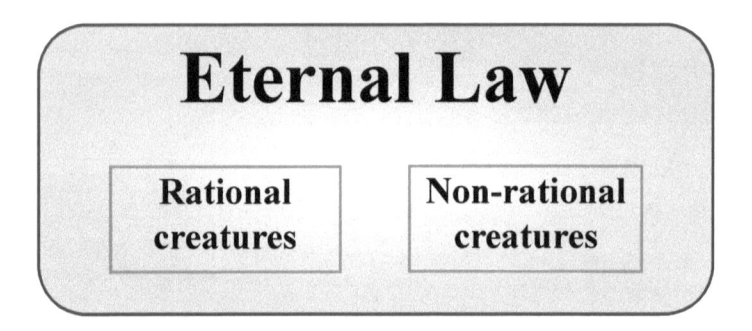

Eternal Law
- Rational creatures
- Non-rational creatures

Relationship between Natural Law and Divine Positive Law

If we return to the diagram on the previous page showing the relationship among the various kinds of law, we will see how natural law and divine positive law relate to each other. Both of these laws govern the moral life of the human person. That is, both of these laws tell us what we *ought* to do if we want to move closer to our Ultimate End. The divine law is a little broader in its content than is the natural law. For example, we know by divine law that we should keep holy the Lord's Day. Natural law tells us that we should keep holy anything that has to do with God, but it does not specifically reveal to us that He has set aside a particular day for Himself.

Because both the natural law and the divine law govern our moral acts, we can usually appeal to either of them when we want to explain why we *ought* to act in a certain way. For example, in explaining why direct abortion is morally evil, we can cite the Fifth Commandment or *Evangelium Vitae*, Pope John Paul II's encyclical on the life issues. However, we could also simply cite the scientific evidence regarding the humanity of the unborn being and point out that any rational person knows that it is wrong directly to kill an innocent human being.

Relationship of Human Law to Divine and Natural Law

Finally, notice the place where human law fits into the diagram. It, too, has something to say about how human beings *ought* to act. For example, human law tells us that we *ought* to drive our cars under a particular speed on certain roads. This human law is binding precisely because what it is telling us to do -- drive so as to protect human life -- is within the command of both the divine and natural law. In other words, diving recklessly violates not only civil law, but also the divine and natural law.

Authority that governs according to reason places citizens in a relationship not so much of subjection to another person as of obedience to the moral order and, therefore, to God himself who is its ultimate source. Whoever refuses to obey an authority that is acting in accordance with the moral order 'resists what God has appointed' *(Rom 13:2)*. Analogously, whenever public authority -- which has its foundation in human nature and belongs to the order pre-ordained by God -- fails to seek the common good, it abandons its proper purpose and so delegitimizes itself.[4]

If a civil law is given which does in fact violate the divine or natural law, then that law is unreasonable and will not lead us to our Ultimate End. Because of this, that civil law would not be binding; *strictly speaking*, it would not be a law. We should not obey it precisely because we have an obligation to obey the moral law. St. Thomas explains:

> Human law is law inasmuch as it is in conformity with right reason, and thus derives from the eternal law. But when a law is contrary to reason, it is called an unjust law; but in this case it ceases to be a law and becomes instead an act of violence.[5]

> Every law made by man can be called a law insofar as it derives from the natural law. But if it is somehow opposed to the natural law, then it is not really a law but rather a corruption of the law.[6]

This is why people were morally correct to disobey the civil law in Nazi Germany. They were actually obeying a "higher law." This is also why in our own country we *ought* not to obey any civil law which tells us to act against the moral law.

"This universal moral law (natural law) provides a sound basis for all cultural, religious and political dialogue, and it ensures that the multifaceted pluralism of cultural diversity does not detach itself from the common quest for truth, goodness and God."
Benedict XVI, *Charity in Truth*, #59

---

[4] *Compendium of the Social Doctrine of the Church*, #398.
[5] St. Thomas Aquinas, *Summa Theologiae*, I-II, q. 93, a.3, ad 2.
[6] Ibid., q. 95, a. 2.

NOTES

Study Guide Questions:

1. How would you explain to someone that the moral law is just as binding as the physical laws of nature?

2. What is the purpose of moral law? If you could, would it be wise to eliminate it?

3. Just because someone in authority makes a statement and declares it to be law, it is not necessarily a law. Explain.

4. What advantage do people have if they are living in a country that is governed by laws that are just?

5. Both rational and non-rational creatures are governed by law. How do they differ in terms of this law?

6. Of what benefit would it be for a person to know how to explain a moral issue from natural law as well as from divine law?

7. How would you draw the diagram (p. 45) showing the relationship among the various kinds of law if the civil law being represented was not in agreement with the moral law?

Chapter III
Moral Law and Freedom

CASES IN POINT

#1 -- The Freedom of Choice Act (FOCA) is legislation that, if enacted, would repeal all federal and state restrictions on abortion, including the ban on partial-birth abortion. It would force all hospitals and health programs offering maternity services to provide abortions. Moreover, it would invalidate any state provisions that protect the speech and the free exercise of religion of those whose conscience is opposed to abortion. Many doctors and nurses would be forced to choose between losing their careers and being compelled to participate in abortions against their moral and religious belief.

- *What would you do if you were a doctor or nurse working in the United States of America?*

- *In Evangelium Vitae, #73, Saint John Paul II tells us that there is a grave and clear obligation to oppose unjust laws by conscientious objection. What good does conscientious objection do?*

- *How would you respond to someone who tells you that the law forced him to participate in some unethical medical practices?*

* * * * *

#2 -- Dr. Martin Luther King, Jr., an important civil rights leader in our nation's history, invoked the moral and natural law to explain just and unjust laws and why civil disobedience is sometimes called for: "One has not only a legal but a moral responsibility to obey just laws. Conversely, one has a moral responsibility to disobey unjust laws. ... An unjust law is no law at all. ... How does one determine whether a law is just or unjust? A just law is a man-made code that squares with the moral law or the law of God. An unjust law is a code that is out of harmony with the moral law. To put it in terms of St. Thomas Aquinas: an unjust law is a human law that is not rooted in the eternal law and natural law. Any law that uplifts the human personality is just. Any law that degrades the human personality is unjust."

- *In light of Dr. King's thinking, what would be his ultimate reason for civil disobedience?*

- *What would Dr. King have thought about the legalization of abortion?*

II. The Law of Our Human Nature

Because the natural law plays such a major role in the science of Ethics, it is essential that we understand it clearly. Let us take a little more time to look at it in depth.

God directs everything that He has created to its proper end. For example, He so ordered the universe that the sun shines; plants grow; birds fly; fish swim; and human beings think and talk. Eternal law expresses this "order towards ends" that God wants to exist in creation. The eternal law itself, however, is *in the mind of God*. As it applies to human creatures it is called **natural law**. In other words, natural law refers to this "order towards ends" as it exists *in the creatures* God made. He stamped it on their natures when He created them. In a sense, we could say that the natural law is an *effect* of the eternal law -- an effect *in time*.

The natural law reveals itself through the very nature of things, that is, through what a thing is, how it acts, the way it is put together, its purpose. As we saw earlier, when the natural law manifests itself through non-rational creatures, we call it the *natural physical law* or the *law of nature*. For example, birds are acting in accord with the "law of their nature" when they fly south for the winter or when they build their nests the way they do.

When the natural law manifests itself through rational creatures, we call it the *natural moral law* or simply the *natural law*. It is this law which is so key to our study of Ethics, because this law has been "stamped into our nature" by the Creator so that we are able knowingly and freely to act according to it, and thus direct ourselves to our Ultimate End. Perhaps we can see now why St. Thomas Aquinas defined the natural law the way he does:

"The natural law is nothing else than the rational creature's participation of the eternal law."[7]

NOTES

"Ever since the creation of the world, God's invisible attributes of eternal power and divinity have been able to be understood and perceived in what he has made."
Romans 1:20

Natural law - the eternal law as it applies to and exists in human creatures.

"What the law requires is written on their hearts."
Romans 2:15

"It follows that the natural law is *itself the eternal law*, implanted in beings endowed with reason, and inclining them *towards their right action and end.*"
Leo XIII,
Libertas Praestantissimum, 219.

Eternal Law

Rational creatures	Non-rational creatures
Natural law	*Laws of nature*

---

[7] St. Thomas Aquinas, *Summa Theologiae*, I-II, q. 91, a. 2.

Notice that all other creatures on the earth are directed *blindly* and *necessarily* to their ends by the laws of nature. For example, trees lose their leaves in the fall and grow them back in the spring. Birds fly south for the winter and return in the spring. Only the human person is able *freely* to move himself toward his End. This testifies to our great dignity: we are actually able to govern our own actions. By means of the natural law we can *know* the eternal law as it applies to us, and then we can *freely* cooperate with God's plan. Thus, human beings are given a certain "partnership" with God in bringing about His eternal will.

Another aspect of the natural law which testifies to our dignity is the fact that it does not come to us by means of something *external* which is imposed on us *from the outside*. Rather, unlike any other kind of law, the natural law comes to us *completely from within*, so to speak. In the case of all law, our intellects *ultimately* promulgate it to us because it is our intellects that come to understand the law as applying to us. In the case of all other law, however, the intellect does this with the aid of some external decree which makes known the mind of the lawgiver. For example, with Divine Law the intellect has the help of Sacred Scripture, and with civil law the intellect has the aid of written documents. With natural law, however, our intellects have no external aid. The intellect promulgates natural law once the intellect itself has rationally reflected *on human nature* and its relation to the Creator. This is precisely why we call it *natural law*: it comes to us from God, not written on stone tablets or in the pages of the Bible, but "on the human heart," that is, deep within the person. Let's see how the process works.

Because the human person has a rational nature, he is able to discover the natural law by using his rational powers as he thinks about his own nature. Reflecting on himself and on others around him, his intellect is able to understand the needs of human nature and to make judgments regarding human acts. If an act helps to meet the needs of his nature, then he knows that it is a good act and that he *ought* to do it. If an act fails to meet human needs or actually works against them, then he knows that that act is bad and that he *ought* not to do it. Notice that it is his own intellect, after rationally reflecting on his own nature, that tells him what he *ought* to do.

For example, a person can come to the conclusion that eating dirt and drinking gasoline is not a good thing for him to do after he reflects on the nature of his digestive system. He could also discover that he should not put food into his ear. If he wants the food to nourish his body, then he needs to put the food into his mouth so that it can be digested.

A further, more serious example of "discovering natural law"

NOTES

"[N]atural law ... is nothing other than the light of understanding infused in us by God, whereby we understand what must be done and what must be avoided."
Saint John Paul,
The Splendor of Truth, #12

"The moral law has its origin in God and always finds its source in him: at the same time, by virtue of natural reason, which derives from divine wisdom, it is *a properly human law."*
Saint John Paul,
The Splendor of Truth, #40

"God provides for man differently from the way in which he provides for beings which are not persons. He cares for man not 'from without,' through the laws of physical nature, but 'from within' through reason, which, by its natural knowledge of God's eternal law, is consequently able to show man the right direction to take in his free actions."
Saint John Paul,
The Splendor of Truth, #43

Called to Happiness ~ Guiding Ethical Principles

NOTES

"...[M]an needs to look inside himself in order to recognize the fundamental norms of the natural moral law which God has written on our hearts."

Benedict XVI,
Charity in Truth, #68

might help to clarify the process. Let us use human sexuality to illustrate. From observing and studying the human body, a person can realize that the male and female bodies are different and that they are both sexually incomplete. Their sexual bodily differences *serve a purpose*: they enable the two bodies to unite in such a way that they can do *together* something which neither of them is able to do alone. They can form one "sexual whole" which has the potential of bringing forth new human life. Our bodily differences -- our sexuality -- are "ordered to an end" that we can figure out: they are ordered to procreation. This is one of the purposes of the sexual differences with which the Creator has fashioned us as human persons.

Any "sexual act" in which a person engages -- if it is to be in line with the order of nature -- *ought* to involve the uniting of two people of the opposite sex so that the procreation of offspring is a possibility. Any use of our sexual powers which does not do this is *"dis-ordered."* This is how we come to understand by means of natural law that masturbation, contraception, and homosexual acts are **disordered** and that we *ought* not to do them if we want to act in accord with the will of God.

Disordered - lack of the regular or proper arrangement.

Virtual - from Latin *virtus* (faculty); possessing the capacity or faculty for producing a thing, even though we do not yet have the thing itself.

Formal - from Latin *formalis* (form); pertaining to the form of a thing; possessing a thing actually.

Insofar as every human person has an intellect which has the potential for reflecting on himself and making moral judgments, we say that we all have natural law -- at least in a **virtual** state. *Virtual* means that we possess the capacity or power to have the natural law, even though that power has not yet been actualized. Regarding those of us who have actually exercised our reasoning power with regard to our own nature and have made correct moral judgments regarding our obligations, we say that we possess the natural law **formally**. *Formal* means that we have actualized our capacity for the natural law; we now possess it essentially. The science of Ethics is designed to help us possess the natural law formally and not merely virtually.

Why Don't We All Know It?

If the natural law is the Creator's way of helping us to our Ultimate End, then why doesn't everyone -- or at least why don't most people -- possess it *formally*? Why are there some who seem to be oblivious to its obligations? Is there a problem with its being made known?

52.

St. Thomas answers these questions by explaining that the natural law is made up of **precepts** which vary in their degrees of importance for the well being of humanity. Those precepts which are more fundamental, and thus more important, are indeed possessed *formally* by all normal and mature people. Those which are derived from these more fundamental precepts are not as widely known, but they are also not as essential for mankind's well being.

The more general a precept of natural law is, the better known it will be, St. Thomas says. There is a much greater chance that people will be ignorant or confused about precepts which are more particular. Let's take a closer look at the various levels of knowledge concerning the natural law:[8]

1. There is the most fundamental precept of the natural law, its first principle: "**Do good and avoid evil**." This precept is *self-evident* to everyone who is able to think. No evidence has to be given to prove this principle. A person can see its truth immediately.

2. There are other general precepts of the natural law which are *based on* the first principle. These precepts express natural inclinations we share with other creatures, such as, "Preserve your own life," "Care for your offspring," "Do not kill an innocent person," "Do not take what belongs to another." These are known by all persons who have normal intelligence, are mature, and have received an adequate moral education. So, for example, if a person is raised by people who teach him that human life has no value, then his moral development might be stunted. Because he is not in a normal condition, it is possible for him not to know that he should not directly kill an innocent person. This just reinforces for us how important adequate moral formation is for everyone.

3. There are other precepts of the natural law that are more distant from the first principle. These are remote conclusions of a longer reasoning process. While these conclusions are certainly true and the reasoning is valid, a person with an untrained mind probably would not be able to know them. Even a person with a trained mind might not know them if he is not really interested in knowing the truth or if he is living in a society which thinks otherwise. Examples of precepts that fall into this category would be the following: "Mercy killing is wrong," "Divorce and remarriage is wrong," "Contraception is wrong," "Artificial human reproduction is wrong." Because even educated people can be ignorant of the truth of these precepts, we see again why the science of Ethics is needed.

---

[8] See Austin Fagothey, S.J., *Right and Reason*, pp. 178-181.

NOTES

Precept - from Latin *praeceptum* (a rule, command); an authoritative command to do some particular act; an order.

"Natural law is nothing else but an imprint on us of the divine light."
St. Thomas Aquinas,
Summa Theologiae, I-II, 91, 2

NOTES

"Inasmuch as the natural law expresses the dignity of the human person and lays the foundation for his fundamental rights and duties, it is universal in its precepts and its authority extends to all mankind."
Saint John Paul,
The Splendor of Truth, #51

4 There are applications of the precepts of the natural law to particular cases. For example, if an employee at a fast food restaurant is asked by a homeless man for a handout just before closing time, it would be wrong for the employee to give away food which would otherwise be discarded unless he either has the permission of his boss to do so or he pays for the food himself. In this example, the precept which tells us that it is wrong to take what does not belong to us is being applied to a specific case. It is possible for normal and mature people who have received an adequate moral formation not to know how to apply precepts correctly to particular cases, even though they do know the precepts of the natural law.

This variation among people in their awareness of the precepts of the natural law and their application to particular cases explains *to some extent* why there is so much disagreement on moral matters. Even though we all possess the natural law *virtually*, those of us who possess it *formally* do so in varying degrees. If we all did possess it formally to the highest degree possible, then there would be no disagreement among us on moral matters. We would readily see the truth about how we *ought* to act. This truth expressed by the natural law would be the same for us all because it is based on the human nature which we all share.

Study Guide Questions:

1. How are the eternal law and the natural law the same? How do they differ?

2. What is the purpose of the natural law?

3. How does the **natural law** differ from the **laws of nature**? Give an example of each.

4. If everything created is governed by eternal law, is there really much difference between the way we are governed and the way non-rational creatures are governed? Explain.

5. How does a person become aware of the natural law?

6. What does it mean to say that a human act is "disordered"? Give an example of a disordered act.

7. What really is the difference between possessing the natural law <u>formally</u> and possessing it only <u>virtually</u>?

8. Give an example of a precept of the natural law which would be considered to be very fundamental and thus also very important for the well being of humanity.

9. If the natural law is so readily available to us all, why is there so much disagreement among us about moral issues?

CASE IN POINT

In an interview with J. Budziszewski, professor of government and philosophy at the University of Texas, Budziszewski was asked why people today so willingly ignore even the basics of the natural law which they apparently "cannot not know." He said the following:

"One reason is latency: It's possible to know something without knowing that you know it. The complementarity of the sexes is like that; it may not even occur to you until someone calls it to your attention.

"Another reason is denial: It's possible to know something and yet tell yourself you don't. Usually, we play such tricks on ourselves either because we know something is wrong but want to do it very much -- or because we've already done it, and conscience is too painful to face. Denial is a much more serious problem than latency, because a person or a culture in denial resists being taught.

"A third reason is rationalization: We make excuses for doing wrong not because we don't know it's wrong, but because we do.... For example, the feminist Eileen McDonagh admits that it's wrong to deliberately take innocent human life, but she says that the fetus isn't innocent -- it's an aggressive intruder in the woman's womb."

"Natural Law in Our Lives, in Our Courts," Part 2, *Zenit.org*, 2004

- *Give an example from your own life or from modern culture of each of these three reasons for ignoring natural law.*

- *What moral responsibility do we have for the evil we do when we use one of the above reasons for being "ignorant" of moral law?*

III. Rights and Duties[9]

Because terms such as "right" and "duty" are mentioned in any discussion of law and justice, it is not surprising that they would have a place in the study of ethics. We have all heard the phrases "human rights," "civil rights," and "animal rights." What are these phrases actually telling us about our responsibility to act in certain ways?

What is a right?

The word *right* has two meanings, both of which stem from the same basic idea referring to what *ought* to be the case:

(a) *Right* as morally good -- that which is in line with the moral norm.
How I *ought* to act: "I am *right* in paying them a just wage."

(b) *Right* as corresponding to duty -- that which is just.
How others *ought* to act toward me: "I have the *right* to an annual vacation."

Because we have an obligation to obey the moral law, we must be guaranteed the *means* we need in order to do so. This entails that we have the *power* to do whatever is necessary to keep the moral law as well as the *power* to keep others from stopping or interfering with us. Rights give us this *power*; they *empower* us to obey the moral law.

There are two kinds of power:

(a) *Physical power (might)* -- This is the bodily strength of one person or of those under his command which enables him to secure the end he seeks. Included in physical power would be not only that of the physical bodies of persons but also that of all of their weapons and machinery. Physical power achieves its end by mere force, regardless of claims of justice. It can be used both to aid or to hinder the observance of the moral law. Thus, in itself, might is morally neutral. Its moral quality will depend on how it is used.

Might does not make *right*!

(b) *Moral power (right)* -- The strength of moral power comes from its appeal to another person's will through his intellect to act in accord with moral law. The *right* tells the person that I am claiming something as mine, and

---

[9] See Austin Fagothey, S.J., *Right and Reason*, pp. 238-262.

he must respect my claim if he is to attain his own Ultimate End. In other words, if he chooses to disregard my right, he does an evil act for which he will be held responsible. A right *morally binds* the free will of another person. It is possible for others physically to infringe on my rights, especially if they have more bodily strength than I have. They cannot do so, however, without taking on moral guilt. This is what we mean when we say that a right is *morally **inviolable***.

Three uses of the term *right*:

<u>First</u>, in the *primary sense* of the term, a **right** is *the moral power to do, hold, or exact something*. The right "to do" includes both the right to act as well as the right not to act. For example, a person might have the right to remain silent as well as the right to speak. The right "to hold" means the right to own or use something, even to hold an office or a job. The right "to exact something" means the right to demand that others act in a certain way. For example, a police officer has the right to direct people who are driving their cars.

<u>Second</u>, we can transfer use of the term *right* from *the one who has* the right to *that over which* he has the right. Thus, we sometimes speak of a person being "denied his rights." No one can take a person's rights away from him, if what we mean by that is the *moral power* he has to claim something as his own. If we could, then he would no longer be able *rightfully* to make the claim to any rights. What we can take away from him, however, is the thing to which he has a right. This is precisely what the person means when he says that his rights were denied: "They did not *respect* my right to claim something as my own."

<u>Third</u>, rights are expressed in law.[10] Law establishes obligations, and rights point out these obligations. Thus, just as there are different names for law, so there are different names for the rights which are expressed in them: natural or positive rights; divine or human rights; ecclesiastical or civil rights. Because the basis of natural law is human nature itself, it can be said that natural rights have their basis in the nature of the human person. The basis of positive law is whatever is truly good for the person.[11]

Components of a Right

A right is made up of four components:
(a) The one possessing a right *(the Subject)*
(b) The one obligated to respect or fulfill a right *(the Term)*
(c) That to which a person has a right *(the Matter)*
(d) The reason why this subject has this right *(the Title)*

Let us take the example of the owner of a house who intends to

---

[10] St. Thomas Aquinas, *Summa Theologiae*, II-II, q.57, a. 1, ad 2.
[11] *Note:* If positive law is unjust, then it fails to meet the criteria for the definition of law, and thus it also fails to establish any true obligations.

NOTES

Inviolable - from Latin *inviolare* (not to do violence to); secure from violation or assault.

Right - the moral power to do, hold, or exact something; an appeal to the will of another through his intellect. to act in accord with moral law.

Called to Happiness ~ Guiding Ethical Principles

NOTES

"Man ... is a *person* -- a spiritual being, a whole unto himself, a being that exists for itself and of itself, that wills its own proper perfection. Therefore, and *for that very reason*, something *is* due to man in the fullest sense, *for that reason* he does inalienably have a *suum*, a 'right' which he can plead against everyone else, a right which imposes upon every one of his partners the obligation at least not to violate it."
Joseph Pieper,
The Four Cardinal Virtues, p. 50

"Where the immutability of human nature is called into question, human rights cannot exist. Human rights are sacrosanct only because they are inscribed in our (immutable) human natures. They can be enshrined in such international conventions as the 1948 Universal Declaration of Human Rights, but they do not derive from such sources."
Alexandre Havard,
Virtuous Leadership, p. 95

sell it. The owner is the <u>subject</u> of the right to a just payment. The buyer of the house is the <u>term</u> of the right for he is obligated to make the just payment. The just payment for the house is the actual <u>matter</u> of the right. The conferring of ownership of the house from the owner to the buyer is the <u>title</u> of the right, for this explains why the owner possesses the right.

<u>Only a person can be the *subject* and the *term* of a right.</u> Rights exist precisely to make it possible for us to observe the moral law and thus to reach our Ultimate End. Only persons are able to know the law and only we have free will whereby we can heed it. All other earthly creatures, because they act without freedom or responsibility, have no need of rights. Nor are they able to fulfill a right.

<u>A person may never be the *matter* of a right</u>. No person may be subordinated to another, to be merely used by him as a means to his own end. All persons are equal in dignity. Each is gifted with an intellect and a will whereby he can establish his own ends. Thus, each person is self-owned, self-possessed, the master of his own acts. Each is ordered directly to *God Himself*. We can use the *labor* of others, if they do the labor willingly and we compensate them for it, for society is based on the constant interchange of goods and services, but we cannot use the persons themselves. Thus human *labor* can be the matter of a right, but not human persons.

Saint John Paul stated this principle in what he called the *Personalistic Norm*: ***A person should not be treated merely as an object of use and, as such, the means to an end. The only proper and adequate way to relate to a person is with love, which means that we must treat him as an equal.***[12]

You do not have to be a Catholic, however, to know this to be true. The German philosopher Immanuel Kant understood it as well:

> Beings whose existence does not depend on our will but on nature, if they are not rational beings have only a relative worth as means and are therefore called 'things;' on the other hand, rational beings are designated 'persons,' because their nature indicates that they are ends in themselves, i.e., things which may not be used merely as means.[13]

---

[12] Karol Wojtyla, *Love and Responsibility*, pp. 40-41.
[13] Immanuel Kant, *Foundations of the Metaphysics of Morals*, section II.

What is a duty?

A **duty** is a person's *obligation to do or not to do something.* We can also speak of duty as that which a person is obligated to do or not do. Thus, we could say that a person has a duty to be honest. We could also say that in telling the truth, a person has done his duty.

Rights and duties always go together -- at least they do for human persons.[14] If I have a *right* to do, to hold, or to exact something, then everyone else has a *duty* to respect my right. Similarly, if I have a *duty* to do or not do something, then someone else has a *right* that I am bound to respect. Even if there is no human person who has a right, I may still be bound by the rights of God Himself. This is why suicide is wrong: It does not respect the rights of my Creator. I have a duty to Him to preserve my life.

Rights are limited by duties. If the exercise of my rights violates the rights of another person, then I have reached the limit of my rights, for my duty to respect the rights of others "trumps" my own rights. For example, I have the right to express my thoughts to others, but not when doing so will harm the reputation of another person. That other person has a *right* to a good reputation, and I have a *duty* to respect that right.

Duties are expressed in law, just as rights are. Thus we can have natural or positive duties, divine or human duties, ecclesiastical or civil duties.

Study Guide Questions:

1) Identify the three meanings of right illustrated in the following sentence: "When a homeless person was unjustly deprived of his <u>rights</u> through his arrest, a lawyer appealed to the code of civil <u>rights</u> and obtained for him a release from jail to which he has a <u>right</u>."

2) "Right and might are two different things because there can be right without might and might without right." Explain.

3) What law is the basis of 'natural rights'? To what do you think the term "God-given rights" refers?

4) In light of what you now understand about the meaning of 'right' and 'duty,' how would you respond to a person who claims that a woman can have an abortion because she has a 'right to do what she wants with her own body'?

5) What is a duty? How does it relate to a right?

6) Are a person's rights unlimited? Explain.

---

[14] God has rights but no duties. Human persons have duties to God, but we have no rights in regard to Him.

NOTES

Duty - a person's obligation to do or not to do something or that which a person is obligated to do or not do.

"...[R]ights presuppose duties, if they are not to become mere licence."
    Benedict XVI,
    Charity in Truth, #43

"An overemphasis on rights leads to a disregard for duties."
    Benedict XVI,
    Charity in Truth, #43

"Duties thereby reinforce rights and call for their defense and promotion as a task to be undertaken in the service of the common good."
    Benedict XVI,
    Charity in Truth, #43

"The animal rights movement is irrational because if animals had rights, the only species that would be required to honor those rights would be people. Animals would not have an obligation to honor each other's rights because they don't understand the concept. Nor do they have the obligation to honor our rights, because they don't have the capacity to understand the concept. Animals cannot be rights-bearing because they are not duties-bearing beings. They're amoral."
    Wesley J. Smith,
    "Nihilism as Compassion"

Called to Happiness ~ Guiding Ethical Principles

CASES IN POINT

#1 -- "I've heard it said that some people like their dogs more than they like most people. I have no doubt that I am one of those people.

"My dog was recently diagnosed with diabetes. If we're conscientious with his treatment program, he will endure daily blood testing, insulin injections, a diet free of sugar and will likely go blind. But if we aren't careful, he's in for much worse: seizures, deafness, even premature death.

"Veterinarian visits, syringes, insulin, special food, rearranged schedules, vitamins, pills, and a blood-testing kit have already cost my family in excess of $1,000.

"This is privileged treatment compared to what I'm willing to give most people, including those starving in Third World countries. If someone were to show up at my door tomorrow asking for $1,000 to save the life of some far-away person, I wouldn't bat an eye before shaking my head and shutting the door."

"I love my dog more than you," by TJ Wihera, in *The Denver Post*, Feb. 17, 2008.

- *Do rights and duties help to clarify the problem with the author's perspective? Explain.*
- *Does the author have a duty which he is failing to respect?*

* * * * *

#2 -- There is a worldwide trend toward granting animals, plants and even things such as streams juridical "rights." For example:

"Spain will soon grant rights to life and freedom to all 350 apes there, making it a penal violation to keep apes for experimentation, circuses, television commercials and filming, among other things.

"The European Court of Human Rights has agreed to hear a case from Austria in which activists want a chimpanzee declared a person [so that it can have the right to receive a monetary gift].

"The country's [Switzerland] Federal Ethics Committee on Non-Human Biotechnology issued a report calling it morally impermissible to cause arbitrary harm to plant life."

"Granting rights to apes, plants, even pond scum," by Thomas A. Szyszkiewicz, in *Our Sunday Visitor*, 10/19/08.

- *What does our world seem to be failing to understand about rights?*
- *Why is it not possible for us to grant rights to animals, plants, and streams?*

* * * * *

#3 -- In his encyclical *Charity in Truth*, Pope Benedict makes the following point concerning "rights and duties," as these are often treated in the world today:

"Nowadays we are witnessing a grave inconsistency. On the one hand, appeals are made to alleged rights, arbitrary and non-essential in nature, accompanied by the demand that they be recognized and promoted by public structures, while, on the other hand, elementary and basic rights remain unacknowledged and are violated in much of the world. A link has often been noted between claims to a 'right to excess', and even to transgression and vice, within affluent societies, and the lack of food, drinkable water, basic instruction and elementary health

Chapter III
Moral Law and Freedom

care in areas of the underdeveloped world and on the outskirts of large metropolitan centres. "

Benedict XVI, *Charity in Truth*, #43

- *What are some of the 'alleged rights' we hear about today?*
- *What basic rights are violated in our country, in the world?*

* * * * *

#4 -- It is not unusual for people today to equate the homosexual's demand for the "*right* to marry" with the struggle of Black Americans for their "civil *rights*." Even the President of the United States had the following comment to make regarding the matter: "I've called on Congress to repeal the so-called Defense of Marriage Act to help end discrimination, to help end discrimination against same-sex couples in this country."

"Voters Won't Decide on D.C. Gay Marriage," from CBN News, July 1, 2009

- *What law provides the basis of a so-called "right to marry"?*
- *What law provides the basis for our civil rights?*
- *Is it reasonable to equate the homosexual's demand for the "right to marry" with the struggle of black people for their "civil rights"? Explain.*
- *Is denying a person with homosexual inclinations the opportunity to "marry" a person of the same sex an act of unjust discrimination? Explain.*
- *What <u>duties</u> do we have regarding marriage that correspond to a person's rights?*

* * * * *

#5 -- The following was a question given to nursing students taking a course at a secular American college in July, 2009:

"Many health-care providers hold strong religious beliefs and/or personal preferences that are culturally bound and that have the potential to exert a significant influence on their practice. Several examples follow:

   * A health-care provider is a vegetarian who does not consume any meat or fish or any product that contains any ingredient derived from these sources. How might the provider's beliefs affect the following: (1) dietary counseling of patients, (2) prescription of cardioprotective supplements such as fish oil capsules containing omega-3 fatty acids.

   * A health-care provider believes that contraception and termination of pregnancy are morally wrong under any circumstance. The provider cares for a culturally diverse group of patients who seek information about and prescriptions for birth control devices and pharmaceuticals as well as pregnancy testing and prenatal care. The Institute for Clinical Systems Improvement's Guideline for Routine Prenatal Care (2002) includes a recommendation that a maternal serum triple screen be offered to all pregnant women, optimally at 16 weeks of gestation, to determine whether the fetus is at potential risk for such conditions as Down Syndrome, neural tube defects such as spina bifida, and so on. If results are abnormal, the Guidelines recommend performing an ultrasound to accurately assess gestational age, presence of a neural tube defect, or other fetal abnormality which require counseling of the woman about the affect of the genetic defect on the fetus and exploring a variety of therapeutic options, including possible elective termination of the pregnancy. What actions should the health-care provider have to take to rectify his or her own moral preferences with the patient's cultural beliefs and right to comprehensive care?"

- *If you were a student taking this course, how would you respond to this assigned question?*
- *In the second example, what would you say about the patient's <u>right</u> to comprehensive care?*

IV. Law and Freedom

Before we complete our discussion of law, we need to investigate one last point: law's relationship to freedom. As Americans we all highly prize our freedom. As human persons, too, we treasure our ability freely to direct ourselves through life as a hallmark of our human nature, and as one of the reasons for our great dignity as creatures made in God's image. The question naturally arises, then: What does law do to my freedom? Many today think that law and freedom are in strong opposition to each other. St. Thomas would not necessarily agree. It all depends on what we understand freedom to be.

There are three different kinds of freedom, and they each correspond to different kinds of bonds or restraints which can limit them. Law is simply one kind of a restraint that *binds* those subject to it. Let's look a little closer at each kind of freedom:[15]

The <u>first</u> kind of freedom is the ability to move around as one pleases. This *freedom of movement* can be curtailed if a person is physically prevented from moving somehow, for example by being tied up, held down, locked up in prison, etc. While these bonds can *physically* force a person to a certain kind of *external* position or behavior, they cannot touch the *inner* act of his free will. In other words, someone might be able to force you to stand up, but he cannot make you *want* to stand up.

A <u>second</u> kind of freedom is the ability we humans have to make our own choices. We call this *freedom of choice* or *free will*. No other creature on this earth enjoys this kind of freedom. All other creatures are wholly bound by the laws of their natures. What they do is completely determined by the *inner physical necessity* of their natural instincts and tendencies. Human persons are different, however: our wills are not bound *from within* by any *physical necessity*. This is what we mean when we say that we can act *freely* or *voluntarily*.

A <u>third</u> kind of freedom is the ability to choose freely without experiencing the *moral* restraint of a commanding authority. This is *freedom from law* or what we usually call independence. Law binds the free will of human persons by imposing upon it a *moral necessity*. We experienced this kind of freedom as Americans after our nation won its independence from England. We became free from English law. A young person experiences this freedom when he becomes 18-years-old and is

---

[15] See Austin Fagothey, S.J., *Right and Reason*, pp. 164-166.

no longer obligated by the authority of his parents.

Notice that these three kinds of freedom do not have to include one another. A person can experience one kind of freedom without experiencing another. For example, a person's free will is still present although he is locked up in prison. A person might also be bound morally by law although he is free from any internal or external physical necessity.

One other point is worth noting as well: The first two kinds of freedom are always *good* for a human being to experience. The third, however, -- freedom from law -- is not *necessarily* good. For example, while it is good to experience independence from a wicked tyrant, it is not a good thing for a person to be free from *all* human law or from the natural moral law. As a citizen of a country or simply as someone living in common with other people, a person is helped by the civil law which governs him, *if it is a just law*. Also, because the natural moral law is there to help him achieve happiness, he will *always* be better off being bound by it. This is why no human being is or ever will be free from the natural moral law while he lives on earth. God wants our happiness; that's why the natural moral law exists in the first place.

Freedom for Happiness

Perhaps the main reason why people think that freedom and law stand in opposition to each other is because they think of freedom only as liberation *from* something. To be free, according to them, is to *not* feel any sort of an obligation to act one way or another. They view freedom as simply the license to do as they please. Thus, since law imposes on them an obligation to act in a certain way, they think it must be opposed to their freedom.

Law threatens *absolute* freedom.

What these people tend to forget about, however, is our natural desire for happiness. The goal is happiness, not freedom. Somehow such persons have fallen into the trap of thinking that the freedom to do as they please -- let's call it ***absolute freedom*** -- is the same thing as happiness. It would indeed be happiness *if* happiness were merely a *subjective* matter which we could determine for ourselves. In that case, whatever we chose to do would be truly good for us and thus make us happy. If happiness is purely subjective, then the freedom to do as we please *would be* happiness.

Chapter III
Moral Law and Freedom

NOTES

"Certain currents of modern thought have gone so far as to exalt freedom to such an extent that it becomes an absolute, which would then be the source of values."
Saint John Paul,
The Splendor of Truth, #32

"If it were possible to conceive of a human being in a state of absolute freedom, he would resemble a fish out of water...."
Andrei Tarkovsky,
Sculpting in Time

Absolute freedom - the ability to do as one pleases.

63.

Called to Happiness ~ Guiding Ethical Principles

NOTES

"This is our freedom, when we are subject to the truth, not merely one good among others; it is the highest good, the good that makes us happy."
St. Augustine,
De lib., II, 13[57], 15[59]

"Truth enlightens man's intelligence and shapes his freedom ...."
Saint John Paul II,
The Splendor of Truth, #1

"The frank and open acceptance of truth is the condition for authentic freedom."
Saint John Paul II,
The Splendor of Truth, #87

Genuine freedom - the ability to do the good act so as to achieve happiness.

"Genuine freedom is an outstanding manifestation of the divine image in man. For God willed to leave man 'in the power of his own counsel' (*cf. Sir. 15:14*), so that he would seek his Creator of his own accord and would freely arrive at full and blessed perfection by cleaving to God."
Gaudium et Spes, #17

"God's law does not reduce, much less do away with human freedom; rather, it protects and promotes that freedom."
Saint John Paul II,
The Splendor of Truth, #35

"Freedom, if it is not to lead to deceit and self-destruction, must orient itself by the truth, that is, by what we really are, and must correspond to our being."
Cardinal Joseph Ratzinger

Since, however, what is truly good for us is not up to us (that is, it is not our subjective choice), then happiness cannot be a purely subjective matter. Absolute freedom should not be what we want. In fact, doing as we please is precisely what can actually keep us from achieving the goal that we are all seeking: the true good that will lead us to happiness. Saint John Paul explains:

> [W]hat does it mean to be free? It means to know how to use one's freedom in truth -- to be 'truly' free. *To be truly free* does not at all mean doing everything that pleases me, or doing what I want to do. Freedom contains in itself the criterion of truth, the discipline of truth. To be truly free means *to use one's own freedom for what is a true good*.[16]

Cardinal Ratzinger[17] expresses this same idea when he writes: "Freedom is tied to a measure, the measure of reality -- to the truth."[18] Both Saint John Paul and Cardinal Ratzinger are simply reminding us that happiness is basically an *objective* matter. Because it is objective, we should try to cultivate a different view of the freedom we want, one which is dependent upon the <u>truth</u> regarding reality. We will call this freedom ***genuine freedom***. Genuine freedom is the ability to do *only* those acts that will <u>truly</u> make it possible for us to be happy. The adjective "genuine" is appropriate for this view of freedom because this freedom is fitting or appropriate for a creature who is bound by a nature which can be fulfilled only in certain *objective* ways.

Law   **Genuine Freedom**   **Law**

Law protects *genuine* freedom.

For example, absolute freedom would say that one could jump off of a 20-story building and try flying like a bird if he wants to. True, I can jump off and try to fly; but doing so will not really make me happy. I have a human nature which cannot be ignored if I want to be happy. My body will find itself crashing to the earth!

Genuine freedom would say that I *ought not* jump off of a 20-

---

[16] Saint John Paul, *Apostolic Letter to the Youth of the World,* 1985, #13.
[17] Cardinal Ratzinger, a long and trusted friend of Pope John Paul II, was elected to be his successor. He was then called Pope Benedict XVI.
[18] Cardinal Joseph Ratzinger, "Truth and Freedom," p. 28.

story building, in order that I can be free to continue living.

Did you notice that word *ought*? That word gives us a clue that law has a role to play in securing genuine freedom. Law and genuine freedom are not at all opposed. In fact, they work hand-in-hand. The moral law keeps us *from* doing bad acts; thus, it actually enhances our genuine freedom. It sets us free *for* achieving happiness. Being restrained from doing evil *frees* us *for* happiness. The moral law, then, *serves* our freedom. It protects our freedom to achieve happiness. Genuine freedom is the means to achieving our goal: happiness.

An easy way to see how these two different views of freedom relate to moral law and happiness is to consider the following story:

A person needs to cut through a piece of property that is about 5 acres in area in order to get to his goal. If he reaches the goal in the time allotted, he will receive a million dollars. There is one difficulty, however: the property is loaded with land mines that will explode and kill him if he steps on them. If you were this person, would you want to have a map accurately telling you where the land mines are located?

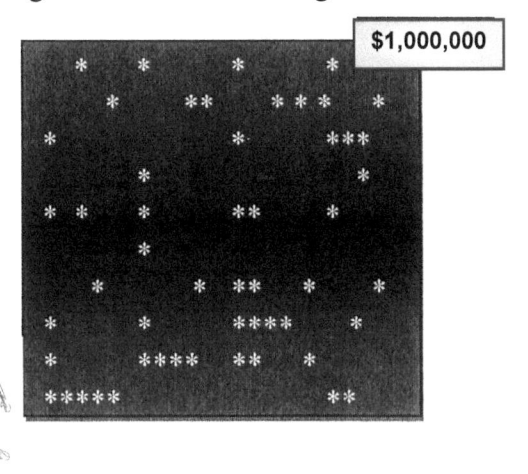

Your answer to this question will depend on what your goal is. If your goal is to be able to step wherever you please, then you will not want the map. The map would *hinder your freedom* to do as you please. If, on the other hand, your goal is to make it safely through the field in order to collect the prize money, then you will surely want the map telling you where *not* to step. The map will actually *set you free* to win the prize.

The field is like our life here on this earth. The goal is heaven. The land mines are the evil acts we could do which would make our achieving heaven impossible. The map accurately telling us where not to step is the moral law. Do you want the map?

Conclusion

Realizing now how moral law *makes possible* our freedom to achieve happiness, we would be foolish to reject it. That is precisely

---

Chapter III
Moral Law and Freedom

NOTES

"Those who live 'by the flesh' experience God's law as a burden, and indeed as a denial or at least a restriction of their own freedom."
Saint John Paul,
The Splendor of Truth, #18

"'You will know the truth, and the truth will set you free.' (John 8:32) These words contain both a fundamental requirement and a warning: the requirement of an honest relationship to truth as a condition for authentic freedom, and the warning to avoid every kind of illusory freedom, every superficial unilateral freedom, every freedom that fails to enter into the whole truth about the human being and the world."
Saint John Paul,
Message for the VI World Youth Day, #5

"Only the freedom which submits to the Truth leads the human person to his true good. The good of the person is to be in the Truth and to do the Truth."
Saint John Paul,
Address to the International Congress of Moral Theology,
4/10/1986

65.

Called to Happiness ~ Guiding Ethical Principles

NOTES

why the Creator gave it to us: He wanted it to act as a guide leading us back to Him, our Ultimate End.

It is very possible that some people today could be confused at this point in our study. Their confusion would come from the fact that they have always been taught that their conscience should be their guide to happiness. So, since we are claiming here that the moral law is to be our guide to happiness, they wonder where the conscience fits into the picture. Why do we even need the conscience if we have moral law? What happens if a person's conscience disagrees with the moral law? Shouldn't we always follow our conscience, no matter what? Our next chapter will answer these questions as we investigate precisely what role our conscience plays in our quest for happiness.

"In the house of the Lord, slavery is free. It is free because it serves not out of necessity, but out of charity…. Charity should make you a servant, just as truth has made you free. … You are at once both a servant and free: a servant, because you have become such; free, because you are loved by God your Creator; indeed, you have also been enabled to love your Creator…. You are a servant of the Lord and you are a freedman of the Lord. Do not go looking for a liberation which will lead you far from the house of your liberator!"
— Saint Augustine

	Absolute Freedom	*Genuine Freedom*
Definition →	The ability to do as one pleases	The ability to do the good act so as to achieve happiness
Goal →	Freedom itself	Happiness
Feelings toward moral law →	Hates it	Loves it
Moral law's relation to it →	Restricts it	Safeguards it
Relationship to truth →	None	Dependent upon it
Relation to *objective* happiness →	Contrary to it	The *means* to achieving it

Chapter III
Moral Law and Freedom

True Freedom ~
An Analogy

"Psssst…psssst…. Turn around, turn around!"

"I turn where I want. Worry about yourself. It's none of your business." This dialogue took place in a field between two big, yellow and orange sunflowers, one of which, while all the others turned their heads towards the sun, insisted on keeping his head turned backwards.

It's not the first time that this sunflower turned his back to the sun. "Ohhhh, if you do this in order to be noticed," commented a swallow, "you're doing a great job." *It's not because I want to be noticed. I have a deep and profound philosophical reason for doing so."* The swallow shook his head. "I suggest that flowers should be flowers and not philosophers. You are a sunflower. Your name says it, you have to turn towards the sun." *"Ahhh, what an intelligent thing you are saying,"* the flower answered, sarcastically. *"You are telling me that we are not free. Even our name tells us what we must do -- to look at the sun. For me it doesn't mean anything. You know what? I'm going to change my name. Don't call me sunflower anymore. Call me 'Against-The-Sun.' Everyone will know that I don't care for the sun. Okay?"*

"Are you always so hypersensitive?" the swallow asked. *"I'm not hypersensitive at all; I just want to clarify things around here. Look at the other sunflowers; just like puppets on a string…. Almost as if they are bound to the sun. They move as he moves."*

"Ohhhh," the swallow said. "It's true, but I think it's awesome! I've often thought that sunflowers mirror themselves in the sun and little by little they become like him. They are like little suns on earth. Isn't it beautiful?" *"It's silly."* Against-The-Sun replied. *"I really think they are simply ridiculous. If I didn't have these roots holding me to the ground, I would go as far as possible where there is no sun."* "Oh, if the roots are your problem, I'd be glad to help you." (The swallow was determined to give the philosopher a lesson.) "I'll take you wherever you want to go." *"Really?!"* "Oh, yeah, really, I'll do it." *"Okay."*

So the swallow flew away to call other swallows and three of them arrived. They uprooted the sunflower and started flying. The sunflower was very happy. *"This is just the most beautiful day of my life. I'm free!"*

After three days, the swallows were dead tired. "Let's stop here," they said. *"No, we don't stop here,"* Against-The-Sun objected. *"There is sun here. I want to go where there is NO sun."* "But you cannot stay far from the ground. You are going to die. Your roots need soil and water." *"Oh listen, I want to go where there is no sun."* "Well, a place like this doesn't exist," one swallow explained to Against-The-Sun. "The only place where we can take you is to the North Pole, where there are six months of darkness and six months of light." *"Oh, that's perfect!"* the flower exclaimed. *"Let's go there."* "But listen, if we go there, the swallows insisted, "You'll freeze!" *"I don't care. I want to go where there is no sun. It's none of your business, just take me there."*

The swallows gave up and flew right to the North Pole. As soon as they saw the ice, shivering and trembling they dropped the flower and went back home. Against-The-Sun was very happy now and said, *"Ahhhh, for six months I can be very happy and at peace because there is no sun around here."*

While he was thinking this, a penguin passed by and said, "Guess what? You are going to get arthritis if you don't watch it. It's very cold around here." *"I don't care about arthritis. I just care about freedom and I am free here. I can do whatever I want and there is no sun."*

"Are you one of those sunflowers that leave their own land to come here where there is no sun?" *"What do you mean 'Are you one of those sunflowers'? Has anybody else come before me?"* "Oh yeah, you are not the only one. Many others have come here for the same reason, but...." *"And what did they do?"* The flower asked. "Well, they went back home after a while."

"Ohhh," Against-The-Sun thought to himself, *"This is good news. I will never go back home. I will be the one who will be here forever."*

As the days went by the sunflower began to be in pain, because trying to put his roots into the ice was very hard. He started to have arthritis, and it was so cold that he couldn't think very much. His mind was a little bit confused, but he was happy. Two weeks later the sunflower couldn't stand anymore. He was lying on the ice, shivering, shaking, without thought. He had only a vague sense of fear in his heart.

A month passed, two months passed and the poor sunflower was exhausted. The only thing he could think was *"I have to do something; otherwise, I'm going to die."* But he was so confused and cold that he couldn't make a decision. Lying down on the ice, he was mumbling strange words; nothing was making sense. Finally one word came to his mind. *"Sun, ...* whispered the flower, *"Sun...."*

Chapter III
Moral Law and Freedom

At that very moment the penguin passed by and heard the sunflower say, *"I need the sun .... Sun .... I need the sun or I'm going to die. I'll die."*

The penguin already knew what to do…. He called 9-1-1 S-e-a-g-u-l-l! The seagull arrived, got the sunflower and flew him back home. When he arrived to the mainland, he dropped the flower on the ground.

"Ahh, home at last," sighed Against-The-Sun. He felt the warmth of the sun's rays, the embrace of the soil, the presence of the other sunflowers. He felt great, but he was ashamed for what he had done. *"What am I going to say? Maybe it's not important now. I'll just enjoy the sun and the soil and maybe there is no need for me to say anything."* In fact, none of the sunflowers made a comment. They were so happy he was back, because it's always a big celebration every time a sunflower comes back home!

That evening, like every evening, the sunflowers turned towards the east to wait for the rising of the sun, as if they were saying a good night prayer to the sun and wishing for the morning.

Before falling asleep, one of them whispered, "I know that you will come again." And another one, "I know you will come back, because you are my everything." The tallest one sighed, "It is in the darkness that we need to believe in the light…." And the little one exclaimed, "Well, I'm sure you are coming back tomorrow because I need you!"

And then the last one, the sunflower who came back from the North Pole murmured, *"I know he will be back ... because the sun loves me and I love him. And where there is love, there is true freedom."*

From *Latte e miele's* by Lauretta (Editrice Ancora)

NOTES

Study Guide Questions:

1. *What does it mean to say that a human person is able to act voluntarily?*

2. *What effect does the moral law have on our freedom of choice?*

3. *Why wouldn't it be a good thing for human beings to be free from all law?*

4. *How do absolute and genuine freedom relate to the moral law and happiness?*

5. *What is the relationship of "truth" to genuine freedom? Where does truth fit into the story about the land mines?*

6. *In "The Analogy," (pp. 67-69) what important lesson did "Against-The-Sun" learn about the freedom he sought?*

7. *Saint John Paul writes in <u>The Splendor of Truth</u> (#103): "He [Christ] has given us the possibility of realizing the entire truth of our being; he has set our freedom free...."*
   Can you explain what the Pope might have meant regarding 'setting our freedom free'?

8. *"Freedom is tied to a measure, the measure of reality -- to the truth." How could you explain to a friend what Cardinal Ratzinger is saying in this statement?*

Chapter III
Moral Law and Freedom

CASES IN POINT

#1 --"In his article entitled "Self-Determination: The Tyranny of Freedom," Barry Schwarz stated that 'modern American society has created an excess of freedom' that has resulted in people being more depressed and indecisive. He suggested that Americans are confused and overwhelmed by their freedom to choose, 'which is not all it's cracked up to be.' … A positive psychology, according to Schwartz, must constrain 'tyranny of choice,' and psychologists should 'deemphasize freedom' because 'American society has created an excess of freedom.'"

Robert Solomon, "In Defense of Freedom," *American Psychologist,* Jan., 2001, p. 79.

- *Does our American society today have an "excess of freedom"? Explain.*
- *What would family life look like if there was an excess of freedom?*
- *Why would it be true to speak of an excess as a kind of "tyranny"? Why would depression and indecision be the fruit of such tyranny?*
- *What criterion should be used in judging whether or not freedom is excessive?*

* * * * *

#2 -- "Facing various possibilities, it is good for us to choose among them. Yet perhaps the highest and most rewarding exercise of freedom is assenting to things we haven't chosen, welcoming in trust realities that transcend us.

"Our real prison is ourselves: our limited perception of reality, our narrow-mindedness and narrow-heartedness. Experience often shows that we break out of this prison and open new horizons in accepting situations we haven't chosen and so come to perceive a deeper dimension of reality, more rich and more beautiful.

"Human freedom is not so much a power to transform as a capacity to welcome. The most rewarding act of freedom ever made by a human being was the *Fiat* of Mary, her trusting, loving Yes.

"We notice, too, that the fundamental question is not whether we have more or less freedom of choice -- freedom that in the end doesn't make much sense in isolation -- but about the reasons that lead us to opt for one choice rather than another. What directs us to our decisions? A simple impulse, a desire? Or is it convention, the desire to do what everyone else does? Or even our fears, our faults, our defense mechanisms? One of the paradoxes of modern life is how often people pretend to be free ("I'm a free man, a free woman," we hear so often on television) when in fact they are only following fashions or whims. Many people think of themselves as original while merely conforming to trends.

"Let's ask ourselves the real question: what values guide and drive my freedom? Are they phantoms, illusions, or lies -- or do they foster authentic fulfillment of my personality and my life?

"If freedom is not directed toward a real good, driven by objective values, it simply ceases to exist. There is no freedom except in relation to a truth that guides it and directs it."

Fr. Jacques Philippe, *Fire & Light: Eucharistic Love and the Search for Peace,* p. 102.

- *How does viewing freedom as a "capacity to welcome" relate to the notion of genuine freedom?*
- *Why doesn't freedom of choice "make much sense in isolation"?*
- *What kinds of acts could a teenager freely choose to do that would demonstrate that he is not in fact very free? What would be examples of the opposite kinds of acts?*

Point to Consider:

"Dear Friends,

[W]hat is the measure of sharing freedom? We see that man needs order, laws, so that he can realize his freedom which is a freedom lived in common. And how can we find this correct order, in which no one is oppressed but rather each one can give his contribution to form this sort of concert of freedoms? If there is no common truth of man as it appears in the vision of God, only positivism remains and one has the impression of something imposed in an even violent manner. From this emerges rebellion against order and law as though it entails slavery.

But if we can find the order of the Creator in our nature, the order of truth that gives each one his place, then order and law can be the very instruments of freedom against the slavery of selfishness. To serve one another becomes the instrument of freedom.... The first reality meriting respect, therefore, is the truth: freedom opposed to truth is not freedom. To serve one another creates the common space of freedom."

Benedict XVI,
Address to the Community of the Roman Major Seminary, 2/20/09

Chapter IV

Conscience and Truth

All law is intended to direct those subject to it to their proper end. In the case of the moral law, which applies only to human beings, the proper end toward which moral law directs us is happiness. This is why we say that the moral law *makes possible* our freedom to achieve happiness. The moral law itself, though, is not enough help for us.

It is not enough for a person to know a general norm or principle -- what we could call "*objective* morality." He also needs to know how that general norm applies to the particular act he is now considering doing. Applying the general norm to a particular act will tell him whether <u>this</u> act that he is now considering is morally good *for him* to do or not. This is where conscience comes in. Conscience gives us the *subjective* basis of morality. Conscience is what enables us personally to apply the moral law to the particular acts we face in our lives each day.

Vocabulary

conscience	synderesis	syllogism	invincible
practical intellect	erroneous	innate	vincible

I. What is Conscience?

The word "conscience" comes from the Latin word *conscientia* meaning literally "knowing with." This Latin word encompasses both the idea of *consciousness* and the idea of *conscience*. *Consciousness* refers to the <u>psychological</u> state of a person who is aware of his own knowing. In a sense, we could say that a person who possesses consciousness is "*knowing with* his own knowing." For example, if Tom is enjoying consciousness, then he is enjoying being aware of his surroundings and aware of himself as knowing them. Likewise, if Tom is unconscious, as when he is sleeping, he is unaware of his surroundings and thus of himself knowing them. **Conscience**, on the other hand, is an <u>ethical</u> term. It refers to a person's act of knowing the moral quality of his free acts. In other words, the conscience is a person's act of "*knowing with* the moral law" the nature of his free acts. The conscience answers the question, "Is this act good for me to do right now?"

NOTES

Conscience: "the proximate norm of personal morality."
Saint John Paul,
The Splendor of Truth, #60

Called to Happiness ~ Guiding Ethical Principles

NOTES

People often think of the conscience as the "voice of God" or as some "inner voice" telling us what we ought to do or avoid doing. Neither of these, if understood literally, however, is correct. There is indeed a very close relationship between a person's conscience and God speaking to us, but it would not be correct to say that the conscience is *literally* God's voice. One problem with this way of speaking or thinking about the conscience is the fact that our consciences can be wrong in their judgments, but we know that God can never be wrong.

Conscience is simply the human intellect functioning in a certain way: judging the rightness or wrongness of a particular act. To be more precise, we could say that the conscience is one of the functions of a person's **practical** intellect. You see, St. Thomas refers to the intellect as being either *practical* or *speculative*, depending on what kind of activity it is doing. If the intellect is dealing with questions about the way things are, such as "Why do the planets revolve around the sun?" or "What does it mean to say that cheating is wrong?" then he refers to it as the **speculative intellect**. If the intellect is figuring out what a person should do or avoid doing, then he calls it the practical intellect.

Should I keep the money I just found without first trying to find its owner?

Conscience — Practical Intellect

Practical intellect - the intellect as it seeks to know reality for the purpose of doing or making something.

"The judgment of conscience is a practical judgment, a judgment which makes known what man must do or not do, or which assesses an act already performed by him."

Saint John Paul,
The Splendor of Truth, #59

Speculative intellect - from Latin *speculari* (to examine, observe); the intellect as it seeks to know reality simply for the sake of knowing it.

For example, it is the practical intellect which wrestles with questions such as the following: how could I do well in school, get the attention of this person, please Mom and Dad? When the practical intellect deals with practical questions that concern moral good and evil, we call it "*conscience*." For example, the conscience answers questions such as the following: If I do this particular act, will I be cheating, will I be truthful, will I be just?

Why do we say cheating is wrong?

Speculative Intellect

Notice, then, that the conscience is not a faculty of the soul distinct from the intellect. To speak about a person's conscience is simply to talk about his intellect when it makes practical judgments about whether a particular act is morally good or bad. Thus, when a person *thinks* that he ought not to do this particular act of copying his friend's

74.

answers because it would be cheating and cheating is wrong, his conscience has "spoken." His intellect has applied the moral norm ("cheating is wrong") to a particular act (copying his friend's answers) and made the judgment: "I should not do this act because it would be morally wrong."

Perhaps now we can understand why St. Thomas defines **conscience** as *the act of applying moral knowledge to a particular act.*[1] The power of the soul which does this act is the practical intellect. Strictly speaking, then, the term conscience refers to the *judgment itself* of the practical intellect. More loosely speaking, we might refer to the intellect, the power which forms that judgment, as the conscience.

How does it actually work?

Let us look a little deeper into this act of applying moral knowledge to particular acts. In forming a judgment of conscience, the practical intellect is actually going through a process of reasoning. **Reasoning** is a step-by-step process whereby the intellect moves from one bit of information it knows to another, and then from these two it draws a conclusion which gives it new knowledge. People who study logic call this 3-step process of reasoning a **syllogism**. When the practical intellect considers how a person should act, its first step -- called *the major premise* -- is to acknowledge a general moral principle or norm. Its second step -- *the minor premise* -- is to identify a particular act as in some way being related to this moral principle. Its third step -- *the conclusion* -- is to make a judgment applying the moral principle to the particular act.

For example, a person is first aware of a moral norm such as "It is wrong to lie." Then he recognizes the particular act he is considering doing as being related to this norm: "My explanation of where I was and what I was doing is a lie." From these two known truths, he logically concludes with the following judgment: "It is wrong for me to give this explanation of where I was and what I was doing." The entire reasoning process proceeds as follows:

1. Major premise → It is wrong to lie.
2. Minor premise → My explanation of where I was and what I was doing is a lie.
3. Conclusion → It is wrong for me to give this explanation of where I was and what I was doing.

---

[1] St. Thomas Aquinas, *Summa Theologiae*, I, 79, 13.

NOTES

Conscience - from Latin *conscientia* (knowing with); an intellectual judgment applying moral law to a particular act.

"The precise nature of conscience: it is a moral judgment about man and his actions."
   Saint John Paul,
   The Splendor of Truth, #59

Reasoning - an act of the intellect whereby it makes one judgment based on another; a step-by-step process of acquiring knowledge.

Syllogism - an argument expressed in the form of two propositions containing a common or middle term, with a third proposition resulting necessarily from the other two.

Premise - from Latin *praemittere* (to put before); a previous statement from which another is inferred or follows as a conclusion.

Let us look at one more example of the reasoning process of conscience:

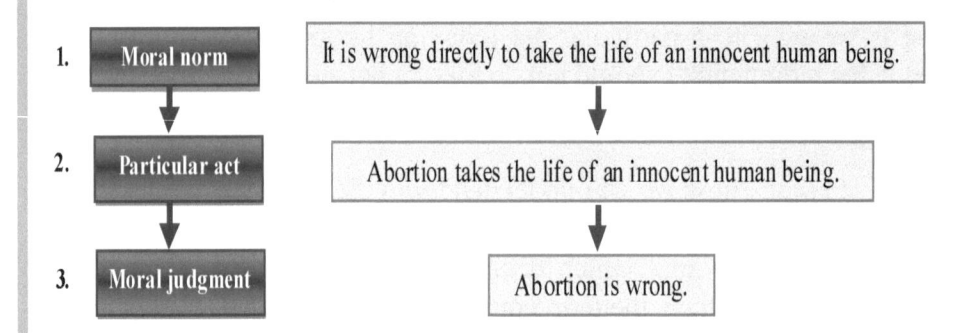

1.	Moral norm	It is wrong directly to take the life of an innocent human being.
2.	Particular act	Abortion takes the life of an innocent human being.
3.	Moral judgment	Abortion is wrong.

Because our minds usually work rather quickly, we tend not to notice this syllogistic reasoning in our thinking. Yet, in every judgment of conscience a moral norm is being applied to a particular act. Our abbreviated acts of reasoning go something like this:

- "Should I go downtown with my friends? No; my parents told me to stay home."
  <u>Syllogism</u>: It is wrong for a young person to disobey his parents.
  My parents told me to stay home.
  I should not go to the mall with my friends.

- "May I keep this? No; it belongs to someone else."
  <u>Syllogism</u>: It is wrong to keep what does not belong to you.
  This does not belong to me.
  I should not keep it.

- "Should I aid this poor person? Yes, I have the resources to do it."
  <u>Syllogism</u>: It is good to aid the poor if you can.
  I have the resources to help this poor person.
  I should aid this poor person.

What are the functions of conscience?

The conscience can make its moral judgment either *before*, *during*, or *after* the act it is judging. When it judges before the act, the conscience often acts as an <u>advisor</u>. It tells us what we *ought* to do or avoid doing. For example, the conscience advises us: "Do not copy that person's answers because copying answers is a form of cheating, and cheating is wrong."

When the conscience judges during the act, it usually simply bears witness to what is happening. For example, the conscience <u>testifies</u> to what is going on: "The cheating I am now doing is morally wrong. I am acting dishonestly."

Chapter IV
Conscience and Truth

When the conscience judges after the act, it <u>assesses</u> or evaluates what has already been done as being good or bad. For example, the conscience assesses my completed act: "I cheated. I acted unreasonably by doing what is morally wrong." The difference between the conscience testifying and assessing an act is simply a difference in timing. It testifies *as the act is being done*; it assesses *after the fact*. The judgment of conscience in both cases, of course, will be essentially the same.

St. Thomas says that the conscience then excuses or accuses, or moves to remorse.[2] We are all probably very familiar with what it feels like when our consciences accuse us of having done evil. We feel badly. We feel that we have let God and ourselves down -- which indeed we have. This is what we mean when we speak of having a "guilty conscience." We refer to this assessing function of conscience when we speak of "examining our consciences."

Part of the assessing function of conscience is also its ability to let us know when we have done a good act. Even if doing good was difficult, the conscience is responsible for the fact that we feel good or are at peace about our act.

Did you notice that St. Thomas says that the conscience can also "move us to remorse"? In other words, conscience has a *positive* role to play in moving the sinner to repentance. We consider it *positive* because the conscience does not simply tell us that we are *not* moving ourselves in the direction of happiness. It can also move us to do something about it. In other words, it can help us to get "back on track." For example, I might have thought that lying to my Mom about where I was going would make me happy because I would get to do what I wanted. My conscience helps me to understand, however, that my lying has hurt my relationship with her and with God. I really do want to be a person who loves and speaks the truth. I regret lying to her, I apologize to Mom for lying to her, and I confess my sin, asking God for His forgiveness.

Conscience does this because -- *even while it tells us that we are doing evil* -- it tells us the right thing to do. In this regard, conscience is something like a road map which tells us both the right and the wrong roads to take. The *Catechism* explains:

> If man commits evil, the just judgment of conscience can remain within him as the witness to the universal truth of the good, at the same time as the evil of his particular choice. The verdict of the judgment of conscience remains a pledge of hope and mercy.[3]

NOTES

"Conscience in a certain sense confronts man with the law, and thus becomes a 'witness' for man: a witness of his own faithfulness or unfaithfulness with regard to the law, of his essential moral rectitude or iniquity."
Saint John Paul,
The Splendor of Truth, #57

"The verdict of conscience remains in him also as a pledge of hope and mercy: while bearing witness to the evil he has done, it also reminds him of his need, with the help of God's grace, to ask forgiveness, to do good and to cultivate virtue constantly."
Saint John Paul,
The Splendor of Truth, #61

[2] St. Thomas Aquinas, *Summa Theologiae*, I, 79, 13.
[3] *The Catechism of the Catholic Church*, #1781.

Called to Happiness ~ Guiding Ethical Principles

NOTES

There is hope in the fact that a person knows where he has gone astray and can avoid doing it again in the future. There is also hope in that the true good he really wants appeals to him through conscience. He realizes that he has sinned and can now repent and ask for mercy.

Can the conscience ever be wrong?

Once we realize that the judgment of conscience is simply our practical intellect reasoning to a conclusion based on the knowledge that it has, we might naturally wonder: Couldn't the intellect make a mistake in its reasoning? As with any reasoning process which involves merely the human intellect, the answer is "yes." Yes, the judgment of conscience can be in error. Its error would arise from either of two sources:

(a) Either it has accepted premises which are false,

or

(b) It has drawn an illogical conclusion.

"In order to have a 'good conscience,' man must seek the truth and must make judgments in accordance with that same truth."
Saint John Paul,
The Splendor of Truth, #62

When the judgment of conscience is in error, we say that the conscience is **erroneous** in that particular judgment. When the judgment is correct, we say the conscience is *correct* in its judgment. Thus, a c*orrect conscience* judges a good act to be good or an evil act to be evil. An *erroneous conscience* judges a good act to be evil or an evil act to be good. A person's conscience can be correct at times and erroneous at other times.

Erroneous - from Latin *erroneous* (straying); in error, not true.

"Conscience is not an infallible judge; it can make mistakes."
Saint John Paul,
The Splendor of Truth, #62

From this we can see that it is possible for a person to do an evil act without knowing that he is actually doing evil. If his conscience is ignorant of the truth about what he is doing, then he does not really know whether he is doing good or evil.

Well, if a person *thinks* that he is doing a good act, then doesn't that automatically make the act good? Let's think about this a little. If Hitler's men thought that their killing innocent men, women, and children was a good thing to do, then would that have made their acts of murder good acts? Surely we would say, "No!" Our *subjective* thinking does not have the power to change the *objective* nature of an act we are doing. Murder is objectively wrong no matter what we think of it.

"Who can discern his errors? Clear me from hidden faults."
Psalm 19:12

One more question about the erroneous conscience: If a person does evil while thinking he is doing good, will he be held responsible for the evil he *unknowingly* does? It might seem at first that he cannot be

78.

held responsible because he does not know he is doing wrong. For example, a 2-year-old will not be held responsible for the damage he does to his mom's papers when he plays with them. He does not know any better, and there is no way to "conquer his ignorance" until he gets older. This is why we would say that his ignorance is *invincible*. ***Invincible* ignorance** does indeed excuse a person from the evil he unknowingly does.

However, it is possible for a person to cause his own ignorance. Take for example a person who is pulled over for speeding. When the police officer asks him if he knows what the speed limit is for that street, the person admits he doesn't know. The chances are good that the officer will give him a ticket because his ignorance does not excuse him. As a driver he is responsible to inform himself of the speed limit. If he chooses not to inform himself, then he is responsible for his ignorance *and for the evil he does through his ignorance*. This kind of ignorance which is "able to be conquered" is called ***vincible* ignorance**. Vincible ignorance does not excuse us from the evil we do because of it.

Do I have to follow it?

Another question arises as soon as we realize that our consciences can be in error: Do we have to follow an erroneous conscience? *If the conscience has no doubts that its judgment is correct*, then the answer is simply and always, **Yes**! The judgment of conscience -- whether it is correct or erroneous -- is always the *best judgment* a person has regarding what he ought to do. A person would be acting unreasonably if he did not follow his best judgment. Even if his best judgment is incorrect, it is still his best judgment. He does not know it is incorrect. If he actually knew that the judgment was incorrect, then the erroneous judgment would no longer be the judgment of his conscience. Conscience is *always* a person's best judgment about what is the morally right thing to do. In other words, the judgment of conscience is what the person thinks the moral law is telling him to do. This is why we are always morally obligated to follow it.

NOTES

Invincible ignorance - from Latin *in-vincere* (not to overcome); ignorance of which a person is not aware and which he is unable to overcome by himself. A person bears no responsibility for this ignorance.

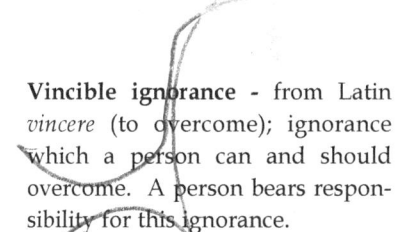

Vincible ignorance - from Latin *vincere* (to overcome); ignorance which a person can and should overcome. A person bears responsibility for this ignorance.

Let's look at some examples of this so that the point is clear:

#1 - Bill's boss tells him to change the numbers on a financial statement of one of their clients so that the numbers reflect a higher cost than the client had originally agreed to for the purchase of some merchandise. The boss does not explain why he wants this change, so Bill's conscience makes a judgment based on the information he has available. His conscience tells him that he should not make the change in numbers without a good reason. To make the change without a good reason is to risk cheating the client. If Bill follows his conscience, then he will ask his boss for an explanation regarding the higher price. If Bill changes the numbers without receiving a reasonable explanation, that is, if he acts contrary to his conscience, then he is guilty of being willing to cooperate in cheating the client.

#2 - Jean thinks that it is all right for her to work with Laura on their math homework. To speed things along, Jean suggests that they divide the problems, so that each of them will do half the assignment. Laura likes Jean and does not want to offend her, but her conscience tells her that splitting the work is not right. It would be like doing only half the assignment and copying the other half. Her conscience tells her that she would be acting dishonestly if she went along with Jean's plan. Even if her math teacher does, in fact, permit his students to divide their work as Jean suggests, Laura is unaware of it. In Laura's best judgment, Jean's plan is dishonest. If Laura does not follow her conscience and does as Jean suggests, then she is guilty of acting dishonestly, for she is agreeing to do what she thinks is dishonest.

#3 - Eliza, a married woman in her late 20's, knows that the Catholic Church teaches that using contraception is wrong. Eliza is a Catholic, but she does not understand why "taking a little pill" is considered to be an ethically bad thing. She has never heard a reasonable explanation nor has she bothered to study the Church's teaching. In *her* best judgment, it seems, there is nothing wrong with this form of contraception. Remember, however, that Eliza is a Catholic who knows that the Church teaches that the use of contraceptives is wrong. Catholics should believe that the Church is guided by the Holy Spirit in all of its moral teaching and is thus the *objective moral authority* of Jesus on this earth. For Eliza not to have bothered to study the Church's teaching to find out why contraception is wrong is for her to *choose* to be ignorant of the truth. If Eliza proceeds to use the pill to contracept, she does an *objectively* evil act. Since she has chosen to be ignorant about why her act is evil, Eliza bears responsibility for her ignorance. Her ignorance is vincible and does not excuse her from responsibility for her evil act.

#4 - Let us change this last scenario and imagine that Eliza has actually studied the Church's teaching on contraception and that she still personally sees nothing wrong with using the pill. If she follows her conscience in its erroneous condition, she does an *objectively* evil act. How responsible is she for the evil act?

It is important to note here that Eliza's conscience is telling her that contraceptive use is good. No one, however, is obligated to pursue all the goods she can pursue. Conscience binds a person to obedience *only* when it judges that doing or not doing an act is evil, i.e., sinful. Thus, since Eliza's conscience is <u>not</u> telling her that it is evil for her to *avoid* using contraceptives, she is morally free not to use them. If she knowingly and freely consents to do an act which the Catholic Church judges to be gravely evil, Eliza is preferring her own personal *subjective* judgment to the Church's. This attitude of hers reflects Eliza's rejection of the belief that the Catholic Church is the infallible teacher of the natural law, endowed by Jesus with his authority to teach morals.

Study Guide Questions:

1. What is the difference between the practical and speculative intellects?
2. What precisely is conscience?
3. Explain the three-step process whereby the practical intellect reaches its moral judgment.
4. Give three of your own examples showing the reasoning process of conscience.
5. What are the three functions of conscience? Give an example of each one.
6. Some people may think of conscience as a threat to their individual happiness and peace of mind; that once a person starts to think too much about conscience he is going to be miserable, and never have any fun, always being worried about whether things are right or wrong. How can the correct understanding of conscience actually be a cause of hope and peace of mind for a person?
7. How could a correct understanding of conscience be a help to a person in admitting he's done wrong and asking God's forgiveness and mercy?
8. How is it possible for a person to do evil without knowing it?
9. What is meant by the terms "vincible" and "invincible" ignorance?
10. Does either type of ignorance excuse a person for the evil he does?
11. Is a person morally obligated to follow his conscience if it is erroneous? Explain.

CASES IN POINT

#1 -- Bill is new to the high school as of three months ago. Since coming, he has begun to hang around with a group of guys who are in many of the same classes he is. They are all smart and like to study together so they can get good grades. In working on their most recent history assignment, they decide to save themselves some time and "divide and conquer" rather than working on the entire assignment as a group as *he thought* the teacher has asked them to do. Bill is uncomfortable putting his name to the assignment because he has not actually done most of it, but he is the only one who raises this concern. Everyone else is fine with the plan, and they say that the teacher doesn't care. Everyone does it this way, they say. Bill decides that because none of the other guys is bothered he shouldn't be either. He knows that they are basically good guys and that they have never cheated since he has been studying with them. Maybe -- he thinks -- his conscience is just too sensitive.

- *What would you do if you were Bill?*
- *Would it be wrong for Bill simply to follow the consciences of the other guys, since his conscience could be wrong? Explain.*

* * * * *

#2 -- Ever since Lisa learned about an erroneous conscience, she has been worried that she could actually be doing evil while thinking it is good -- and vice versa. She prefers to think that her conscience is *always* giving her a correct moral judgment.

- *Is there any advice you could offer Lisa that might ease her worries?*
- *What danger is there in thinking that your conscience is always correct?*

* * * * *

#3 -- Susan was absent from school the day the teacher assigned the project for biology. Specific instructions were given out on a piece of paper regarding how the project needed to be done, but the teacher also announced some changes to those written instructions. When she returned to school, Susan asked both a classmate and the teacher about what she had missed. She received the paper with the instructions for the project, but no one told her about any of the changes that had been made orally. When Susan received her project back, she noticed that the grade was lower than she had expected because she had not followed the instructions. When Susan went to talk to the teacher about it, he told her that she was irresponsible for not being fully informed about the project. It was her responsibility to get all of the information.

- *Was the teacher correct in his assessment of Susan? Explain.*

What if conscience is not sure?

Did you notice in that last section where we were talking about following an erroneous conscience, that we said a person must follow his conscience *as long as he has no doubts that its judgment is correct?* We call a conscience that has no doubts a "***certain* conscience**." One which has moral doubts we call a "***doubtful* conscience**."

When a person has a doubtful conscience, then he must not act. The reason for this is simply because **we do not want to risk doing evil!**

What, then, should a person with a doubtful conscience do? He should resolve his moral doubt. He should find out what is the morally correct thing to do. Another way of saying this is to say that he should *inform* his conscience. He should inquire and seek advice from moral authorities. He should find out the *moral truth* about the act he is considering doing so that he can act with a certain conscience.

If after consulting moral authorities a person is still unable to resolve his doubt, then there are two different guidelines:

<u>First</u>, if he is certain about his moral obligation but doubtful about the means of carrying it out, then he should take the means he is *certain* about: he should take the morally safer course of action. This means that he should do that which more surely preserves moral goodness, more certainly avoids wrongdoing. Fagothey explains:

> One is always *allowed* to choose the morally safer course. If a man is certainly not obliged to act but doubts whether he is allowed to act, the morally safer course is to omit the act; thus if I doubt whether this money is justly mine, I can simply refuse it. If a man is certainly allowed to act but doubts whether he is obliged to act, the morally safer course is to do the act; thus if I doubt whether I have paid a bill, I can offer the money and risk paying it twice.
>
> Sometimes we are *obliged* to follow the morally safer course. We must do so when there is an end certainly to be obtained to the best of our power, and our doubt merely concerns the effectiveness of the means to be used for this purpose.[4]

An example of this latter case where a person is obliged to follow the morally safer course is the following: A hunter goes out to shoot deer. After some length of time, he hears movement in the brush about 200 yards away.

---

[4] Austin Fagothey, S.J., *Right and Reason*, 6th Edition, p. 45.

Chapter IV
Conscience and Truth

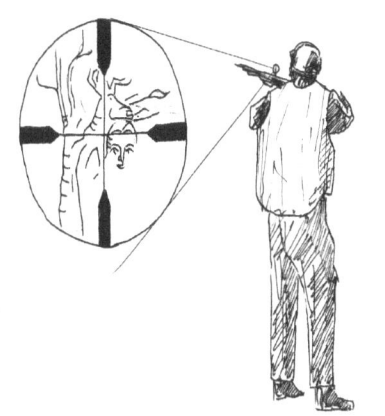

NOTES

Certain conscience - a moral judgment about which a person has no doubts.

Doubtful conscience - a moral judgment about which a person has doubts.

He lifts his rifle to shoot, but he is not sure if the noise he hears is caused by a deer or by another hunter. Because the hunter is *certain* that he should not kill an innocent person, he is morally obligated to take the morally safer course of action and not shoot his gun.

<u>Second</u>, if a person is doubtful not about the means of achieving his end but about the moral obligation itself, then the following principle holds true: *A doubtful obligation does not bind.* This principle applies whenever a person doubts whether or not he is bound by a law or obligation. Because it is essential to law that it be promulgated (made known), if a person is sufficiently unaware of it, then the law cannot bind him.

For example, I may doubt whether the speed limit on this new road is 35 mph; whether the fruit that fell from the neighbor's tree into my yard is mine or his; or whether my boss will permit me to make a personal telephone call. If after trying to find out my obligation, I am still in doubt concerning it, then I am morally justified in acting according to my own preferences.

II. The Objectivity of Conscience

Contrary to what some people think, the judgment of conscience is <u>not</u> a person's *subjective* opinion about what is morally right or wrong. The only thing subjective about conscience is that it is a particular person's own intellect which makes the moral judgment. The judgment itself, however, is fundamentally *objective* because it is based on the moral law which is the same for us all. In fact, it is the purpose of conscience to put a person in contact with and to keep him in contact with the objective moral order. Cardinal Joseph Ratzinger expresses it this way:

> "<u>Conscience</u> ... a window through which one can see outward to *that common truth* which founds and sustains us all."[5]

We see proof of this *objectivity* of the conscience every time it makes a judgment we do not like. For example, a person who loves chocolate does not want to be told by his conscience that he ought to stop eating the chocolate right now because he has had more than enough. If the judgment of conscience were identical with his personal wishes and tastes, that is, with his *subjective* opinion, then he would never experience it telling him to do something that he does not want to do. But we

---

NOTES

"Conscience is like God's herald and messenger; it does not command things on its own authority, but commands them as coming from God's authority, like a herald when he proclaims the edict of the king."
St. Bonaventure

"Conscience is the witness of God himself, whose voice and judgment penetrate the depths of man's soul, calling him *fortiter et suaviter* to obedience."
Saint John Paul,
The Splendor of Truth, #58

"Conscience signifies the perceptible and demanding presence of the voice of truth in the subject himself. It is the overcoming of mere subjectivity in the encounter of the interiority of man with the truth of God."
Cardinal Joseph Ratzinger,
"Conscience & Truth"

---

[5] Joseph Cardinal Ratzinger, "Conscience & Truth."

all have experience of the conscience telling us something we do not really want to hear.

Cardinal Ratzinger offers us two standards for recognizing the *real* voice of conscience:

<u>First</u>, conscience is not identical to personal wishes and taste.
<u>Secondly</u>, conscience cannot be reduced to social advantage, to group consensus, or to the demands of political and social power.⁶

Rather than being the reflection of personal or popular opinion, conscience is our *link* or *connection* to the objective truth of the moral law. It is this "connection to truth" which enables the conscience to be the invaluable guide it was designed to be in leading us to our Ultimate End. Safeguarding this "connection to truth" is what we mean when we speak of informing our consciences.

How does a person inform his conscience?

To inform one's conscience is to become more knowledgeable of the truth of the objective moral law and its application to the particular act under consideration. Without this knowledge, the intellect is "blind" in its moral judgment. Without this knowledge, the judgment is nothing but a person's subjective opinion. This is why the conscience is so dependent upon the **truth** of the moral law.

Conscience without truth is like eyes without light: It is worthless! Informing the conscience is like "turning the lights on" so that the intellect can make a correct judgment about the nature of the act a person is considering doing.

How can the intellect get access to the *light*, that is, to the truth of the moral law? There are a number of ways:

The **<u>first</u>** way is one to which all people have access because, as St. Thomas tells us, it is "stamped into our nature" as human beings. Remember our discussion about the natural law in the precious chapter? We said there that the intellect is able to reflect on human nature itself and draw conclusions from its reflection. St. Thomas explains that we can do this because every person has present within him, as an aspect of his human nature, a basic awareness of general moral principles, that is, the principles of natural law.

---

⁶ Ibid.

NOTES

"A man of conscience is one who never acquires tolerance, well-being, success, public standing, and approval on the part of prevailing opinion, at the expense of truth."
Cardinal Joseph Ratzinger, "Conscience & Truth"

"It is always from the truth that the dignity of conscience derives."
Saint John Paul, *The Splendor of Truth*, #63

Truth - the agreement between a person's thinking and objective reality.

"Deep within his conscience man discovers a law which he has not laid upon himself but which he must obey. Its voice ever calling him to love and to do what is good and to avoid evil, tells him inwardly at the right moment: do this, shun that. For man has in his heart a law inscribed by God. His dignity lies in observing this law, and by it he will be judged. His conscience is man's most secret core, and his sanctuary. There he is alone with God whose voice echoes in his depths."
Gaudium et Spes, #16

NOTES

Habit - from Latin *habere* (to have); a firm and permanent disposition to act in a certain way.

Synderesis - from the Greek word meaning "guarding or preserving closely;" the natural or innate habit of the mind to know the first principles of the moral order without recourse to a reasoning process. Developed by Aristotle, the term was introduced to the West by St. Jerome who referred to it as the "spark of conscience." St. Thomas later accepted the term to explain the intellect's natural habit of knowing very basic moral truths.

Innate - from Latin *innatus* (inborn); existing in a person from birth.

St. Thomas refers to this basic awareness as a **habit** of our nature which he calls **synderesis**.[7] That word "habit" comes from the Latin word *habere* which means "to have." To say that this basic moral awareness is a *habit*, then, simply means that it is something that we have within us from our creation because of the godlike creatures we are. This abiding awareness of the first principles of the moral law identifies us as moral beings. This awareness, however, is more an inner sense than a knowledge we can clearly express in words. This *inner sense*, or synderesis, is what initiates our attraction toward the good and our repulsion for evil. Cardinal Ratzinger explains:

> It [synderesis] is so to speak an inner sense, a capacity to recall, so that the one whom it addresses, if he is not turned in on himself, hears its echo from within. He sees: That's it! That is what my nature points to and seeks.[8]

St. Thomas considers synderesis to be the *foundation* or *basis* of conscience. It is the "law of our intellect"[9] to which the conscience looks in order to begin its moral reasoning. This is why, in the diagram to the right, the arrows are pointing *from* the conscience *to* synderesis. Synderesis, as the habit of basic moral awareness, is present in every human being. However, it can go unnoticed unless the person chooses to *"look to it."* When the intellect makes its moral judgments, that is, when it acts as conscience, it needs to *look to* the moral law present within if it wants to be informed with moral truth.

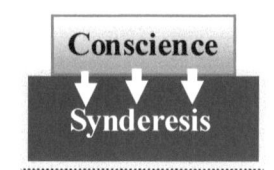

The most foundational moral principle of synderesis is that good is to be done and evil avoided. In other words, the Creator designed us in such a way that **innate** in every person is the "light of objective truth." This is why Cardinal Ratzinger refers to conscience as "man's openness to the ground of his being, the power of perception for what is highest and most essential."[10]

If every person has this "light of objective truth" within him as a habit that is continuously present, then how is it possible for the conscience to make an error in its judgment? The conscience can err if the intellect does not "turn to" this inner source of truth. The light of truth within us is like a small, flickering flame which can easily be overlooked. Endless activity, faulty moral upbringing, a depraved will, or social pressures can make it easy for us not to see it. Sometimes our blindness to this truth is our own fault: we do not see the truth because we do not want to see it.

---

[7] St. Thomas Aquinas, *Summa Theologiae* I-II, 94, 1, 2.
[8] Joseph Cardinal Ratzinger, "Conscience & Truth."
[9] St. Thomas Aquinas, *Summa Theologiae* I-II, 94, 1, 2.
[10] Joseph Cardinal Ratzinger, "Conscience & Truth."

Chapter IV
Conscience and Truth

In order to "see" the light of truth, we must *want* to see it. It will not impose itself on us. This means that we must *want* to know the truth, even when it is inconvenient or unpopular. Seeing it will require a certain *silencing* of "external distractions." It will require that we take time for reflection, for self-examination and introspection, and that we foster within ourselves a love for truth.

It is precisely because we can easily be unaware of the light of truth within us that we need further help. The One who instilled synderesis in us offers us added "light" to help us inform our consciences.

A **second** way we have of gaining access to the light of moral truth is a way that is not readily available to everyone. Only those who have the *true* faith have access to this light. It is the light of *Divine revelation.* God actually spells out for us the moral law in language that we can understand. The Ten Commandments are an example of this in the days of ancient Israel. Although the Hebrews could know from natural law that they should not directly kill an innocent human being, God spelled it out more clearly for them in the Fifth Commandment: Thou shalt not murder! This added "light" they were given should have made it easier for them to judge correctly about how they should act.

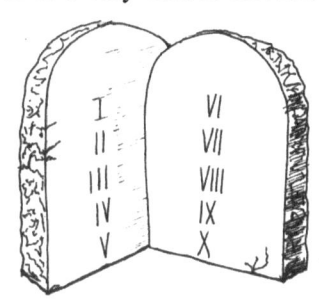

Divine revelation did not stop with the Hebrews, however. The fullness of revelation came when the Second Person of the Blessed Trinity took on our human nature in the Person of Jesus Christ. His teaching is the **third** way we have of knowing the moral law. It is Jesus who said,

> I am the light of the world. Whoever follows me will not walk in darkness, but will have the light of life.[11]

So it is in Jesus that we are given more "light" to assist us in determining right and wrong acts. For example, the Jews already knew from natural law and from the 6th Commandment that adultery was wrong, but Jesus clarified even further for them when he said,

> Everyone who looks at a woman with lust has already committed adultery with her in his heart.[12]

"Being aware of this, young people of today and adults of the new millennium, let yourselves be 'formed' in the school of Jesus."
Saint John Paul,
Message for the 14th World Youth Day, #14

---
[11] John 8:12
[12] Matthew 5:28

87.

Called to Happiness ~ Guiding Ethical Principles

NOTES

"The Church puts herself always and only at the service of conscience, helping it to avoid being tossed to and fro by every wind of doctrine proposed by human deceit, and helping it not to swerve from the truth about the good of man, but rather, especially in more difficult questions, to attain the truth with certainty and to abide in it."
Saint John Paul,
The Splendor of Truth, #64

"Do not conform yourselves to this age but be transformed by the renewal of your mind, that you may discern what is the will of God, what is good and pleasing and perfect."
Romans 12:2

"The eye is the lamp of the body. So if your eye is sound, your whole body will be full of light; but if your eye is not sound, your whole body will be full of darkness. If then the light in you is darkness, how great is the darkness!"
Mt. 6:22-23

The Jews would also have known from the 5th Commandment that murder is wrong, but Jesus sheds more light on the matter when he tells them that anger and cruel name-calling are ways of "killing" people.[13] It follows, then, that those people who know Jesus are better off than those who do not, for there is more "light" to guide them on their journey to Heaven.

The added help given to us through divine revelation does not stop with Jesus present with us in human flesh. It continues as Jesus makes Himself present to us through the power of the Holy Spirit, whom Jesus promised would be present in His Church to guide us to all truth. The **fourth** way we have of knowing the moral law, then, is through the Catholic Church. The Church makes Jesus' guiding light readily available to help guide us through any new moral questions that might arise since His death until He returns in glory.

In summary, then, we can say that informing one's conscience is a matter of educating it with the truth of the moral law. That truth is accessible to us naturally through the habit of synderesis innate in each of us. It is most perfectly available through Divine revelation as expressed in the Ten Commandments and in the moral teachings of Jesus and his Catholic Church. If we want to know the truth, then we need to go to these sources. We can encounter these sources directly or through the counsel of good, holy and moral people who are familiar with them.

Perhaps an analogy will make the point here even clearer. Consider a person who has just entered a room which is pitch black. There is no light at all in the room. Although the person has 20-20 vision, he is unable to see his hand in front of him because of the darkness. This person needs to walk to the other side of the room where there is a door that he can exit. However, between him and that door are numerous razor-sharp objects and traps that can mortally wound him if he is not careful. He is desperately in need of some light.

One of the lights available to him is the glow of a cell phone which he could use if he moves very slowly and carefully. It does not

---
[13] Matthew 5:22

give off much light, but it is enough if he moves very slowly. There's also a light from a small flashlight which sheds more light. In addition to that, there is a desk lamp available. Finally, he could turn on the overhead fluorescent light.

The dark room with the dangerous objects and traps is like our world. The person's eyes which have 20-20 vision are like his conscience. The eyes are there to help guide him through the world so that he can avoid all that would harm him. The eyes are of no use, of course, without some light -- the light of the moral law. The glow of a cell phone is similar to the help he can receive from the natural law to which he has access through synderesis. The light from a small flashlight is like the added help he could receive from the Ten Commandments. The desk lamp is like the help he could receive from Jesus' moral teachings which would enable him to see with so much more clarity. The overhead light is like the help which the teachings of the Church would offer him, as Jesus continues to guide the Church to make his teachings more clear to us here and now.

The moral of the story: Just as eyes need light, so too does the conscience need the truth of the moral law. With his conscience informed by truth, the person is truly free to move himself closer to the happiness for which he longs. This informing of conscience, however, like the education of the mind, is a lifelong task.

Does lack of guilt mean innocence?

Because a conscience which does not have the "light of truth" can be in error, it is possible for a person not to realize that what he is doing is evil. Thus, he will not *feel* guilt regarding his evil actions. We see this in a mentally handicapped person who takes something from a store without paying for it. The person does not know that he has done anything wrong and so he feels no guilt. His lack of knowing the truth about his actions, in this case, excuses him from any responsibility for his evil act. His ignorance is invincible. He does not sin.

This lack of feeling guilt, however, does not always mean that the person is innocent of sin. It could indicate just how morally sick the person really is: The person is so sick that he does not even know that he is sick. Soldiers under Hitler who did horrible things to innocent people *without feeling any guilt* for their actions are examples of such a sickness. So too is the Pharisee Jesus talks about who, *free of any feelings of guilt*, is nevertheless held responsible for his sinfulness.[14]

---
[14] Luke 18:9-14

NOTES

"With respect to conscience, an objection can arise: Is conscience not enough on its own as the norm of our conduct? Do not decalogues, the codes, imposed on us from outside, not undermine conscience...? This is a delicate and very current problem. Here all we will say is that subjective conscience is the first and immediate norm of our conduct, but it needs light, it needs to see which standard it should follow, especially when the action in question does not evidence its own moral exigencies. Conscience needs to be instructed and trained about what is the best choice to make, by the authority of a law."
Paul VI, *General Audience*,
March 28, 1973

Pope Benedict XVI speaks about this great sickness of conscience and its consequences:

> The 'delusion of innocence,' i.e., the inability to recognize guilt, is a destructive sickness, a sleeping-sickness of the conscience. Where, however, conscience falls asleep -- we have seen it happen in the last century -- man destroys both himself and the world. Hence the sleeping-sickness that can affect man's conscience mustn't be ignored; rather his conscience must be awakened so that he can seek forgiveness.
>
> This is, in fact, an essential manifestation of love, whereas to allow one's neighbor to become religiously forgetful, or to let his conscience wither and die, is to show a lack of love towards him. In other words, it is a sign of love for one's neighbor to harass him, so that he wakes up to God, so that he himself can once again become a loving person.[15]

One Final Question

Have you ever noticed that some peoples' consciences are more sensitive or alert than others? Even though these people might have had the very same moral formation and upbringing, there can be great differences between them. What accounts for these differences?

We know that some aspects of the conscience are the same for everyone: We all have the innate habit of knowing basic moral principles (synderesis), and we all also have a practical intellect. So the "raw material" for making correct judgments of conscience is present within us all. Why one person's conscience is more sensitive than another's or why one makes correct judgments more readily than another can be explained by looking at what each person has done with his "raw material."

Conscience is like a muscle. It needs to be exercised. If we let it remain unused over time, it will atrophy, just like a muscle does. If we exercise it, however, we will find that it becomes more and more sensitive or alert to the Law-Giver Himself. The first and most important exercise conscience can do is to *listen honestly*, to be *genuinely open* to the will of our Creator.

People who do not realize there is a Creator, however, will not be inclined to listen. They will think that any moral "voice" they hear from within themselves is simply a reflection of society's opinion or their own

---

NOTES

"Dear young people, do not let the culture of possessions and pleasure lull your consciences! Be vigilant and alert 'sentinels,' in order to be genuine protagonists of a new humanity."

Saint John Paul,
Angelus Address, July 7, 2002

[15] Pope Benedict XVI, *Sermon*, September 4, 2004.

subconscious thoughts which they are free to disregard if they so choose. Because of their lack of faith, they are unable to recognize the "voice" of conscience as a moral authority which they are obligated to heed.

This is probably why people of faith -- those who know there is a Being superior to themselves who created them and loves them -- tend to have more sensitive consciences. To the degree that their faith is strong, their conscience will be more sensitive. The more they are convinced there is Someone superior to themselves to Whom they are obligated in some way, the more they will want to know His law and heed it.

Love also plays a major part in this. Have you ever noticed how attentive a person is to those whom he loves? The degree to which a person listens and is open to another has everything to do with how much he loves him. We are truly attentive to those we love because we are eager to please them. Perhaps, then, the reason why some consciences are more sensitive than others is simply a matter of the degree of love a person has for the One who reveals His will to us through the conscience.

Conclusion

Conscience is the ability each of us has of applying the general moral law to the particular acts we are considering doing. Making correct moral judgments about these acts is going to be the key to our freedom. If we judge correctly, then we can navigate through the "mine fields" of this life and reach the goal we seek. In other words, conscience and its link to truth make it possible for us to achieve the happiness we seek.

With this understanding of the role conscience plays in our search for happiness, we are ready now to proceed with our study of ethics by investigating the voluntary human act itself.

Study Guide Questions:

1. *What is conscience?*
2. *Why do we think conscience is more than a feeling or an opinion a person has?*
3. *What accounts for the fact that the judgment of conscience is fundamentally objective? What makes us think it is subjective?*
4. *What is a doubtful conscience and what are our moral obligations regarding it?*

"To be truly free means to be a person of upright conscience...."
Saint John Paul,
Apostolic Letter to Youth, 1985, #3

Called to Happiness ~ Guiding Ethical Principles

NOTES

5. How does a person "form" his conscience? Where can a person find the truth of the moral law which he needs to inform his conscience?

6. What is the relationship between conscience and truth?

7. What is "synderesis"? Why does St. Thomas speak of it in relation to conscience?

8. If every human person has the light of truth within him, how is it possible for his conscience to make an error in judgment?

9. In light of what you have read in this chapter, how would you respond to someone who said, "I am better off not being Catholic because I don't have to follow so many laws"?

10. Of the two men of normal intelligence who commit murder, the one who does not recognize that murder is wrong is sicker than one who does. Explain.

11. Using what you have learned about conscience, how would you explain why Jesus might have been critical of the Pharisee in the parable from Luke 18:9-14?

12. If two people have the same moral upbringing, why might one of them have a more sensitive conscience than the other?

Chapter IV
Conscience and Truth

CASES IN POINT

#1 - After the terrorists' attack on the World Trade Center 9/11/01, we found letters the terrorists had written. Some of these letters indicated that they viewed their actions against us as "good" acts in accord with the wishes of their god.
- *Because they thought they were doing good, were their acts good? Explain.*
- *Does the fact that their consciences did not tell them they were doing wrong excuse them from the evil they did? Explain.*

* * * * *

#2 - A 36-year-old Austrian layman, Franz Jaegerstaetter, was executed by guillotine on August 9, 1943, for his refusal to serve in the Nazi army. As a devout Catholic, Jaegerstaetter viewed his Christian faith as being completely irreconcilable with Nazism. When he was called upon to serve, he presented himself to the military authorities as a conscientious objector. They condemned and executed him. He left behind a wife and three young children.
- *If he were simply to follow the orders of his commanding officers, then wouldn't that excuse Jaegerstaetter from moral responsibility for his actions in the military? Shouldn't the responsibility lie with those who issue the orders? Explain.*
- *Jaegerstaetter knew that he could be killed for refusing to fight for the Nazi army. Wouldn't that fact have excused him from any evil act he would do as a soldier?*
- *What would you have done if you had been Jaegerstaetter?*

* * * * *

#3 - Tony has just heard about artificial human reproduction from one of his coworkers at the office who has used it to have a child. Because he loves children, Tony's first reaction is to think that it is a marvelous thing for infertile couples to be able to have a child of their own. After giving it some more thought, however, he begins to have some doubts. Not too long after this, someone else asks him for his opinion about a married couple using artificial human reproduction to have a baby they want.
- *What should Tony say or do in response to the question?*
- *Would it be ok for him to simply give his own personal opinion and leave it at that? Explain.*

* * * * *

#4 - "I am not conscious of anything against me, but I do not thereby stand acquitted; the one who judges me is the Lord. Therefore do not make any judgment before the appointed time, until the Lord comes, for he will bring to light what is hidden in darkness and will manifest the motives of our hearts...." *1 Cor. 4:4*
- *In view of what we have studied about conscience, why might St. Paul be unwilling to consider himself without blame?*

"Man's real strength is seen in the fidelity with which he is capable to render witness to truth, resisting blandishments and threats, incomprehension and blackmail, including harsh and merciless persecution."

Saint John Paul,
March 24, 2002

NOTES

"Truth means more than knowledge: knowing the truth leads us to discover the good."
Pope Benedict XVI, 4/17/08

Point to Consider:

"Dear young friends!

"... Christ asks you about the state of your moral awareness, and at the same time he questions you about the state of your conscience. This is a key question for man: it is the fundamental question of your youth, one that concerns the whole plan of life which must be formed precisely in youth. Its value is the one most closely connected with the relationship of each of you with moral good and evil. The value of this plan depends in an essential way on the authenticity and rectitude of your conscience. It also depends on its sensitivity.

"So we find ourselves here at a crucial moment, when at every step time and eternity meet at a level which is proper to man. It is the level of the conscience, the level of moral values: the conscience is the most important dimension of time and history. For history is written not only by the events which in a certain sense happen 'from outside;' it is written first of all 'from within:' it is the history of human consciences, of moral victories and defeats. Here too the essential greatness of man finds its foundation: his authentically human dignity. This is that interior treasure whereby man continually goes beyond himself in the direction of eternity. If it is true that 'it is established that people would die only once,' it is also true that man carries with him the treasure of conscience, the deposit of good and evil, across the frontier of death, in order that, in the sight of him who is holiness itself, he may find the ultimate and definitive truth about his whole life: 'after that comes judgment.'

"This is just what happens in the conscience: in the interior truth of our acts, in a certain sense, there is constantly present the dimension of eternal life. And simultaneously the same conscience, through moral values, imprints the most expressive seal upon the life of the generations, upon the history and culture of human environments, societies, nations and of all humanity.

"In this field how much depends on each one of you!"

Pope Saint John Paul the Great,
Apostolic Letter to the Youth of the World, 1985, #6.

Chapter V

The Human Act

We have seen that the human person seeks a good that will fulfill all of his desires and thus make it possible for him to enjoy complete happiness. To secure the freedom he needs to reach this happiness, the Creator has provided him with both moral law and conscience. The moral law serves as general guide, while the conscience *specifically* directs him regarding each and every free act. Thus equipped, he is ready to set off on the journey.

With this understanding of what has been provided to help us in our journey to complete happiness, we are ready now to turn our attention to those *free acts* which are the means by which we reach this goal. *Free* acts are those which only the human person is capable of doing. You see, it is by means of acts which are under our control here and now that we can actually play a role in becoming worthy of the happiness we seek.

The fact that we human beings have this role to play in our own destiny points to our great dignity. According to St. Thomas Aquinas, it is in our free will that the true image of God can be perceived in us, for we show forth his image precisely in our mastery, or control, over our actions.[1] Let us turn now and see what we mean by the "human act" -- that act over which we, as human persons, have mastery.

Vocabulary

voluntary	human act	antecedent passion	consent
deliberation	imputable	consequent passion	merit

It is not unusual to hear people speak about the *behavior* of animals as well as the *behavior* of human beings. We never hear them speak, however, about the *conduct* of animals. That word "conduct," then, must imply something more than "behavior," for we use the word "conduct" *only* in reference to human activity. For example, we might hear parents tell their son to conduct himself as a gentleman. Not all human activity, however, would be referred to as conduct but only that

---

[1] St. Thomas Aquinas, *Summa Theologiae*, Prologue, I-II.

Human act - an act for which a person bears responsibility because he deliberately chose to do it.

activity over which the person has control. For example, we would never speak about how a person conducts himself while he is sleeping.

When we are speaking about how a person *conducts* himself, we are speaking about "**human acts**," that is, acts which are unique to human persons. In other words, we are talking about those ***acts over which a person has mastery*** ("human acts") as opposed to other acts which occur without his conscious control ("acts of man"). For example, *deliberately choosing* to go to bed in order to sleep is a "human act" but unconsciously dozing off because of drowsiness is an "act of man." The difference between the two is based *solely* on whether or not the act was done knowingly and willingly. Because animals lack an intellect and a free will, they are not capable of acting knowingly and willingly; that is, they are not capable of doing "human acts."

The term "human act" does not refer only to the external activity of our bodies. It also refers to our thoughts, our words, and our "omissions." Anything that is the result of the free choice of the will is included as a "human act." For example, a person may choose to *think* impurely about another person, or he may choose *not to talk* to someone with whom he works closely. He could also choose to *remember* a past kindness of someone who has just made an angry remark to him so that he could more easily forgive him, or to *speak* a welcoming word to someone who tends to isolate himself from others. These are all human acts because they were freely chosen by a human will.

From this explanation, you should be coming to realize that the term "human acts" is a technical term with a restricted meaning. St. Thomas explains:

> Of actions done by man, those alone are properly called human which are ***proper to man as man.*** Now man differs from irrational animals in this that he is master of his actions. Wherefore ***those actions alone are properly called human of which man is master.*** Now man is master of his actions through his reason and will …. Therefore those actions are properly called human which proceed from a deliberate will. And if any other actions are found in man, they can be called actions of a man, but not properly human actions, since they are not proper to man as man.[2]

---

[2] St. Thomas Aquinas, *Summa Theologiae*, I-II, q. 1, a. 1.

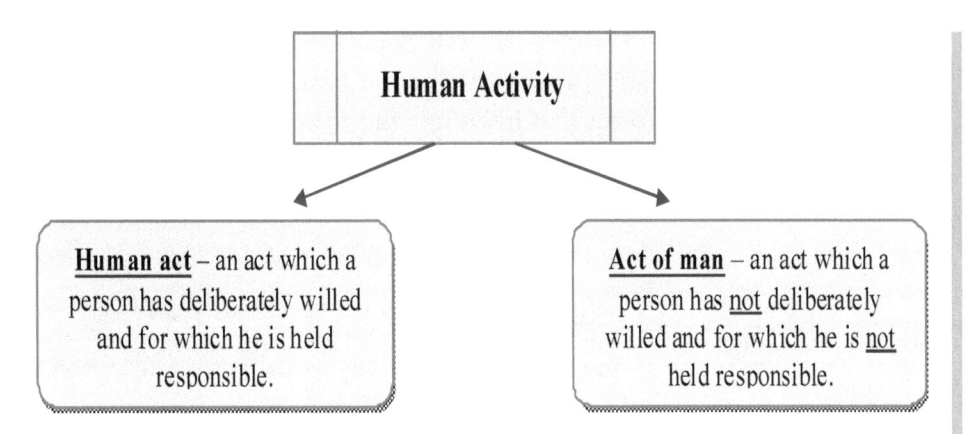

```
                    ┌─────────────────────┐
                    │   Human Activity    │
                    └─────────────────────┘
                       ↙             ↘
```

Human act – an act which a person has deliberately willed and for which he is held responsible.

Act of man – an act which a person has <u>not</u> deliberately willed and for which he is <u>not</u> held responsible.

Human acts are the subject matter of the science of Ethics. Because we have conscious control of them, we want to be sure that we choose the kind of acts that will move us closer to the happiness we seek.

Analyzing the Human Act

As St. Thomas says, a human act is one which is *proper to man as man*. This means that it is an act which only a human being can do. Thus a human act must involve the two faculties of the rational soul: the intellect and the will. When these two powers work together, the person has the ability to will *freely*. Let us see what this cooperative process involving the intellect and the will in the human act looks like. We are going to "slow the act down" and "pull it apart" in order to get a really good look at it.

No human person acts unless he is attracted by something which he thinks is good. So it is this attraction to the good which begins every human act. Because the will itself is blind, it is the intellect which starts the process. Once the intellect knows something as good, the will can respond with a liking for it. If the intellect knows it as a good *for the person,* then the will can respond with a **wish** or desire for it. If the intellect thinks it is actually possible to obtain this good, then the will can "tend toward" it by forming an **intention**, although the will is free not to form the intention. Thus far in the process, we have considered only the person's response to the good *as an end* or goal.

Let's look at an example of this first step. The intellect begins by realizing that it is a good thing to get ready for tryouts for the baseball team. The will can respond to the intellect's realization of this good with its own liking of it. The intellect then proceeds to realize that getting ready for tryouts would be a good thing *for the person* himself to do. The will can respond to this intellectual thought with a <u>wish</u> or desire to get ready for tryouts. The intellect might then think that it is actually possible for the person to do this.

Chapter V
The Human Act

NOTES

97.

Called to Happiness ~ Guiding Ethical Principles

NOTES

As a response to this thought, the will could form its <u>intention</u>: "I'm going to try to get ready for tryouts for the baseball team." The will could also, however, reject that intention and form another one.

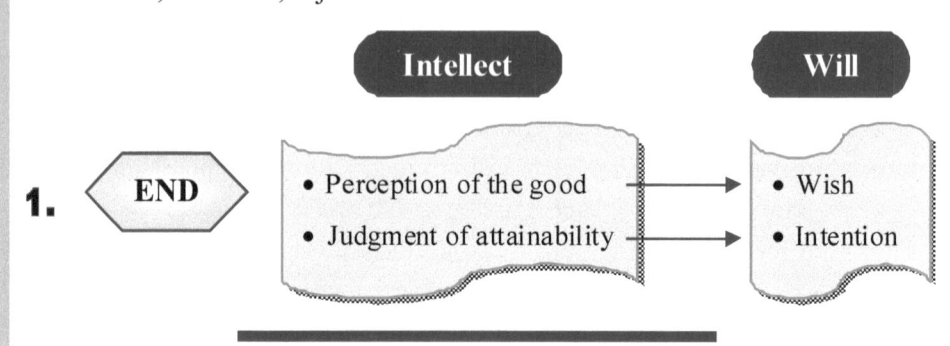

1. END — Intellect: • Perception of the good • Judgment of attainability → Will: • Wish • Intention

The next step in the human act is for the intellect to begin considering the various *means* which are possible for carrying out the intention of the will. This act of the intellect is called its **deliberation**. When the intellect finishes its deliberation, it reaches its final outcome, its *last practical judgment*: "This is what I should do now." The will is free either to accept this last judgment of the intellect about what to do here and now, or it can reject it and direct the intellect to think about something else.

Deliberation - the act of weighing a thing in the mind; careful consideration with a view to decision.

"Truly human behavior is *considered* behavior, behavior which bears everywhere on it the mark of intelligence."
D.Q. McInerny, *Thomistic Ethics*, p. 57

For example, following the will's intention to get ready for tryouts for the school's baseball team, the intellect *deliberates* about a number of ways of doing this. Perhaps the person could practice at the batting cages. Or maybe he could ask his older brother who is on the team to practice with him. Or perhaps he could begin to lift weights after school. The intellect finishes its thinking about these various possible *means* with the *practical judgment*: "It would be best to begin lifting weights after school."

Aware of the intellect's decision to begin lifting weights, the will could agree with the intellect and make that decision its own by giving its **consent**. If the intellect does not made a decision but instead offers two options to the will, then the will could select between these two options and make a **choice**. For example, the intellect could have decided that both lifting weights and practicing at the cages are good *means* to getting ready for baseball tryouts. The will, then, could have *chosen* between these two *means*. *Consent* and *choice* are really two names for the same act of the will: To consent to one option is to choose it over another, if there is another one.

Consent - from Latin *consentire* (to feel with, agree); to agree or approve through an act of the will.

Choice - a selection between at least two options.

"Our choices have objects, and the object of our choice will determine the moral status of the act of choice itself."
D.Q. McInerny, *Thomistic Ethics*, p. 54

The will could also reject completely what the intellect suggests and simply tell the intellect to keep thinking, that is, to find some other *means* or to consider more fully one option that it has already proposed.

98.

2. MEANS

Intellect:
- Deliberation
- Last practical judgment

Will:
- Consent
- Choice

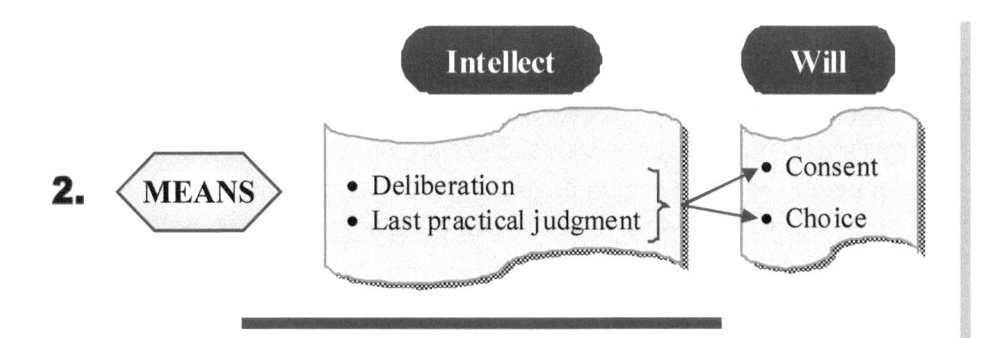

In the final stages of the human act, the intellect tells the will that its decision needs to be carried out; that is, it needs to be executed. This act of the intellect is called its **command**. (St. Thomas thinks that the command must be the work of the intellect because it involves a directing which requires an *understanding* of how means lead to ends.[3] The command of the intellect is not carried out, however, until the will acts.) The will then directs that the *means* it selected be used. We call this act of the will its act of **use**. Then, when the intellect becomes aware that the person has attained the *end* he was after, the will responds with its **enjoyment** of that *end*.

With regard to our example, the final stages of the human act would look like this: The intellect tells the will that the person needs to go down to the weight room after school. In response to this command by the intellect, the will directs the powers of the soul to do what needs to be done in order to walk down there. Thus, the will tells the leg muscles to walk, the hand to open the doors, and other parts of the body to do what is necessary to lift the weights. When the intellect is aware that the person is actually lifting the weights, the will responds with its enjoyment of having attained the goal it sought.

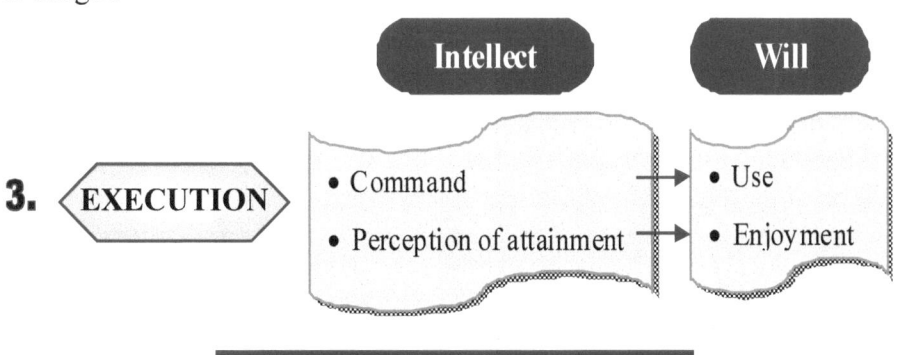

3. EXECUTION

Intellect:
- Command
- Perception of attainment

Will:
- Use
- Enjoyment

Before we complete this analysis of the human act, let us highlight a few points:

---
[3] St. Thomas Aquinas, *Summa Theologiae,* I-II, q. 17, a. 1.

Called to Happiness ~ Guiding Ethical Principles

> "A human act, precisely as human and moral, flows from a person's 'heart,' from a person's will. This is why human actions have an existential and religious significance and why they are primarily specified by the object chosen."
> Saint John Paul, *Splendor of Truth*, #79

Interior act - an act elicited from the will; an act of willing as such.

Exterior act - an act commanded by the will carrying out the command of reason but executed by the other powers of the soul and the bodily members.

◆ Did you notice that we said that the will acts in forming its <u>intention</u> regarding the end *as well as* in consenting to or choosing the <u>means</u>? There are two steps, then, in the human act before the person actually executes it. In the will's first step, the will can either respond to a perceived good which begins the process of deliberation or it cannot. In its second step, at the end of deliberating, the will can <u>consent</u> to or <u>choose</u> the means to achieving its end. Both of these steps are acts for which the will bears responsibility.

◆ Notice that the act becomes a human act *as soon as* the will forms its intention and gives its <u>consent</u>. Actually "doing the act" or "not doing the act" only adds to the act's "perfection." Thus, a person who <u>intends</u> to harm another and <u>consents</u> to murder him but is unable to carry it out because of circumstances beyond his control is responsible for the sin of murder, even though he never carries out the act. In like manner, a person who <u>intends</u> and <u>consents</u> to an act of charity but dies before he can accomplish the act will receive **merit** for his act of charity.

◆ Did you also notice that there is an interior and an exterior dimension to the will's act? The **interior act** is the act of willing itself, that is, the will's acts of forming its intention and consenting or choosing. The **exterior act** is the act commanded by the will but executed by the other powers of the soul and the bodily members.

◆ *A human act is any act over which the human will has control.* This includes not only the will's own acts but also the acts of the other faculties of the soul over which the will has control. We see this in the example above. The will is responsible for its own acts of forming an intention and giving consent to the idea of getting ready to tryout for the baseball team. The will is also responsible for the other acts that it commands the various powers of the soul to do: telling the legs to walk, the hands to turn the door knobs, the intellect to consider which weights to lift, the arms to lift the weights, etc. Thus, in addition to its own acts, the will commands both internal mental acts as well as external bodily acts.

Our analysis of the human act pulled apart what actually exists altogether as a whole. We have taken a very complicated process -- the human act -- and broken it down into its parts. The analysis shows, though, that the human act is the work of both the intellect and will cooperating together. While it is surely true to say that the human will is the controlling faculty of the person, the will is blind without the aid of the intellect.

Study Guide Questions:

1. How does a "human act" differ from an "act of man"?
Which of them is of interest to the science of Ethics? Why?

Chapter V
The Human Act

2. *Within the human act, what two steps does the will take before it actually executes the act?*
3. *Where in the analysis of the human act would the judgment of conscience fit in?*
4. *If it is the intellect's role to deliberate and to make the last practical judgment about what we should do, then why do we say that the will is in control?*
5. *Where in the analysis of the human act would sin occur?*
6. *Why will a person be held responsible for the sin of stealing if, when he attempted robbery, he found that the man he was robbing had no money?*
7. *Why would a person who planned to visit the elderly in a nursing home but was unable to do so because he got the flu be worthy of any merit?*
8. *List five acts you have done in the last half an hour that have been commanded by your will.*
9. *Of the two faculties -- the intellect and the will -- which is man's highest power? Justify your answer.*

CASES IN POINT

#1 - Once in awhile when he is out shopping, the idea spontaneously pops into Rob's mind that he could easily shop lift an item or two from the stores and never get caught. Rob has never given into these ideas, but he did once consent to thinking about shop lifting. He mulled it over for about 10 minutes and then decided not to do it, but he felt guilty for even thinking about it.

- *Was Rob's act of thinking about shop lifting something he should be concerned about? Explain.*

* * * * *

#2 - Sarah wanted to get a good grade on the up-coming algebra exam, but because of activities at school and at home she didn't have much time to study. As she was taking the exam, she found it to be much more difficult than she had expected and she panicked. In considering her options, she realized that there was a very bright student sitting next to her whose answers could be seen if she took the trouble. Just as she turned her eyes to look in that direction, however, the teacher walked next to her and remained there until the test was finished. Sarah was unable to cheat, and she failed the algebra test.

- *Is Sarah guilty of the sin of cheating? Explain.*
- *What do you think happened to her conscience in the above scenario?*

NOTES

It is possible to sin through our thoughts as well as through our words, deeds, and omissions. The heart of sin is the act of the will. As we learn more about sin, it is important to remember that God is supremely merciful if we are sorry and turn to Him for forgiveness.

The Voluntary Act

Every *human act* is a **voluntary** act. That means that it is a *willed* act. Because the will is blind and needs the intellect to show it the end, however, every voluntary act must also be an act which is guided by knowledge. St. Thomas speaks of the voluntary act as an act whose cause is "within the agent," along with some knowledge of the end or goal.[4]

In other words, the voluntary act cannot be forced on a person by someone who overpowers him, nor can it be an automatic response that arises from within him. It must be *an act that originates in the will and is guided by knowledge of the end.*

This is precisely why the voluntary act is so very important: it is the act whereby a person freely moves himself toward an end that he knows. He is master of his voluntary act. Whatever *he* chooses to do or not do gets done or remains undone because of his choice.

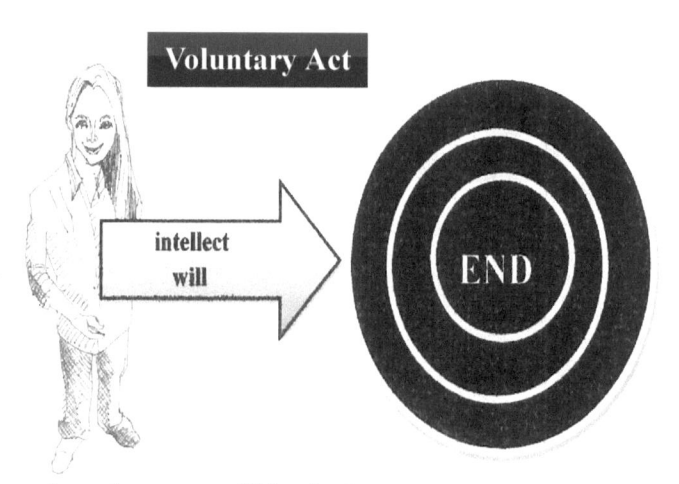

It is because he both knows what he is doing and freely chooses to do it that a person is held *responsible* for his voluntary acts. What he wills to be done is done <u>because</u> he wills it. For example, the ball breaks the window because a person freely chose to hit the ball in the direction of the window. The person who freely chose to hit the ball is held responsible or accountable for the window <u>he</u> broke. This is what it means for a person to be master of his voluntary act. Whatever that act produces will be **imputed** to him as its cause. Because he is its cause, he is the one who **merits** to be either praised or blamed for it. He is the one who deserves the reward or the punishment for what his act accomplished. The degree of his reward or punishment will depend on the extent to which his act was voluntary.

In the science of Ethics, the voluntary act is also called the *moral act*. Simply because the intellect and the will are involved, an act takes on a moral quality. It will be either morally good or morally evil,

---

NOTES

Voluntary - from Latin *voluntarius* (freely undertaken); performed or done knowingly and freely, with one's own free will.

"The soul shows its royal and exalted character ... in that it is free and self-governed, swayed autonomously by its own will. Of whom else can this be said, save a king...?"
 St. Gregory of Nyssa

Impute - from Latin *imputare* (to charge); to attribute or ascribe to a person; to charge with a fault.

Merit - from Latin *mereri* (to earn as pay; deserve); that which is deserved; due reward or punishment.

---

[4] St. Thomas Aquinas, *Summa Theologiae*, I-II, q. 6, a. 1.

depending on whether the act takes the person closer to the True End, that is, to the Happiness that he seeks. This again is why the voluntary act is so important. Because we are the master of our voluntary acts, their moral quality will be totally our responsibility. If we freely choose to do morally evil acts, then we will merit punishment for them. In the same way, if we freely choose to do morally good acts, then we also merit for ourselves a reward.

One added point about voluntary acts: In *almost* all cases, the voluntary act is also a *free* act. Since the term "voluntary" means something different than "free," however, it is possible to have a voluntary act which is *not* free. In a free act, the will is able to choose between at least two options. The person who acts freely understands that he can choose differently than he does. A voluntary act, on the other hand, is simply one which originates in the will and is guided by knowledge.

An act could be voluntary but not free *if the will were offered a choice that was infinitely good, that is, good without limit.* In such a case, a person would knowingly and willingly choose this unlimited good which is offered to him, but he would not be free to choose differently since there would be no other real options.

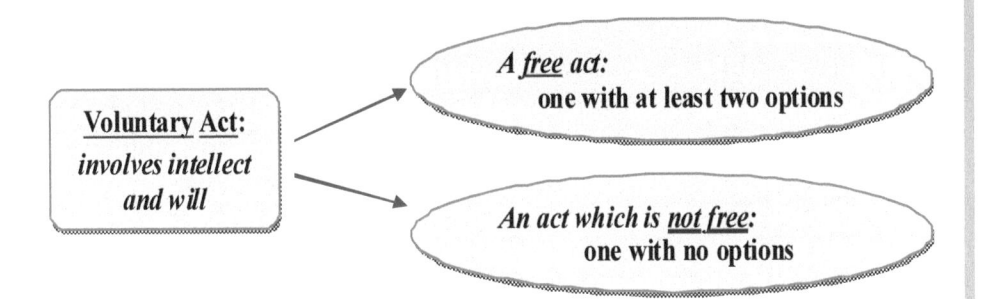

Voluntary Act: *involves intellect and will*
→ *A free act:* one with at least two options
→ An act which is *not free*: one with no options

Does this ever happen? Not in our life here on earth because we never find a good which is *so good* that we cannot reject it. The goods here are always limited or finite goods. In the next life, however, when we behold *Infinite Goodness Himself*, we will have found a Good which far surpasses anything our wills could desire. Our movement toward this Great Good will indeed be voluntary, for we will know and will it, but our acts of choosing it will <u>not</u> be free. We will not be able to move ourselves in any other direction than toward it because we will have found the complete happiness for which we long.

Limitations of the Voluntary Act

Because we are responsible for our acts only to the degree that they are voluntary, it will be important for us to know what things could make an act less voluntary. There are several.

Called to Happiness ~ Guiding Ethical Principles

NOTES

Ignorance -- Would ignorance make a person's act involuntary? It all depends. While it is true that knowledge is essential to the voluntary act, it is *not* always true that a lack of knowledge makes an act involuntary. Let us see why this is so.

Ignorance does not always remove a person from responsibility for the acts he does. It will all depend on *why* he is ignorant. Is the ignorance itself voluntary? If it is, then anything a person does in voluntary ignorance will to some extent be voluntary, and he will bear responsibility for it. If his ignorance is not voluntary, then his actions done in involuntary ignorance will *not* be voluntary, and he will bear no responsibility for it.

As we learned in the previous chapter, these two types of ignorance are commonly referred to as vincible and invincible ignorance. "Vincible" comes from the Latin word *vincere*, meaning to overcome or conquer. **Vincible ignorance** is ignorance that we could have overcome if we had wanted to do so. For example, Susan, a student returning to school after a day's absence is ignorant of the math assignment for that day. Her ignorance is *vincible*, however, because it easily could have been overcome by asking the teacher or a fellow student for the assignment.

Vincible ignorance - from Latin *vincere* (to overcome); ignorance which a person can and should overcome. A person bears responsibility for this ignorance.

Invincible ignorance - from Latin *in-vincere* (not to overcome); ignorance of which a person is not aware and which he is unable to overcome by himself. A person bears no responsibility for this ignorance.

Invincible ignorance is ignorance that could not have been overcome. For example, Matt was called away from football practice for five minutes by one of the school counselors. When he returned, he asked his fellow players if he has missed anything, but none of them told him about a change the coach made in one of the plays. When it came time to run the play, Matt messed up the play because he was ignorant of the change. Matt's ignorance was invincible, though, because he was unaware of it.

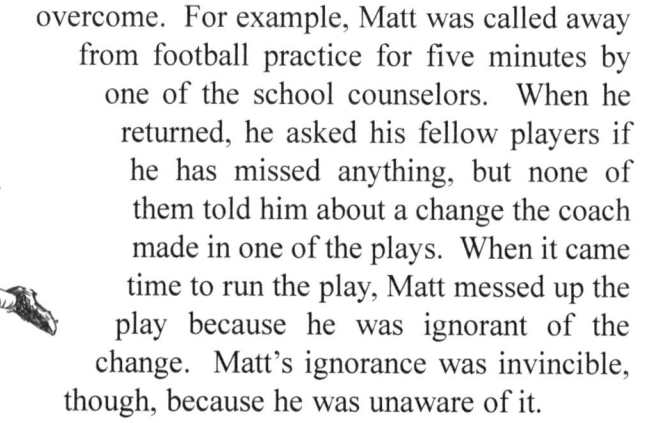

Vincible ignorance does not make an act involuntary. Because the ignorance is voluntary, the act done in ignorance will also *to some extent* be voluntary. Vincible ignorance does *lessen* the voluntariness of an act, however. To the degree there is less knowledge, an act will always be less voluntary.

Consider the example of a person who voluntarily drinks too much alcohol. In his drunken state, he wrecks his car and damages another's. Because his drunkenness was voluntary, the damage he does in his drunken state is to some extent voluntary. However, because he was not fully aware of the effects his drunken acts would have when he chose to drink too much, we would have to say that wrecking the car was not *fully* voluntary. He would be held less responsible for his wrecked car than if he had *deliberately* planned to wreck his car. He would, of course, be held *totally* responsible for choosing to drink in the first place, knowing full well that he intended to drive in that condition.

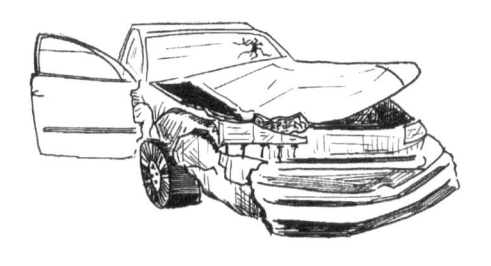

Invincible ignorance, however, does make an act completely involuntary. For example, if a salesman is unaware that the merchandise he is selling is stolen, then he does no wrong. His ignorance excuses him. He voluntarily sells merchandise, but he does not voluntarily sell *stolen* merchandise.

Passion -- Would strong emotion (passion) affect a person's voluntary act? Yes. Emotion is a movement of the sensitive appetites. A voluntary act involves a movement of the rational appetite. Both appetites are "moving powers" within a human person. Having the sense appetites (emotions) moving strongly would only make it *easier* for the rational appetite to move as well, *if they were moving in the same direction*. In cases such as this, the passion makes an act *more voluntary:* the will moves more easily.

> My feelings come *without* my wanting them to be here. I do forgive him for the hurt he caused me.

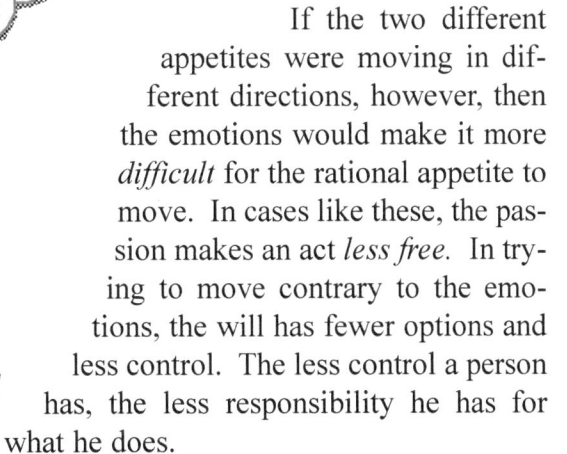

If the two different appetites were moving in different directions, however, then the emotions would make it more *difficult* for the rational appetite to move. In cases like these, the passion makes an act *less free*. In trying to move contrary to the emotions, the will has fewer options and less control. The less control a person has, the less responsibility he has for what he does.

Passion can be either "antecedent" or "consequent" -- depending on when it is aroused. If the passion is aroused spontaneously *before* the will can act, then it is called **antecedent passion**. If the passion is delib-

Antecedent passion - from Latin *antecedere* (to go before); an emotional response which precedes an act of the will.

NOTES

Consequent passion - from Latin *consequeri* (to follow closely); an emotional response which follows an act of the will.

erately aroused by a person, then it is called **consequent passion** because it comes *after* a choice of the will. It is possible for antecedent passion to become consequent passion if the person freely chooses to foster the passion once it is has been aroused.

Antecedent passion can, on rare occasions, make an act completely *not* free. This happens when the passion blocks the person's use of his intellect. Without the use of his intellect, the person cannot perform a voluntary act. Usually, however, antecedent passion does not prevent a voluntary act; it simply *lessens* the person's freedom and control. Because a person is not in as much control of his act, his responsibility will be less. An example of antecedent passion affecting the voluntary act would be the case of a person who witnesses someone he loves get hurt in a car accident due to the drunkenness of another driver. In his anger, the witness might grab the drunken driver and begin to hit him. The passion of anger actually makes the witness less free and less in control of his actions.

Consequent passion does not make an act less voluntary. On the contrary, it makes an act *more* voluntary because the passion is *deliberately* aroused or fostered. Since the presence of the passion makes it easier for the will to act and the person freely chose to arouse the passion, the act will be *more* voluntary. For example, a person who deliberately chooses to brood over hurtful remarks that another has said chooses to stir up within himself strong anger. The presence of this anger makes it easier for him to do what he wants to do to him: cause him bodily harm. Because he freely chooses to arouse the anger that makes it easier for him to do bodily harm to a person, he is held *fully* responsible for his act because it was *completely* voluntary.

Fear -- Would an awareness of an approaching evil affect the voluntary act? The fear we are considering here is not the emotion of fear. It is an *intellectual fear* which comes from understanding the presence of a threatening evil. For example, a person may lie because he fears being caught in his wrongdoing, or a soldier may desert because he fears the enemy will win.

To illustrate this fear, St. Thomas uses the example of the sea captain who throws a sizable portion of his valuable cargo overboard in order to save his ship during a violent storm. Does the captain do this voluntarily? St. Thomas answers, "Yes" and "no." Yes - the captain freely chooses to dump his cargo, even though he knows that he could keep it and try to survive the storm. In other words, the captain does have an option from which to choose. No -- it is not voluntary, St. Thomas says, in that the captain would not choose to throw away his valuable cargo *if his life was not being threatened by the storm.* The fear of losing his life influenced the captain's actions, but it did not completely make them involuntary.[5]

According to St. Thomas, then, fear can make a voluntary act *less* voluntary, but it cannot make it *completely* involuntary. In fear, we still freely choose to act one way or another, though we would probably not make that choice if we were not aware of the approaching evil.

We often see examples of fear in cases of bullying. A bully may threaten a young boy with a fight if the boy doesn't give him his lunch every day. So the boy surrenders his lunch daily. Does he do this voluntarily? Yes and no. Yes, he freely chooses to give his lunch rather than go through the trouble of trying to keep it for himself. No, it is not voluntary in that he would not choose to give his lunch away if he were not being threatened with bodily harm.

Force -- What does external physical force do to the voluntary act? For example, what if a person does not want to stand up, but a bigger, stronger person physically pulls him to an erect position and then holds him there? Does the external physical force of this strong person affect the voluntary act of the weaker one? No, the person still does not want to stand up. His will has not at all changed. External physical force cannot touch the will. The will is *within* a person. It is impossible for someone other than the person himself to get to it in order to influence it directly. Thus, a stronger person may be able to make me be in an upright position when I do not want to be there by physically making my body do what I do not want it to do, but he cannot make me <u>want</u> to have my body be in an erect position if I do not choose to want it. Only the person himself has direct control of the will.

Habit -- A habit is a disposition or inclination to act in a certain way which a person acquires because of his repeated acts. Would the presence of a habit affect the voluntary act? It all depends.

If we deliberately acquired the habit and have done nothing to get rid of it, then yes the habit itself is voluntary and any acts that follow

"We can be forced to act against our will, but we cannot be forced to will against our will."
D.Q. McInerny,
Thomistic Ethics, p. 36

---

[5] St. Thomas Aquinas, *Summa Theologiae,* I-II, q. 6, a. 6.

from it would be voluntary. The habit of playing a musical instrument would be an example of this. A musician works long hours trying to acquire the habit of playing his instrument well. Once the habit of playing has been acquired, the acts of playing the instrument, which follow with ease and enjoyment, are no less voluntary than is the habit itself. The musician would be fully responsible for his musical acts.

If we did not intend to acquire a habit, but we did intend to repeatedly do acts that we knew would cause us to form a habit, then the habit itself as well as the acts that follow from it would be voluntary. The habit of smoking is a good example of this. A person knows that smoking is a habit-forming act. If he chooses to do this act repeatedly, then the habit he forms would indeed be voluntary and so would the acts of smoking that follow from having acquired the habit. He would bear full responsibility for them.

If we acquired a habit *unintentionally* by doing things in the same way so often that a habit is formed, then the habit is not voluntary. Neither are the acts that follow unintentionally from it. However, once we are aware the habit exists, the choice to keep it or to get rid of it becomes voluntary. For example, a person might develop the habit of eating in-between meals because the people he lives with do it all the time. However, it is not his intention to develop the habit, and he regrets when he finds himself looking for something to eat without even being hungry. He is not responsible for the habit he has unintentionally developed, even though he is responsible for each of the acts that led to forming the habit. He is also not responsible for his inclination to look for food when he is not hungry. The habit causes him to do this. Once the person is aware that he has developed this bad habit, however, he will become responsible for what he decides to do about it.

Conclusion

The human act is an awesome thing! It is the one dimension of our lives over which we have control. This indeed is an important aspect of our human dignity: we are masters of our own acts! Accompanying this tremendous dignity of ours, however, is a weighty responsibility. We must choose to act in such a way as to do what is *truly* good for us so that we will secure our genuine happiness.

In our next chapter we will look more in depth at the human act in an attempt to determine what it is that makes the act to be a morally good or evil one.

Study Guide Questions:

1. What does it mean to say that an act is voluntary?
2. Why is the voluntary act so important?
3. What does it mean to say that an act is free? Is every voluntary act of a human person also a free act? Explain.
4. Explain the difference between vincible and invincible ignorance.
5. Why does vincible ignorance make a person's act less voluntary?
6. How can passion make a person's act more voluntary? How can passion make an act less free?
7. Why is consequent passion a more serious ethical matter than antecedent passion?
8. Does fear completely excuse a person of all responsibility for his actions?
9. What effect does external physical force have on the voluntary act of a person?
10. Does a person's habit of smoking make his act of smoking less voluntary? Explain.

Called to Happiness ~ Guiding Ethical Principles

NOTES

CASES IN POINT

Discuss the level of responsibility the persons have in the following scenarios:

♦ One of Pete's responsibilities at home is to make sure that the dog has food and water in its bowls outside. When his parents noticed that the dog had lost weight, they asked Pete about it. Pete explained that he did not voluntarily choose not to fill the dog's bowls. He just did not usually think about doing it. He admitted that there were days when the dog went without food and water.

♦ Sam hates going to school ever since the new kid Will arrived. Sam is small for his age, and Will towers over him by about a foot. It's not unusual for Will to shove Sam around to get him to do what he wants. Yesterday at break between classes, Will tripped Sam so that he fell flat on the ground. Later, when the teacher was asking Will and Sam what happened, Will explained that Sam had tripped on his own feet. When the teacher turned to Sam for his version, Sam said he had tripped on his own feet.

♦ Rebecca has always been a little vain about her good looks, and likes to look through popular fashion magazines for ideas about new hair styles and outfits so she can share them with her friends. One day, as they're talking about this at lunch in the cafeteria, Laurie comes to sit at the end of their table. Rebecca can't resist calling attention to the fact that Laurie just does not have a sense of how to dress. "It wouldn't help anyway," Rebecca laughs, "since someone with Laurie's looks needs more help than just a cool outfit!"

♦ Three prisoners were taken from their cells and led to the interrogation room. On the table before them were papers with typed confessions waiting for their signatures. The prisoners were threatened with torture unless they signed the papers. Two of the prisoners signed. When the third refused, the guards broke his hand and then forced his broken hand to hold the pen as the guards themselves moved the hand to sign the man's name.

Point to Consider:
*"God created man a rational being,
conferring on him the dignity of a person
who can initiate and control his own actions....
'Man is rational and therefore like God;
he is created with free will and is master over his acts.'"*
<u>Catechism of the Catholic Church</u>, #1730

110.

Chapter VI

The Moral Act

The human act is indeed an awesome thing! With the consent of our will, we are able to bring about an effect not only in the external world around us but within ourselves as well. Our choices have a profound impact on us, for it is precisely through our choices that we form our character. As masters of our voluntary acts, we can use them to move ourselves either closer to true happiness or farther away from it.

In the last chapter, we saw how the intellect and will work together to produce the voluntary act. Now we will focus on understanding how we can evaluate the voluntary act morally, that is, how we can judge whether the act is good or evil.

> **Vocabulary**
>
> object of the act · formal cooperation · physical evil
> intrinsically evil act · material cooperation · circumstances
> moral object · intention · end

I. The Interior and Exterior Acts

As we saw in the previous chapter, moral acts are voluntary acts. Without the use of his intellect and will, a person cannot perform a moral act. Knowledge and consent are essential for an act to be voluntary. We also saw in our previous analysis that the human act has both an internal and an external dimension. Both the *interior act* of our will seeking a good and commanding other powers to achieve it and the *exterior act* of those other powers carrying out the will's command have moral ramifications.

Although the interior act is the primary "**seat**" of morality, the exterior act is also within the moral scope. The two acts involve different faculties of the soul and occur at different times, yet they form <u>one moral whole</u>. The exterior act which the will commands becomes good or bad by sharing in the morality of the will's interior act. Thus, the exterior act of taking what does not belong to me is morally evil *because* it accomplishes or completes what I deliberately chose in my interior act.

NOTES

"Morality is not a matter of accident but of deliberate will."
Austin Fagothey, S.J.,
Right and Reason, p. 159

Seat - the place in which something belongs, occurs, or is established.

Called to Happiness ~ Guiding Ethical Principles

NOTES

One Moral Whole

| **Interior Act:** the will's consenting to an act with its object, end, and circumstances | → | **Exterior Act:** the execution of the will's decision |

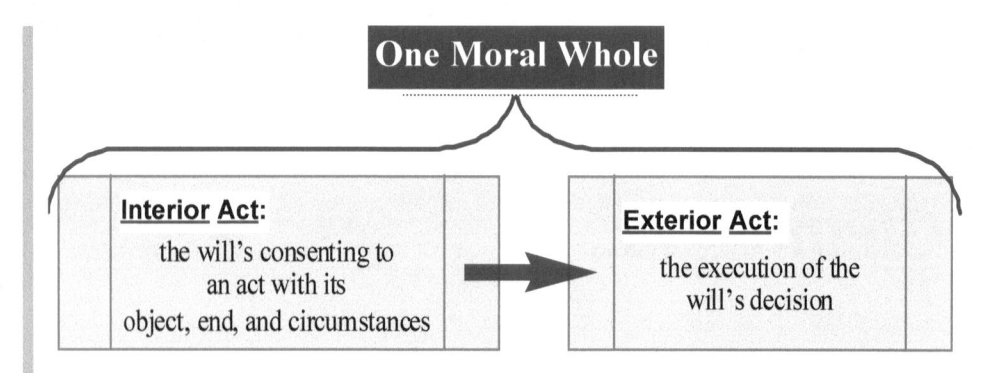

Execution - carrying out or performing the act.

Actually doing the exterior act merely completes or perfects the interior act; it cannot *essentially* change its moral quality. The exterior act could be an occasion for the person to continue or to repeat the interior act. For example, having broken into a person's home and located his money, a thief may be encouraged by his success and decide to continue what he set out to do: take the money for himself. Once an exterior act has been completed, a person might find it easier to do the act again. In ways such as these, the exterior act can *accidentally* have an effect on the interior act.

Essentially - the essence of a thing.

Accidentally - nonessentially.

Because the interior act of the will is the primary seat of morality, the inability of someone to do the exterior act which he deliberately intended does not change the moral goodness or badness of his interior act.

> One who has made up his mind to murder or steal, but cannot bring off the crime successfully, is saved by his failure from civil punishment, not from moral guilt. One who risks his life to rescue a drowning man, only to bring ashore a corpse, will receive the full merit of his heroic deed, even though it was fruitless. Effort is our gift to God, success His gift to us. In this life He does not always give success, but His justice demands that no sincere effort go unrewarded forever.[1]

Sin of omission - from Latin *omittere* (to lay aside); a deliberate failure to do what one can and ought to do.

The interior act as the seat of morality also explains how we can be guilty of **sins of omission**. Through a sin of omission, a person knowingly and freely decides <u>not</u> to do something that he knows he should do. For example, a teenager might choose <u>not</u> to do his homework, or <u>not</u> to respond to his parents, or <u>not</u> to pray when he knows he should. In each case, an evil interior act must be present for sin to occur.

Evil interior act — *Sin!* → **No exterior act**

If it is possible to have an evil interior act without having *any* exterior act, we might reasonably wonder if the opposite is also true: Is it possible to have an evil exterior act without having *any* interior act? If such a thing is possible, then is the person who does the evil exterior

---
[1] Austin Fagothey, S.J., *Right and Reason*, p. 159.

act without having an evil interior act, guilty of sin? In other words, can a person sin without an interior act of his will?

No interior act → ? → Evil exterior act

First of all, yes, it is possible to have an evil exterior act without having an interior act that corresponds to it. This happens when a person does evil *unknowingly*. The person who unknowingly uses counterfeit money to pay his bills is an example of this. Another example would be that of a student unknowingly taking a book that is not his. The acts of passing on counterfeit money and taking what does not belong to him are evil, but because the person does not **know** and ***freely choose*** his evil act, he is not morally responsible for it -- ***if*** *his ignorance is invincible*. There are three requirements for sin:

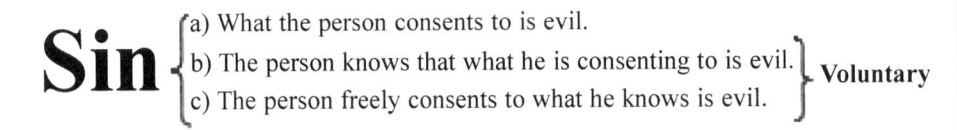

Sin
a) What the person consents to is evil.
b) The person knows that what he is consenting to is evil. } Voluntary
c) The person freely consents to what he knows is evil.

Thus, it is **not** possible to sin without an interior act of the will. The simple fact of doing an exterior evil act does not constitute a sin. The doing of wrong must be voluntary.

No interior act → **No sin!** → Evil exterior act

All of this just reinforces the point we made above that the interior act is the primary seat of morality. There is no sin without an interior act of the will because without an interior act, the person's exterior act is not voluntary.

Saying this is **not** the same thing as saying that all that matters is the person's *intention*. What a person actually does is also morally important. In order see why this is so, we need to understand the *sources* of the moral quality of an act.

Study Guide Questions:

1. *What is meant by the "interior act" and the "exterior act"?*
2. *Why is the interior act called the "primary seat of morality"?*
3. *What effect does the exterior act have on the moral quality of the interior act?*
4. *Why must a sin of omission have an interior act?*
5. *Give an example, other than one mentioned in this text, of a person doing an evil exterior act* **without** *an evil interior act.*

II. The Sources of Morality

Those aspects of the voluntary act which actually make it possible for us to determine whether the act is morally good or bad are usually referred to as the *sources* or *founts* of morality. Since the time of St. Thomas Aquinas, the three sources of morality have been called the *object*, the *end*, and the *circumstances*.[2]

The Object of the Human Act   (*What* is being done)

The term "object" refers to "that toward which a power is directed." It is a relational term implying a subject or agent that is doing the directing. Thus, subjects direct themselves to objects, but they do so by means of their powers or faculties. For example, with my power of sight, I direct myself to colored objects. This explains why we often speak of powers and objects together; every power of the soul has its own object. *Power* and *object* are correlative terms.

Correlative - so related that each implies or complements the other.

Power ➤ Object

The rational power we call the will has for its proper object the universal good. The universal good is the *term* or end of the will's act; it is what the will is *going for*, so to speak, whenever it acts. Whatever the will *goes for* is always in some way good; otherwise, the will would not find it attractive.

Now, because the will cannot of itself obtain the good, it must command other powers to act in order to acquire it. Thus, every moral (voluntary) act entails two dimensions:

(a) the *interior act of the will itself*, which aims at the good and commands other powers, and

(b) the *exterior act of those other powers* acting on the will's command, by which the subject acquires the good.

When we speak about what "those other powers" are *going for* in the exterior act, we are talking about the **object of the act**. Because it is the will that directs those other powers, we can also say that the *object of the act* is what the will itself is *going for* through its exterior act. For example, my will directs my hand to pick up the medicine and my mouth to swallow it. The object of my act, then, that which I'm *going for*, is the medicine. This object is <u>what</u> my will deliberately chooses to be united with through its exterior act. Another example: In the act of helping an injured friend, my will has as its object my friend who is in need.

Object of the Act - the object of the exterior act; the *matter* of the act.

The *object of the human act* is the primary factor in determining the goodness or evilness of an act.[3] The object of the act <u>*materially*</u> con-

---

[2] St. Thomas Aquinas, *Summa Theologiae*, I-II, q. 18, aa. 2-7.
[3] Ibid., I-II, q. 18, a. 2.

tributes to making the act to be the *kind of act* that it is because it tells us what good the will is seeking to obtain by its exterior act. Sometimes this good, as it is perceived by the will, is a reasonable object of a particular exterior act; but sometimes it is an unreasonable object of a particular exterior act. For example, it is reasonable for a person who is ill to have medicine as the object of his act of ingestion. It is unreasonable, however, for a healthy person to have poison as the object of his act of ingestion.

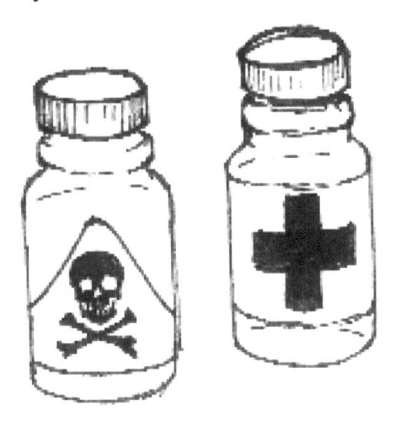

An act which is evil *because* its object is unreasonable for a particular kind of exterior act is said to be an ***intrinsically evil act***. To say that an act is intrinsically evil is <u>not</u> to say anything about its degree of evil. It simply says that what makes the act evil is something at the very "heart or center" of the act. The very kind of act that it is -- that is, as understood by the exterior action and its object -- makes it bad, apart from any further reason why the act is being done.

For example, telling a lie is an *intrinsically evil act* because the person who lies wills that his words (the object of his act) contradict his thoughts. The liar, then, bears a disorder within himself. The liar wills that another person hears words which are not true. This voluntary act of lying is evil *in itself*, that is, apart from any further reason for the lie. The lie can concern a small matter like not telling the truth to someone who asks for your opinion about how she looks, or it could concern an important matter like lying under oath on the witness stand. Both are intrinsically evil acts because the objects of both acts (false words) are disordered since words signifying what I know to be false are not the reasonable objects of the act of speech.

THE LIE

Interior act #1: the intention to escape criticism

Interior act #2: the choice to speak false words *(in order to escape criticism)*

Exterior act: speaking

Object of exterior act *(Object of the act)*: false words

The End *(<u>Why</u> it is being done)*

The second *source* or *fount* of the moral quality of an act is the *end*, the reason why the act is being done. The good that the will seeks

---

NOTES

"The primary and decisive element for moral judgment is the object of the human act, which establishes whether it is capable of being ordered to the good and to the ultimate end, which is God."
Saint John Paul,
Veritatis Splendor, #79

Intrinsically evil act - from Latin *intrinsecus* (inwards); an act considered to be evil in itself with the proximate end that is willed, apart from any further intentions of the will to which the act is ordered.

"If acts are intrinsically evil, a good intention or particular circumstances can diminish their evil, but they cannot remove it. They remain 'irremediably' evil acts; *per se* and in themselves they are not capable of being ordered to God and to the good of the person."
Saint John Paul,
Veritatis Splendor, #81

NOTES

Proximate End - the end which is the act itself.

Remote End - from the Latin *remotus* (removed); the end which is removed from the act itself.

Intention - the end for the sake of which the exterior act is done.

Motive - from Latin *movere* (to move); the goal of a person's actions.

"A good intention (for example, that of helping one's neighbor) does not make behavior that is intrinsically disordered, such as lying and calumny, good or just. The end does not justify the means. Thus the condemnation of an innocent person cannot be justified as a legitimate means of saving the nation. On the other hand, an added bad intention (such as vainglory) makes an act evil that, in and of itself, can be good (such as almsgiving)."
Catechism of the Catholic Church,
#1753

---

is its *end*. In its interior act of choice, the will *"goes for"* the exterior act with its object and circumstances. In other words, the exterior act itself is the object of the will; it is the *proximate end* the will seeks.

The exterior act, however, is chosen as a *means* to achieve a further *end*, the *remote end*. It is this *end*, the reason *why* a person does the exterior act, which is the second *source* or *fount* of the act's moral quality. We sometimes refer to this end that the agent has in mind as his goal as his **intention** or **motive**. For example, a person might walk *for exercise*, he might sing *for money*, or he might steal *for drugs*.

The end which is the object of the will's intention can have an effect on the moral quality of an act:

a) The end can make an act evil which is morally good *in itself*. For example, the good act of giving money to a collection for the poor is made evil if it is done simply to receive praise from others. What could have been an act of charity becomes an act of vanity.

b) The end can give a moral quality to an otherwise morally neutral act. For example, the person who receives money with the intention of never returning it steals, while one who borrows money in order to pay a friend's debt does a just act.

c) The end can intensify or weaken the moral quality of an act. For example, one who lies in order to appear better than he is *compounds* his deceit, while one who speaks the truth out of love for those who are listening *intensifies* his good act.

The end is the most important cause of an act because it moves the agent to do the act in the first place. It has such a powerful influence on the act that the end actually "colors" the entire act, <u>*formally*</u> making it to be the certain *kind of act* that it is.[4] Thus, the person who steals in order to pay for his drug habit is more an addict than he is a thief. This is what St. Thomas means when he speaks of an act in terms of its formal and material components.[5]

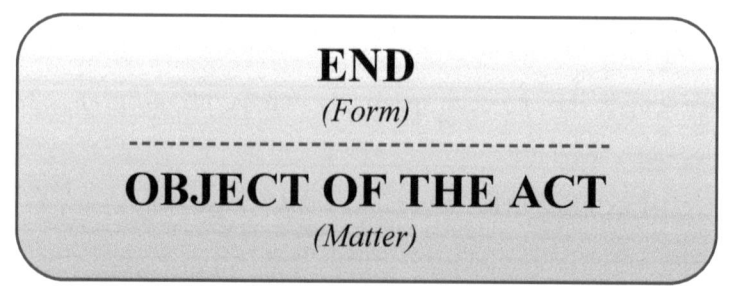

END
(Form)
- - - - - - - - - - - - - - - - - - - -
OBJECT OF THE ACT
(Matter)

The end, however, has its limitations. It cannot make an intrinsically evil act a good act. In other words, **the end cannot justify the means**. Deliberately killing an innocent person because I want to end his suffering is still murder, even if I have a good intention for doing it.

---

[4] St. Thomas Aquinas, *Summa Theologiae,* I-II, q. 7, a. 4, ad. 2.
[5] Ibid., I-II, q. 18, a. 7.

If the act is to be a morally good act, then both the means and the end must be good. What a person does *as well as* why he does it must be good. This is an essential fact to remember, and one often misunderstood today.

> ### The Moral Object
>
> With our knowledge of the meaning of *object* and *end*, we are in a good position to understand what St. Thomas refers to as the **moral object**. The *moral object* can be understood in three different ways: **1)** as that which the will goes for, in its entirety; **2)** as that which (materially) makes the act to be the kind of act that it is; the matter of the act; **3)** as that which contributes to the moral good or evil of the act as a whole.
>
> **Meaning One** refers to *everything that the will goes for* in its act of choosing. This means that the exterior act, with its object and all of its circumstances (morally relevant or not), as well as the intended end all form the one object we call the *moral object*.
>
> **Meaning Two** refers to all that is considered when determining whether, materially speaking, the act is morally good or evil: the exterior act, its object, and circumstances. The circumstances also have to be considered because sometimes a circumstance is morally relevant. According to this meaning, what is included in the moral object will depend on where the intellect finds its first fittingness or repugnance to reason. This meaning specifically tries to avoid any confusion with further intentions -- the formal dimension of the act. The *moral object* is thus distinct from the intention or remote end.
>
> **Meaning Three** refers to the objects, circumstances, and intentions which actually do contribute to an act's being good or evil. Thus, all morally indifferent objects and morally irrelevant circumstances would not be included in this meaning of *moral object*.
>
> Because St. Thomas and most people today use *moral object* in accord with **Meaning Two**, that is the meaning that we will presuppose as we proceed in this text.

The Circumstances *(When, where, how, to whom it is being done)*

The third *source* or *fount* of the moral quality of an act is the circumstances which modify the act in some way. The word "circumstance" comes from the Latin word *circumstare*, meaning "to stand around." The **circumstances** of an act are those conditions of an act which "stand around" it, either:

a) having no moral bearing on the act whatsoever, or

b) changing only the degree of the act's moral good or evil.

St. Thomas refers to the circumstances as "accidents" of the act in contrast to the object and end of the act which are more like the act's essence or substance.[6]

---
[6] Ibid., I-II, q. 7, a. 1.

NOTES

Moral Object - all that is considered when determining whether, materially speaking, the act is morally good or evil: the exterior act, its object, and circumstances.

Circumstances - from Latin *circumstare* (to stand around); those conditions of an act which have no moral bearing whatsoever on the act or which merely increase or decrease the act's moral quality. Those conditions which actually change the moral quality of the act would *strictly speaking* not be circumstances.

Called to Happiness ~ Guiding Ethical Principles

NOTES

"Now, a circumstance names that which stands around the act, as if considered extrinsically outside the substance of the act. And, indeed, this is in one way on the part of final cause, when we consider *why* he did it; or on the part of the principal agent cause, when we consider *who* did it; or on the part of the instrument, when we consider *by what instrument* or *by what assistances*. In another way, it stands around the act on the part of a measure, for example, when we consider *where* or *when* he did it...."
St. Thomas, *De Malo*, 2, 6.

"Certain conditions are identified as circumstantial in relation to what is being considered. Thus, if a certain condition is considered insofar as it gives species to the act, it will be considered no longer as a circumstance, but rather as a 'principal condition of the object.'"
Kevin F. Keiser,
p. 249

CIRCUMSTANCES
END
OBJECT OF THE ACT

The circumstances of an act answer questions about the act such as: *who? where? when? how? to whom? how often?* Although the answer to the question *why?* can also be a circumstance, St. Thomas handles it as a separate moral source: **the end.** He does this because of its importance.

The remote reason why someone does an act is a circumstance of his moral act because it does not have any direct bearing on the exterior act. Thus, robbing a bank *in order to pay bills* or *in order to give to the poor* is merely circumstantial to the act of robbing a bank.

The *proximate end* of the act, however, is never merely circumstantial, because the proximate end *is* the exterior act. Thus, the robber's proximate end of taking money that is not his is of the essence of his act.

It can at times be challenging to understand properly the role the circumstances play in determining whether an act is morally good or evil. This is because what may be merely a circumstance if the act is considered one way could be a defining feature if the act is considered another way.

For example, consider the acts of killing an innocent person and killing one who is guilty. If the acts are being considered simply as the kind of acts they are, *naturally speaking*, then we would say they are the same. Both are acts of killing a human being. The innocence or guilt of the persons killed is merely a circumstance which has no bearing on the kind of act it is, *naturally considered*.

However, if we consider the acts *ethically*, that is, if we consider whether they are reasonable or not, then the guilt or innocence of the person becomes part of the *object of the act* and as such, is no longer a circumstance of the act. Killing a guilty person can be a morally good act, while killing an innocent person is intrinsically evil.

Any circumstance which ethically changes the act's moral quality is *strictly speaking* no longer a circumstance. It becomes part of the *object of the act* and thus helps to define the act morally. For example, lying *on the witness stand* is not just lying; it is a violation of religion and justice. Giving generously to the poor *with money that should be used to pay debts* is an act of irresponsibility, not a work of charity.

Some conditions of an act, however, do not change its moral quality; they merely affect the <u>degree</u> of its goodness or badness. Whether a person steals *from a rich* or *from a poor* man, whether he does a kind deed *for an enemy* or *for a friend* -- these circumstances of an act affect the moral quality of the act as would mere accidents of the act. Taking time to visit the sick and elderly *when I have a busy schedule* could be a greater act of charity than doing so *when I have nothing else to do.* Speaking the truth *when I am threatened with persecution* is a greater good than speaking the truth *to people who already know and agree with it.* Breaking into the *principal's office* and stealing from his files is a greater evil than breaking into a *classmate's locker* and stealing from him.

Finally, some conditions of an act have no bearing whatsoever on the ethical quality of an act. For example: whether a person lies *in Spanish* or *in English*, whether he gives to the poor *on Monday* or *on Tuesday*, whether he kills *with poison* or *with a gun*.

Insofar as a person foresees or should have foreseen the circumstances of an act he is willing to do, he is held responsible for those circumstances. In willing the act, he also wills the circumstances that he foresees. However, if a person is *invincibly* ignorant of some circumstances of an act he willingly does, then he is not held responsible for those circumstances. For example, if a person passes on counterfeit money without knowing that it is counterfeit, then he is not responsible for any evil doing. He willingly pays money, but he does not willingly pay with *counterfeit* money.

All Three must be Good

A long-standing rule in ethics holds that all three sources of morality -- the object, the end, and the circumstances -- must be good in order for the voluntary act to be good. If just one of them does not conform to moral norms, then the entire act is morally wrong.

Looking at a water fountain as an analogy might help us to understand this rule: Every source of water to the fountain must be clean for the water in the fountain's basin to be clean; so too with the human act. (The picture of the fountain on the next page depicts this comparison.) The water in the basin of the fountain represents that part of the agent's *moral object* which shapes his act ethically -- that is, it is all that the will deliberately *goes for*, which is ethically significant, in its interior act. The two main sources of water flowing down into the basin represent the *object of the act* and the *end*. The fountain spray that shoots out the top of the fountain and falls either in the basin or outside of it represents the various *circumstances* of the act -- some becoming part of the *moral object* because of their ethical significance and others not.

Called to Happiness ~ Guiding Ethical Principles

NOTES

"If one element of the whole structure of the act is bad, the act cannot be said to be good. If you dial a phone number and miss it just by one digit, you still have a 'wrong number'."

Andrew Varga,
On Being Human, p. 91

"Circumstances which diminish guilt are only those circumstances that in some way diminish the voluntariness of the agent (e.g., fear, passion, ignorance). A good intention or a due external circumstance does not diminish the evil of an action, although it may seem like it since people normally do a given action for more depraved ends. For example, to kill one's grandparent for mercy's sake does not diminish the evil of killing, but it seems to since people normally murder for entirely utilitarian purposes."

Kevin Keiser

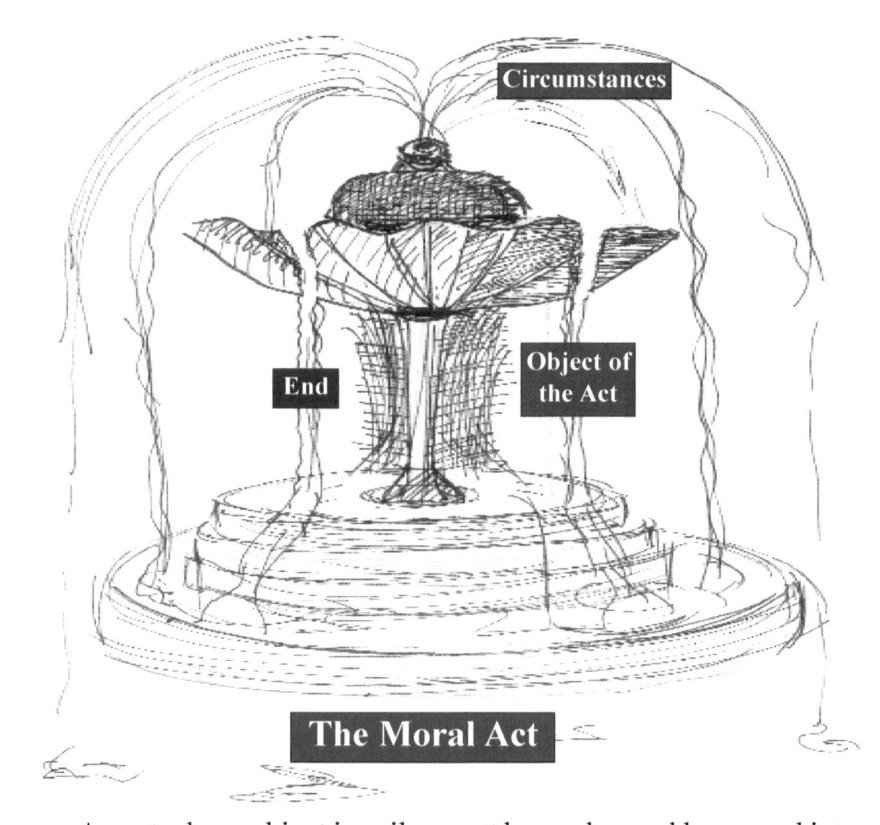

The Moral Act

An act whose object is evil cannot be made good by a good intention or by good circumstances. The principle that *the end justifies the means* is a false ethical principle. The intrinsically evil act remains evil, even if a good intention or concern for due circumstances may indicate something praiseworthy in the will of the agent. ***We may never do evil in order to obtain some good.*** For example, to kill an aging grandparent whom one loves because she is suffering with the progression of cancer is still murder. The good intention of ending her suffering does not change the nature of the act itself. If an act which is intrinsically evil also has an evil end and circumstances, then the evil act is all the more evil.

An act whose object is good is made all the better by a good intention and good circumstances. However, an act whose object is good is made evil by an evil intention. For example, a person's good act of offering a ride to someone in need of one becomes an evil act because of his intention to rob the person.

What about a good act which has a number of intentions -- some good and some evil? For example, a person who takes an hour of his time to help tutor a fellow student in math does this good act for a number of motives. His chief motive is to help out the student, but he would also like to impress the teacher who will observe them working together. The mixed motives of this person do not make his act a bad act. Rather, they make his act *imperfect*. Because his chief intention is a good one, however, and his other intentions are not wholly contrary to reason, his act as a whole remains a good act.

Or what about a good act which has a bad circumstance of minor importance? Consider the case of a person who has been hired to do a job. He does his job, but he does it in a rather negligent and lazy manner. Is his act good, in light of the circumstance regarding how he did his job? Answering this question will depend precisely on how negligent the person was in doing his job. If his negligence was so great that he didn't really do his job, then his act was evil because he was paid for a job that he did not do. In this case, what might at first seem a mere circumstance actually becomes part of what colors the act morally (the object of the act) because of its opposition to reason, which demands that just wages be paid for services done. If, however, he basically did do his job, but because of his negligence it was imperfectly done, then his act remains good but imperfect.

Every act which is morally neutral *in itself* will be made morally good or evil depending on the intentions of the person doing the act or on any circumstances of the act that become part of the object because of their agreement with or opposition to reason. For example, picking up a pen off the classroom floor is a morally neutral act in itself. If a person does this act in order to help the person who dropped the pen, then the act is morally good. If, however, the person does this with the intention of making fun of the disorderliness of the person who dropped it, then his act becomes a bad act of ridicule.

Morally Evaluating Voluntary Acts

In morally evaluating the voluntary act, one should proceed as follows:

<u>First</u>, identify the act *(i.e., What am I doing?)*. To do this, refer to the powers that execute the act and to the object the powers are *going for (Examples: throwing a rock; speaking words; stabbing a person)*. This will provide knowledge of the act itself.

<u>Second</u>, having identified the basic act, consider the object of this exterior act in relation to reason. If it is contrary to reason, the act is sinful. If it is not contrary to reason, then move on to the next consideration.

<u>Third</u>, are there any circumstances that have a special opposition to reason? *(Examples: The words I am speaking are false; the person I am stabbing is innocent.)* If there are, then the act is sinful if the will chooses to do the act under these circumstances.

<u>Finally</u>, why is the act being done? *(Examples: I am throwing the rock to move it out of the way of traffic, or I am throwing the rock in an attempt to break an enemy's window.)* If my intention is evil, then the act is evil because I choose it for an evil end.

> *Another example*:
>
> <u>First</u>, the act is one of "carving." The object of my act of carving is my school desk. I am carving into my school desk.
>
> <u>Second</u>, carving into my school desk would normally be contrary to reason, unless there are some circumstances that might enter into the moral object.
>
> <u>Third</u>, the carving is occurring while the teacher is out of the room.
>
> <u>Finally</u>, I am carving because I am upset about the low grade I have in this class.
>
> This is an example of the sin of vandalism.
>
> ♦ *Think of three other examples demonstrating this process of ethically evaluating a moral act.*

Study Guide Questions:

1. To what does the phrase "object of the act" refer? How does the object of the act give us knowledge about the moral quality of an act?
2. What are we saying when we say that an act is "intrinsically evil"? Give three examples of intrinsically evil acts.
3. How is it possible that <u>both</u> the object of the act as well as the end make an act to be the kind of act that it is?
4. What is the difference between the proximate and remote ends of the will's act?
5. Explain the meaning of the saying, "The end justifies the means." Is the saying necessarily true?
6. What is meant by the "moral object"? How do the circumstances stand in relation to it?
7. What is meant by the circumstances of an act? Give an example of a circumstance which is merely a circumstance.
8. How does the end differ from the other circumstances of an act?
9. What is the rule regarding the three sources of morality of an act?
10. Give an example of each of the following situations:
    a. A person's intention making a morally neutral act evil.
    b. A person's intention making an intrinsically evil act good.
    c. A person's intention making a morally good act evil.
    d. A circumstance changing the moral quality of an act.
    e. A morally good act where the agent has both a good and a bad intention.
    f. A morally evil act where the agent has both a good and a bad intention.
    g. A circumstance intensifying the evil of a morally evil act.
    h. A circumstance intensifying the goodness of a morally good act.

Chapter VI
The Moral Act

The will's act of choice is *going for* the exterior act with its object and all of its circumstances (including the end).

WILL

Intention

Choice

When we say "moral object," we are speaking of the exterior act, its object, and circumstances -- all that defines the act morally *apart from the intention*.

When we say "object, end, and circumstance," we mean *object* as *object of the exterior act*.

Exterior Act
↓
Object of the Exterior Act

circumstance

circumstance

circumstance

circumstance

circumstance
(End)

Moral Object

The end is often separated out only because it is the only circumstance that is related to the exterior act merely through the will.

123.

Called to Happiness ~ Guiding Ethical Principles

CASES IN POINT

#1 -- In his book *Making Choices* (p. 31), Peter Kreeft writes about the three parts of a moral act:

"Three popular systems of ethics today emphasize just one of these three factors and ignore the other two. Unthinking legalism concentrates on only the first factor [the action], the objective moral law, ignoring the subjective motive [why he did it] and the relative circumstances. Moral subjectivism concentrates on only the second factor, the subjective motive [why he did it], and ignores the other two. (This is probably the most popular morality today: 'if only your motive is sincere and loving, nothing else matters.') Finally, situation ethics says the situation [the circumstances] (or the situation plus the motive) determines everything. This denies factor one, the objective nature of the act itself."

- *Provide an example of each of the three popular ethical ways of sizing up an act. Be sure to point out the ethical difficulties each example entails.*

* * * * *

#2 -- *Determine whether the following brief descriptions reveal an ethically good or bad act. Explain why you make the judgment that you do about the act.*

a. The legitimate leader of a nation sincerely believes that he is helping women by making it possible for them to receive abortion services.

b. A very wealthy man gives a million dollars to build shelters for the homeless people in his city, but he does this only because he wants to receive the city's honorary title of "Man of the Year."

c. A research scientist whose specialty is studying the cells of the human body is asked to extract stem cells from the body of a 2-week old human embryo. He is told that these cells offer great hope of curing disease. Even though he himself has a disabled son who might benefit from his study and with the realization that his response might cost him his job, the scientist refuses to destroy a human embryo.

d. A teacher asks his class to write out the answers to the questions at the end of the chapter. One of the students, because he is especially pressed for time, asks his friend for his answers in order to copy them.

e. A 15-year-old is raped one night when she goes with friends to a party. Because she knows that her parents would be so distraught over the incident, she doesn't tell them when they ask her about the party.

f. A teacher takes extra time after school to work with a few students who are struggling in his classes. He does this even though he receives no pay for it and the students seldom express gratitude.

NOTES

"St. Paul urged us to do everything for the glory of God *(1Cor. 10:31)*. It is not possible to attach an openness towards the greater glory of God to an action that directly attacks the dignity of the human person, because the glory of God is the living person flourishing in its humanity."

Rev. Wojciech Giertych, O.P.
L'Osservatore Romano, 4/29/09

III. Evaluating the Moral Act

Now that we have a basic understanding of the sources of morality, we are ready to turn our attention to the ethical evaluation of the moral act. The evaluation will focus on the moral object of the act because that is the object of the will's choice. The moral object includes both the *object of the act* (what is being done) and the agent's *end* (why he is acting). These two dimensions of the act are as *matter* and *form* in giving us the act's substance.

We evaluate the form of the act, the *end,* in light of what the will ultimately seeks, that is, in light of what will truly fulfill it. Thus, the will must always wrestle with the question: *"Is the end of this particular act in accord with my Ultimate End?"* In other words, *"Is this desire of mine compatible with my desire for God?"*

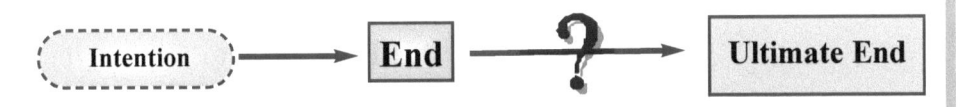

```
Intention ──▶ End ──?──▶ Ultimate End
```

Is the end my will seeks in its intention in accord with my Ultimate End?

We evaluate the matter of the act, the object of the act, according to the objective norms which the intellect grasps. The intellect asks the question: *"Is the object of this exterior act good?"* In other words, *"Is what I am doing in accord with objective moral norms?"*[7]

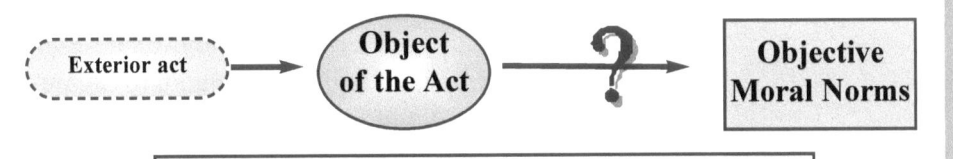

```
Exterior act ──▶ Object of the Act ──?──▶ Objective Moral Norms
```

Is what I am doing in this exterior act good?

St. Thomas looks at the moral act in its entirety: both the formal and the material dimensions are important. Both *where a person is going* (his end) and *what he is doing* (his means / the object of the act) are ethically significant dimensions of the voluntary act. The two dimensions unite as form and matter to give us the *full* ethical picture. Thus, the man who steals money (the object) in order to support his drug addiction (the end) is more a drug addict than a thief. What the man considers to be more important is his drug use, not his stealing.

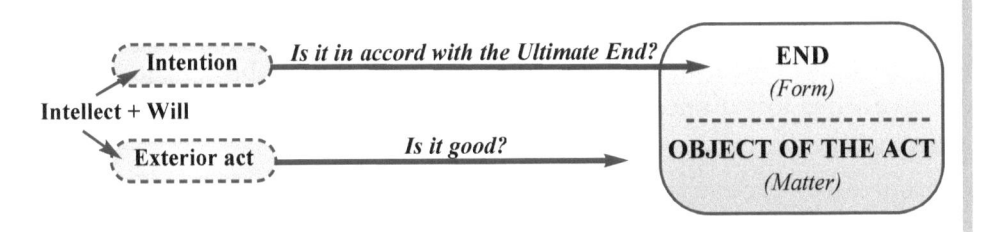

```
Intellect + Will
    Intention ──Is it in accord with the Ultimate End?──▶ END (Form)
    Exterior act ──Is it good?──▶ OBJECT OF THE ACT (Matter)
```

To Judge or Not to Judge

With this understanding of the difference between the interior and exterior acts, we are in a good position to see why there are times when we **should** judge the actions of others and times when we **should not**.

We should judge those aspects of human acts which are *objective*, that is, those that are reasonably accessible to us because they exist *independent of a particular person*. The objective aspects of a human act are the object of the act and some of its circumstances -- those aspects which usually make up the *external act*. For example, a person giving a portion of his salary to the poor, or an unmarried couple engaging in sexual intercourse, or a person deliberately thinking impure

---

[7] St. Thomas Aquinas, *Summa Theologiae*, I-II, 18, 6.

NOTES

"The movement of the interior act is the focus of virtue. What is it I desire most profoundly? Sometimes desires are illogical, immature, spontaneous, but what is important in the spiritual life is the interpenetration of God in our innermost motives."
Rev. Wojciech Giertych, O.P.
Class notes

"Sometimes people focus exclusively on the sins they've committed. They never stop to wonder whether they're going in the right direction."
Rev. Wojciech Giertych, O.P.
Class notes

"The discovery that both the interior and the exterior acts of the will have their appropriate objects teaches that the fullness of the picture will not center exclusively on the object. We need to look at virtue to get the whole picture."
Rev. Wojciech Giertych, O.P.
Class notes

> *I can and should judge **external** acts.*

thoughts, or a teacher taking extra time to work with a struggling student are actions belonging to the *objective* order.

To the degree that we are able to determine, through the use of our senses, the nature of the act being performed and we know its morally significant circumstances, to that degree we can and should judge its moral quality in view of a legitimate standard. The legitimate standard against which we judge voluntary human acts is the moral law.

We can expect our judgments of an exterior act to be the same for anyone making the judgment because the outer reality with which we are in contact through our senses is the same for everyone and because the moral law is the same for all people. What would interfere with this judgment would be if, for some reason, our senses were unable to give us accurate information or if we were ignorant of the moral law.

It is in light of this ability of ours to judge exterior acts that we are able to say that giving money to the poor is good, engaging in sexual activity before marriage is wrong, thinking impure thoughts is wrong, or taking extra time to help a struggling student is good. If we fail to make these kinds of judgments, then we will be unable to direct ourselves, our loved ones, or our society toward the *true* good and away from evil.

It is because we have the ability to make judgments *in this sense* that St. James' exhorts Christians to "bring back a sinner from the error of his way."[8] Such a correction is only possible if the Christians have made a prior judgment regarding his behavior. St. Paul advises us,

> Do not conform yourself to this age but be transformed by the renewal of your mind, that you may judge what is the will of God, what is good and pleasing and perfect.[9]

Even Jesus Himself asked the question, "Why do you not *judge* for yourselves what is right?"[10]

There are, on the other hand, acts which we should <u>not</u> judge. We should not judge those acts which are *subjective*, that is, those which we

---

[8] James 5:20
[9] Romans 12:2
[10] Luke 12:57

Chapter VI
The Moral Act

do not have access to because they are *dependent on a particular person*. The subjective aspects of a human act involve the *interior acts* of the will -- the person's intention as well as the inner activity of his intellect and will in knowing and freely choosing. We really cannot be sure why people do what they do unless they honestly tell us. We also do not know to what extent they really know what they are doing or how free they are in acting.

Thus, while we can judge that a person giving a portion of his salary to the poor is a good thing to do, we cannot judge whether the act was morally good or evil *for that person* because we do not know *why* he did it. He may have done it in order to avoid taxes, or to gain the approval of other people, or perhaps because he truly loves the poor. We also do not know how voluntary his act was -- that is, how knowledgeable and free he was in acting. To make a negative judgment about another's motives for acting without adequate information is to commit **rash judgment**. To avoid rashly judging others, we should always assume the best possible motives for their actions.

If a person chooses to reveal his motive to us, then we can evaluate that particular motive according to moral standards. Thus, we can judge that giving money to the poor merely to appear generous is a bad act, but that giving money because of your concern for the poor is good. Even in making these judgments, however, we must keep in mind that people can have various motives for acting, even motives of which they may not be fully aware. Because of this, we must *always* refrain from judging the state of a person's soul. Not only do we not have access to the various motives of his heart, but we are also ignorant of the role that his good and bad habits have played or the effect that grace has had on him.

Our ignorance of this internal subjective realm of human action is the reason why we cannot judge the sinfulness of another by his action alone. Of the three conditions for sin, only the first are we able to judge objectively; that is, we can judge whether or not an act violates the moral law. The other two conditions are in the subjective realm and, as such, cannot be judged by us who lack the knowledge of this realm.

> I should **not** judge a person's intentions or the condition of his soul.

NOTES

Rash judgment - forming a judgment of another person without sufficient evidence.

"... In judging others we should respecct the fact that we do not know everythng about them. Even if a system of justice has to do it, for the sake of keeping order -- it never judges persons, but only certain acts, and tries to find an appropriate response -- we ought always to respect what is secret, the fact that there are things hidden from us, which only God can judge."
Joseph Cardinal Ratzinger,
God and the World, p. 287

Called to Happiness ~ Guiding Ethical Principles

NOTES

Sin
a) What the person consents to is evil. } **Objective**
b) The person knows that what he is consenting to is evil.
c) The person freely consents to what he knows is evil. } **Subjective**

An example might help us to see the distinction we are making. The terrorists' act of flying planes into the New York Trade Center in 2001 was a grave offense against the moral law; however, we do not know how knowledgeable or free the terrorists were in doing their act. Yes, we may have a glimpse into their motivation due to evidence left behind, but we do not have full knowledge of their motivation nor do we have access to the psychological or emotional factors that may have impaired their knowledge or freedom. Any factor that lessens a person's knowledge or freedom could also lessen his responsibility for the evil he does. Neither must we forget that we do not know their final state of mind as their planes impacted the building. Perhaps there was a moment of profound sorrow unknown to anyone else but God. Thus, while we can and should judge that the terrorists' act was gravely evil, we cannot judge that they will necessarily be in hell because of it.

Making the distinction between the interior and exterior acts is extremely important. It allows us to cultivate our capacity for making sound moral judgments about *objective* good and evil. At the same time, however, it enables us to heed Jesus' command in regard to the *subjective* dimension of human acts: "Stop judging, that you may not be judged."[11] Thus it frees us to hold the mystery of each person in deep respect, reverencing that sacred space within each of us where only God can enter and only God can judge.

"... We should always recall that we are going to be judged and that we will be judged according to the standard that we ourselves have applied. In this way it exhorts us to use a true standard, to keep a limit, to have a proper respect for others."
Joseph Cardinal Ratzinger, *God and the World*, p. 287

Study Guide Questions:

1. *What does it mean to say that the matter and form of the human act are morally evaluated by different criteria?*

2. *If the interior act is the primary seat of morality, then why does the interior act of willing a good end not justify an evil means?*

3. *What is meant by the objective and subjective dimensions of the human act?*

---
[11] Matthew 7:1

4. What may we judge and what may we not judge with regard to the human acts of other people? Why?

5. What is rash judgment? Give an example. How can we avoid rashly judging other persons?

CASES IN POINT

#1 -- The *Catechism of the Catholic Church* teaches the following: "'A *lie* consists in speaking a falsehood with the intention of deceiving.' ... The *gravity of a lie* is measured against the nature of the truth it deforms, the circumstances, the intentions of the one who lies, and the harm suffered by its victims." (#2482, #2484)

"Truth is primarily a self-regarding virtue: it is something which man owes to his own rational nature, and no one who has any regard for his own dignity and self-respect will be guilty of the turpitude of a lie."
("Lying," from *The Catholic Encyclopedia*)

• The <u>Catechism</u> explains that when the good and safety of others requires that information not be known, a person may either remain silent or use discreet language. Can you think of circumstances when this might be required? What discreet language could be used in these circumstances?

* * * * *

#2 -- Determine what we can and should judge in each of the following situations. Note also what we cannot judge.

a) A person commits suicide and leaves a note explaining his sadness over a broken relationship.

b) A friend fails to keep his word and tells someone what I told him to keep strictly confidential between the two of us.

c) One of my teachers goes out of his way to help a student who is struggling.

d) A classmate always has his hand up in class ready to respond to the teacher's questions. He also seems to enjoy getting up in front of the class to give presentations.

e) I see another person in class using the pen I have been missing for two weeks.

f) My older brother is living in the same apartment with his girlfriend.

g) My friend tells me that he lied to his parents.

Chapter VI
The Moral Act

NOTES

"By its every nature, lying is to be condemned."
Catechism of the Catholic Church, #2485

IV. The Principle of Double Effect

Sometimes it happens that the acts we consider doing contain some evil which lies neither in the act nor in any of its immediate surroundings. Rather, the evil is found in an *effect* or *consequence* that *follows from* the act. When this happens, some questions naturally arise: Is it morally acceptable for a person to do an act which has an effect that is evil? Does it matter whether or not a person *foresees* the evil effect of his voluntary act?

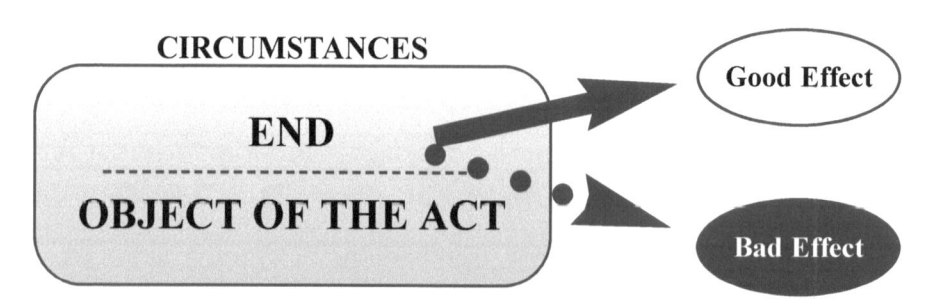

The answers to these questions are given to us through an ethical principle known as the **Principle of Double Effect**. According to this principle, a person is morally permitted to do an act which has *both* a good and an evil effect. He can do so, however, *only if* there is no other way to get the good effect and if the following four conditions are met:

1. The act itself must be morally good or neutral.
We are never allowed deliberately to do evil -- either as an end or as a means to an end. We may never do an intrinsically evil act.

2. The person must *directly* intend the good effect and *only tolerate* the evil effect.
We may never *directly* intend to bring about evil. If we did, then our act would be unethical because of our evil intention.

3. The good effect must be greater than or equal to the evil effect.
We may not tolerate a great evil in order to achieve a small good effect. There needs to be a certain proportion between the good and evil effects. If there is not, then the act becomes evil because of its evil circumstances.

There must be no other way to achieve the good effect than to do this act. If there is another way to get the good effect, then there is no good reason to tolerate the evil effect. It would be evil, therefore, to do the act.

4. The good effect must not be obtained by means of the evil effect.

Chapter VI
The Moral Act

We may never do evil in order to achieve a good. If we do, then the evil would be *directly* voluntary. A good end does not justify the use of an evil means.

Notice that each of the first three conditions guarantees that all three aspects of a voluntary act -- the object of the act, the intention, and the circumstances -- are good. The fourth condition seeks to guarantee that the evil effect plays no role in the agent's getting the good effect. If *any* of these four conditions of the *Principle of Double Effect* are <u>not</u> met, then the act would be morally evil and should not be done.

One other point is worth noting about the *Principle of Double Effect:* The evil which is tolerated by the Principle of Double Effect -- precisely because it is merely tolerated and not chosen -- is always a **physical evil** of some kind, not a moral evil. A physical evil is an evil which does <u>not</u> involve directly a free act of the will. Evil which does involve a free act of the will is called **moral evil**. We may never do a moral evil, but we may under certain conditions tolerate a physical evil. The *Principle of Double Effect* helps us to know what those appropriate conditions are.

An example of the use of the Principle of Double Effect might help to clarify its meaning. A young woman is expecting her third child when she is diagnosed with uterine cancer. The cancer is advanced, and without an immediate hysterectomy the expectant mother will die. Her unborn child, however, is unable to survive outside of the womb at this stage of his development. Since the cancer is in an advanced stage, the doctor thinks that both the mother and the child will die if she waits for the baby to be viable. However, the proposed operation will also certainly cause the child's death, though it will save the mother's life.

To determine if it would be a morally good act for her to have her cancerous uterus removed, we must find out if the four conditions of the *Principle of Double Effect* are met.

1. The act itself -- removing the cancerous uterus -- is a morally good act.

2. The young woman's *direct* intention is to save her life from the threat of cancer. She knows, however, that the child in her womb will die if she has the surgery. She foresees the evil effect of the baby's death, but she does not directly will it. If she could remove the cancer without harming her baby, she would.

NOTES

Physical evil - evil which does not involve directly a free act of the will.

Moral evil - evil which does involve directly a free act of the will.

"The evil that double effect allows us to tolerate refers to something that normally would be a moral evil were we to choose it directly or immediately as a principal object of our will."

Kevin Keiser

131.

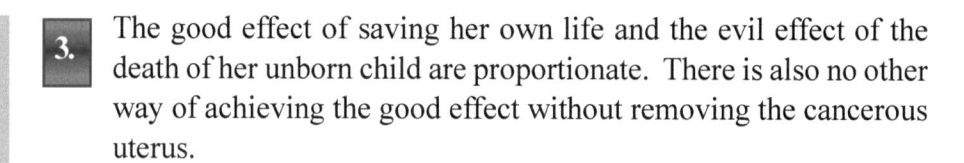

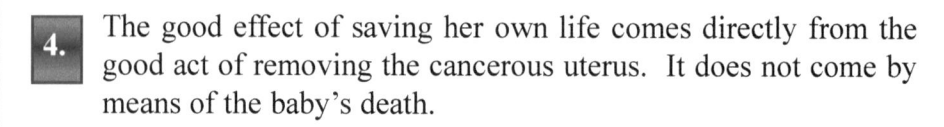

Called to Happiness ~ Guiding Ethical Principles

NOTES

3. The good effect of saving her own life and the evil effect of the death of her unborn child are proportionate. There is also no other way of achieving the good effect without removing the cancerous uterus.

4. The good effect of saving her own life comes directly from the good act of removing the cancerous uterus. It does not come by means of the baby's death.

Because all four of the conditions of the *Principle of Double Effect* are met, the young woman is free to proceed because her act will <u>not</u> be morally evil.

Though we may not have been aware of it before now, the *Principle of Double Effect* is at times used in the ordinary acts of our lives. Policemen and firemen who risk their lives to save others are justified in doing so by the *Principle of Double Effect*. Precisely because the *Principle of Double Effect* can be used in ordinary acts of our lives, we want to be sure that we do not misuse it.

CASES IN POINT

#1 -- The following scenarios present a variety of cases where a person might try to apply the principle of double effect. Determine whether the principle can be <u>correctly</u> applied in each case. Justify your answer.

a) An employee working at a large department store takes home various articles of clothing for his wife and children without paying for them. He does this because his family has had some unexpected medical bills which have set them back financially. They are in need of the clothes, but they do not have the money to pay for them right now. The employee intends to reimburse the store once his family becomes financially stable. The employee's act has both a good and bad effect: meeting the needs of the family and depriving the store of its merchandise. Is the employee's act of taking merchandise morally justified?

b) A man offers to pay a very good amount of money to a poor young woman to clean his apartment every week. He does not care about the poor woman, but he wants her present in his apartment in order to make his girlfriend jealous. This man's act has two effects: the good effect of the poor woman getting some much needed money and the evil effect of giving the impression of immoral activity. Is the man's act of paying the woman to clean his apartment morally justifiable?

c) Firemen are called to the scene of a house fire. When they arrive, they find that every member of the family has escaped from the burning building. They are told, however, that the family's pet cat is still inside. In spite of the fact that the house is extremely dangerous because of the extent of the fire, one of the firemen runs into the house to find and save the cat. Is the fireman's attempt to save the cat morally justified?

d) A 40-year-old woman who lives with her severely diabetic mother goes out of her way to provide sweets for her mother to eat. She does this because she is fully aware that she will inherit a large sum of money upon her mother's death. Thus, her act of providing sweets has both a good and a bad effect: the death of her mother and the gaining of a large sum of money. Is the woman morally justified in providing sweets for her mother?

e) A key military target needs to be destroyed for the common good of one's country (presuming the country is fighting a just war). But the key target is near an orphanage, and it is certain that some innocent people will be killed. Is the military morally justified in destroying its target?

f) A soldier needs to blow up a bridge to prevent a massive force of the enemy from crossing, thereby saving many lives. Just as the army is about to approach on one side of the bridge, however, a little child enters the bridge from the other side. If the soldier waits for the child to cross, the enemy will have already passed, or passed in great part, and presumably cause far more damage. Is the soldier permitted to blow up the bridge?

g) Consider the soldier blowing up the bridge once again. If the soldier's remote TNT does not work, but he has a spare switch on the bridge, and he sees that the child is right next to the switch, such that if he shot the child, the child would fall on the switch and destroy the bridge and prevent the enemy from crossing. Is the soldier morally permitted to shoot the child?

*****

#2 -- Gianna Molla *(1922-1962)* was a wife, mother, and doctor. She happily embraced the married life, dedicated herself to forming a truly Christian family, and served mothers, babies, the elderly and the poor in her medical clinic. She is probably best known, however, for her sacrifice of her own life for her fourth child.

Early in her fourth pregnancy, Gianna was diagnosed with a large benign tumor in her uterus. It caused her considerable pain and was large enough to threaten the continuation of the pregnancy by compressing the fetus. Large tumors can also cause other serious complications during pregnancy.

Gianna had three options:

1. Because of the dangers, she could have chosen to have her uterus removed in order to remove the tumor from her body. This would be a fairly low-risk solution to the problem, but it would result in the death of her 2-month-old fetus, and remove the possibility of future pregnancies.

2. She could have removed the tumor as well as terminated the pregnancy. Doing this, she would have retained the possibility of future pregnancies.

3. She could have had the tumor removed and risked the continuation of her pregnancy. Several risks remained: the surgery on the uterus might threaten the pregnancy and cause a spontaneous abortion; there might be uncontrollable blood loss; and there might be a re-opening of the scarred wound from the surgery.

Gianna chose the third option for the benefit of her child, and she insisted that the maximum care be used so as not to harm the developing fetus. The surgery was successful and her pregnancy continued. At the end of her pregnancy, the doctors delivered a healthy baby girl. Soon after giving birth, Gianna got severely sick. Amid unspeakable pain and after repeated exclamations of "Jesus, I love you," Gianna died 7 days later of an infection of the lining of her abdomen. She was 39-years-old. Pope John Paul II canonized her in 2004.

(See http://www.saintgianna.org/medicalcircum.htm)

- *Why is Saint Gianna Molla considered by many to be a pro-life witness?*

Called to Happiness ~ Guiding Ethical Principles

NOTES

Consequentialism - ethical system which determines the moral quality of an act based solely on the foreseeable consequences of the act.

Proportionalism - ethical system which determines the moral quality of an act based on the proportion between good and evil effects which come from the act.

"Christians, like all people of good will, are called upon under grave obligation of conscience not to cooperate formally in practices which, even if permitted by civil legislation, are contrary to God's law."
Evangelium Vitae, #74

Contemporary Ethical Systems

Two contemporary ethical systems -- Consequentialism and Proportionalism -- offer similar approaches to determining the moral quality of an act. **Consequentialism** calculates the foreseeable consequences of the act. If there are more good consequences than evil ones that will come from the act, then the act is judged to be good. If there are more evil consequences than good ones, then the act is evil.

Proportionalism weighs the good and bad effects that will come from an act to determine the proportion between them. If the good effects outweigh the evil effects, then the act is judged to be morally good. If the evil effects outweigh the good effects, then the act is judged to be morally evil. Proportionalists often speak of trying to find the "greater good" or the "lesser evil."

- *One of the conditions of the Principle of Double Effect requires that the good and evil effects of an act be proportionate. Is there any difference between using the Principle of Double Effect to judge the moral quality of an act and using the Proportionalist system? Explain.*

- *Do you see anything problematic about using Consequentialism or Proportionalism in judging an act's moral quality?*

- *Explain how a Proportionalist might judge the act of a 16-year-old girl getting an abortion.*

Cooperating in an Evil Act

One important application of the *Principle of Double Effect* concerns the act of cooperating in evil. May a person do an act which in itself is not wrong but which is used by others for an evil purpose? Take for example a robber who orders a bank teller to hand over the money in the safe. In itself, handing money to a person is a morally neutral act. In this case, however, the act has a double effect: one good and one evil. If the teller cooperates with the robber, the good effect will be that her life is spared. The evil effect that comes from her act of cooperating with the robber is that he will take the bank's money.

If the bank teller is working in partnership with the robber, then she is a *formal* cooperator in his evil act. This means that she is in agreement with it.

Chapter VI
The Moral Act

Formal cooperation in evil is never permitted because the one who cooperates formally in the evil act of another *directly* intends and thus consents to the evil act. This intention and consent to do evil violates the *Principle of Double Effect*.

If the bank teller does not agree with the evil act of the robber, but she nevertheless hands over the money to him because she is coerced into doing so, then she is a *material* cooperator in his evil act. She is neither directly intending the evil effect of the robber's act nor is she doing an act which is in itself wrong. However, the circumstance of her act is that she is aiding the robber in his evil act. According to the *Principle of Double Effect*, her **material cooperation** in this evil act can be morally permitted as long as there is a grave reason for permitting the evil effect of her act. In this case, her grave reason would be to avoid being killed.

Material cooperation can be further divided into the categories of *immediate* (*direct*) and *mediate* (*indirect*). If the person cooperates in the execution of the evil act itself by providing resources or instruments essential to its execution, then his material cooperation is *immediate* or *direct*. If he provides instruments or resources that are not essential to the commission of the evil act, then his material cooperation is *mediate* or *indirect*. For example, the bank teller lifting the money from the drawer and putting it in the robber's bag would be *immediate* or *direct* cooperation in the robbery. If she had closed the blinds as he directed her to do, she would be guilty of *mediate* or *indirect* cooperation.

We can also distinguish between material cooperation that is *proximate* and that which is *remote*. This distinction depends on the "distance" between the act of cooperation and the evil act committed. "Distance" can be either in terms of time (temporal space) or material connection. For example, providing the combination to the safe when the robber demands it would be *proximate* mediate cooperation. Filling his get-away car with gas would be *remote* mediate cooperation. *Immediate material* cooperation is always *proximate*, while *mediate material* cooperation can be either *proximate* or *remote*.

The closer a person's cooperation is to the evil act, the greater the reason one needs to be able to cooperate in it. For example: In a hospital in which occasional abortions are performed, the doctor doing the abortion would be the principal agent while the patient requesting it would be a *formal* coop-

NOTES

Formal cooperation - from Latin *cooperari* (to work together); working together with another while agreeing with the other in the act they are doing together.

Material cooperation - from Latin *cooperari* (to work together); working together with another because of duress, although not agreeing with the other in the act they are doing together.

Immediate (direct) cooperation - assistance in the execution of the evil act itself by providing resources or instruments that are essential to its execution.

Mediate (indirect) cooperation - assistance in the evil act by providing instruments or resources that are not essential to the commission of the evil act.

Proximate cooperation - assistance given which is "close" to the evil act either in terms of time or material connection.

Remote cooperation - assistance given which is "far" from the evil act either in terms of time or material connection.

135.

Called to Happiness ~ Guiding Ethical Principles

NOTES

"To refuse to take part in committing an injustice is not only a moral duty; it is also a basic human right. Were this not so, the human person would be forced to perform an action intrinsically incompatible with human dignity, and in this way human freedom itself, the authentic meaning and purpose of which are found in its orientation to the true and the good, would be radically compromised."
Evangelium Vitae, #74

"But let's remember that, during the Holocaust, one man ran the trains, another man opened the doors, and another man loaded the prisoners, so that none of them had to take responsibility for the evil being done. Those who want you to violate your conscience will first seek to misinform your conscience, and then try to deaden its voice."
Randall Smith
"No Cooperation with Evil"

erator. Nurses *directly* participating in the abortion procedure would be either *formal* cooperators (because they approve of and assist in the doctor's action) or *immediate material* cooperators (because they disapprove of but nevertheless provide essential assistance). *Immediate material* cooperation which concerns grave attacks on human life will always be unethical because of the high value of human life.

Proximate material cooperators would need a very strong reason for their involvement. If, however, a hospital employee who works in the laundry neither approves of the abortions performed by the principal agent nor is involved directly in them, then his *remote material* cooperation might be morally acceptable if he has a serious reason for cooperating and if he does what he can to avoid the possibility that others may conclude that he approves of the abortions. Perhaps the employee desperately needs a job and has no other means of employment. Perhaps, too, whenever this employee is asked about where he works, he always points out his opposition to the abortions that are performed there. Because he has serious reasons for his remote material cooperation, and because he does what he can to avoid giving scandal, his employment at the hospital could be morally acceptable.

A person also needs a greater reason for materially cooperating in an evil act if his cooperation is *indispensable*. This means that if he could actually prevent this act from happening by not cooperating, then he needs an even greater reason to cooperate than if the evil would happen even if he did not cooperate. Cooperation is considered to be <u>not</u> indispensable when someone else could be substituted for the person cooperating so that the evil will be done no matter what.

The third condition of the *Principle of Double Effect* requires that the good and evil effects be proportionate. With regard to cooperating in evil, two considerations should guide us:

a) The amount of evil that my cooperation will enable others to do.

b) The amount of evil that I will suffer if I refuse to cooperate.

With regard to these two considerations: A person is not required to suffer a greater evil than he is trying to spare from others. Thus, a person whose life is threatened if he does not hand over the money of others may hand over the money. The loss of life is a much

136.

greater evil than is the loss of money. Charity does require, however, that a person be willing to suffer a small evil in order to prevent others from suffering a greater evil. Thus, a person should tolerate being ridiculed by his peers rather than himself cooperating in their act of sabotaging the bus of the opposing football team.

Charity also requires that a person be willing to give his life rather than to cooperate in an act which would bring about a huge evil to many people. Thus, a flight controller at an airport should suffer death rather than cooperate in an act that would bring down a plane loaded with people.

One final distinction can be made regarding the types of cooperation in evil: cooperation can be either *active* (*positive*) or *passive* (*negative*). *Active* cooperation happens whenever a person does something that aids another person in doing his evil act. *Passive* cooperation happens when a person does not do that which he ought to do to prevent the evil act of another person. All of the examples of cooperation we have considered thus far have been of *active* cooperation. Examples of *passive* cooperation would be the bank manager who chooses not to press the button alerting the police of the robber, or a student who does not report the conversation he overhears of his classmates planning to sabotage the bus, or the friend who does not offer any ethical advice to her friend who is considering an abortion. Passive cooperation can be formal or material, immediate or mediate, proximate or remote.

Active (positive) cooperation - assistance given by the performance of an act.

Passive (negative) cooperation - assistance given by the failure to perform an act which the person is morally bound to perform.

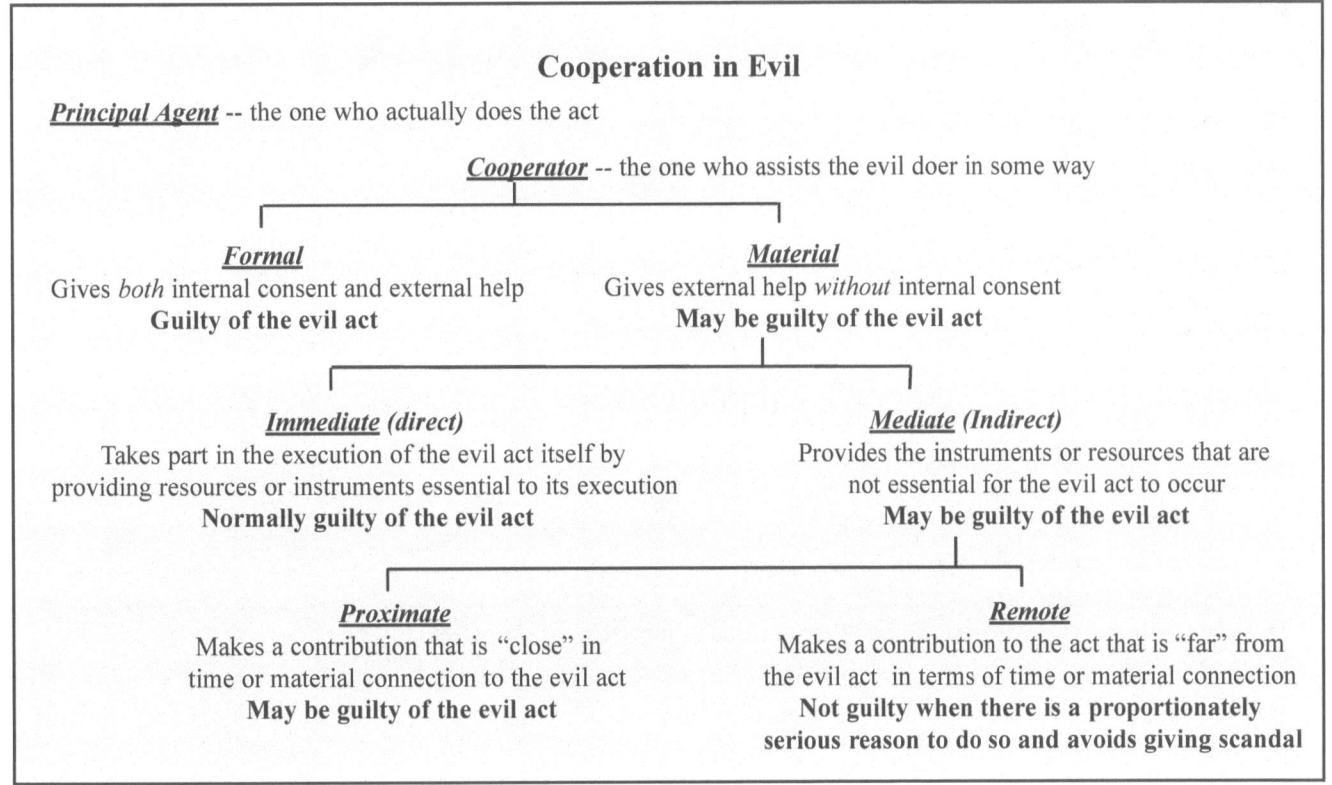

Cooperation in Evil

Principal Agent -- the one who actually does the act

Cooperator -- the one who assists the evil doer in some way

Formal
Gives *both* internal consent and external help
Guilty of the evil act

Material
Gives external help *without* internal consent
May be guilty of the evil act

Immediate (direct)
Takes part in the execution of the evil act itself by providing resources or instruments essential to its execution
Normally guilty of the evil act

Mediate (Indirect)
Provides the instruments or resources that are not essential for the evil act to occur
May be guilty of the evil act

Proximate
Makes a contribution that is "close" in time or material connection to the evil act
May be guilty of the evil act

Remote
Makes a contribution to the act that is "far" from the evil act in terms of time or material connection
Not guilty when there is a proportionately serious reason to do so and avoids giving scandal

Called to Happiness ~ Guiding Ethical Principles

Study Guide Questions:

1. What is the difference between a cause and an effect?
2. May a person do an act if he foresees that it will cause some evil? Explain.
3. What does each of the four conditions of the Principle of Double Effect safeguard?
4. How does a physical evil differ from a moral evil?
5. Can you think of an example from your own life where the Principle of Double Effect would apply?
6. Identify the type of cooperation involved in the publication of an immoral book by each of the following:
    a. The person who writes the book.
    b. The publishers who accept and edit the book.
    c. The typesetters, proofreaders, and others who prepare the actual text and who personally approve of it.
    d. Those who run the presses, bind the books, and prepare them for delivery, but who do not personally approve of them.
    e. The heads of bookselling firms that stock the books.
    f. Hired clerks who sell them and who approve of them.
    g. Secretaries who handle the business correspondence concerning them but who don't approve of them.
    h. The person who buys and reads the book for enjoyment.
7. Give three examples of situations where teenagers could be involved as cooperators (passive/active) in the evil acts of others.

CASES IN POINT

#1 -- In July, 2009, Tim Roach (38-years-old) was laid off his job as an electrician. In the year and a half since then, Tim and his family struggled because of his unemployment. Unexpectedly in February, 2011, Tim received a call from his local union offering him a job. The timing could not have been better as Tim's unemployment benefits were due to run out that month. The job offer: foreman, with a salary of $65,000 to $70,000 a year. "Perfect!" Tim thought, until he heard the bad news -- he would be job foreman for a crew working on a new Planned Parenthood Clinic in St. Paul on University Avenue.

The union representative who offered Tim the job down-played the fact that Planned Parenthood is the number one abortion-provider in the country. The union rep said he wasn't sure if there were going to be abortions there, probably in order to entice Tim to take the job. Without even a second thought, however, Tim declined the offer. He, his wife, and their two children would make do on his wife's salary rather than take this job.

When Tim's pastor from Divine Mercy parish heard of Tim's decision, he was inspired by Tim's pro-life witness. He commented, "Here at Divine Mercy, the words, 'Jesus, I trust in You' are written on our baptismal font, and that's what it's all about."

Tim's ultimate goal is to start up his own company, but in order to make that happen he will need to earn and save money. In the meantime, he is eager to take any work he can find.

Taken from "Out-of-work electrician offered major job ...," theCatholicSpirit.com.

* If Tim had chosen to cooperate in building a Planned Parenthood clinic, could he have ethically justified his decision? Explain.

Chapter VI
The Moral Act

#2 -- Carol, a recent college graduate with a degree in film production, wrote a letter asking for advice concerning an ethical problem she is facing. She is working as a film production assistant, and describes her job as one of "basically getting people coffee and running copies and doing errands for higher ups on set." She likes her job so far, but she explains that "it's a business built 100% on connections. It's all about who you know and recommendations, and so bad impressions go really far in stopping your career."

Her current job is to finish out a show called *Miracle Workers*. Carol explains: "I was told it was a show about heaven, similar to *Bruce Almighty*. But I now know that this isn't true. This series is highly offensive; it portrays God as an illiterate, lazy, careless, rude and selfish man who is incapable of anything.

"I just don't know what to do. The show is not meant to be real at all, but it does directly mock God, a very real action, and that's not ok at all. So, I'm trying to figure out the material/formal cooperation of my working on this show.

"I'm primarily concerned with staying so I don't burn bridges by quitting suddenly. As dumb as it seems, that could blacklist me and set me back months from finding work again. As far as income, I am able to provide for myself in other ways, but quitting would be a *really* hard hit to my career, but probably eventually salvageable. But loyalty and dependence are not taken lightly in this field, and a person is categorized as an asset or a waste depending on whether he shows up and does the work.

"At the same time, I can't figure out my level of cooperation and the proximity to the evil act of mocking God through this series. Is my getting people coffee wrong? -- No.

"Is my getting people coffee so they can use their energy to creatively and 'tastefully' insult God, then share that with others through the media wrong? -- I don't know. Also, my level of ability is so low that I would be quickly replaced without much effort, but I think that is beside the point.

"Basically, quitting based on religious viewpoints would blacklist me. And I know there are some lines I won't cross (I've already had to turn down work for a Planned Parenthood project which stopped my getting job offers from one employer), so should this be one of them? Am I overreacting?

"I know you can't make a decision for me, but I'd appreciate any advice you have."

- *For what kind of cooperation would Carol be responsible if she agreed to continue working on this project?*
- *What advice would you offer Carol?*

* * * * *

#3 -- I once asked the vice president of a major pharmaceutical firm, a good Catholic family man, whether he had faced any major moral quandaries in his job. "Well, there was this pump. It *could* have been used for a lot of things, but we all knew it was used primarily for abortions. And that bothered me quite a lot."

What did you do? "A female colleague organized a prayer group," which gathered regularly to, as he put it: "pray that pump off the face of the earth." And indeed, when the FDA eventually changed the specifications on the pump, the company decided it would cost too much to re-tool the plant, so they decided to stop making it....

But another little story about that pump. It turns out that whenever the production line would go down, it would take much longer than usual to repair. So this man's boss asked him to fly down and find out why. When the vice president asked the plant manager about the problem, the manager answered, somewhat sheepishly: "Oh, yeah, that's that *pump*! My head of maintenance is a Catholic, and he knows what that pump is used for, so he won't work on it." And he didn't. ...

The plant manager didn't fire him -- one has to assume he had previously built up some real credibility with his boss in terms of honesty, decency, and hard work. The Catholic vice president who told me this story didn't insist on it. And the executive vice president to whom he reported undoubtedly grumbled, but for some reason, he let it go too. Then eventually God stepped in and made the pump go away.

Randall Smith, "No Cooperation with Evil, *The Catholic Thing*, March 4, 2012

- *What could have been the ramifications of the head of maintenance's refusal to work on the pump?*

V. Emotion & the Moral Act

As we pointed out in Chapter Five, emotion (passion) can make an act more or less voluntary, depending on whether the emotion is *antecedent* or *consequent*. Here we would like to take our investigation one step further and seek the answers to the following two questions:

1. Is a movement of the sense appetites (an emotion) a human act?

From our previous study of the human person, we know that our two sense appetites -- the Concupiscible Appetite and the Irascible Appetite -- provide us with *automatic* or *spontaneous* responses to our sense knowledge. Thus, if we hear beautiful music, we *spontaneously* experience the emotion of joy. If we smell cookies baking, we *automatically* experience the emotion of desire. If we are betrayed by a friend, we respond *without thinking* with the emotion of anger.

With this previous knowledge of what the sense appetites are and with our understanding now of what a human act is, we are in a good position to answer our first question. A movement of the sense appetites *in itself* cannot be a human act. A human act is one which a person *deliberately* wills. It requires that the person be free. This explains why a movement of the sense appetites (an emotion) *in itself* is neither ethically good nor bad. It is *morally neutral* because the free will is not involved.

An emotional response only takes on an ethical quality to the extent that the free will is involved in it. Thus, if a person *deliberately* chooses to sense something that he knows will "turn on" his sense appetites, then he is morally responsible for the fact that he is experiencing an emotion. He freely chose to experience the emotion when he chose to sense something that he knew would activate it. When this occurs, we would have to say that experiencing the emotion is indeed a human act.

As a human act, experiencing an emotion will be judged to be ethically good or bad according to the three sources of morality: the object of the act, the end, and the circumstances. The object of the act cannot be evil because experiencing an emotion -- any emotion -- as a *natural* experience for human persons is good. What will make it evil in any particular situation will be either the person's *intention* in choosing to experience the emotion or a *circumstance* regarding it that might be ethically significant.

NOTES

"We cannot say that an emotion is a *moral* good, for the emotion itself is not an act, and only acts can be said to be morally good or evil."
Conrad Baars, p. 63

"When an emotion leads us to do something, and, of course, all emotions by their very nature tend to move us toward some kind of action, even if it is the decision to abstain from any external action, then what we do is subject to moral judgment."
Conrad Baars, p. 63

Chapter VI
The Moral Act

NOTES

For example, if a person -- in order to feel anger -- chooses to dwell on an insult he suffered so that he can more easily become worked up to commit an act of vengeance, then experiencing the anger is evil because of the person's *end* or *motive*.

Consider also the case of a person who chooses to arouse his anger over an injustice his boss did to him last week. He deliberately remembers the injustice, stimulates his anger, and expresses his anger to his co-workers rather than to his boss. Experiencing the emotion in this case is evil because of the *circumstances*. He chose to experience it at a time when the emotion made it easy for him to gossip or detract from his boss' good reputation. If he had roused his emotion just before going in to talk to the boss himself and used it to help him communicate the seriousness of the boss' offense, then he would not have done an evil act.

2. What effect does emotion have on the moral quality of a human act?

In determining the answer to this second question, we need first to distinguish between situations where the emotion is deliberately aroused (consequent passion) and those where it is not (antecedent passion). If the emotion is present because we *chose* to "turn it on," then its presence can simply *add to* the moral good or evil of the human act that we are doing. The emotion or passion makes it possible for us not simply to do good or evil, but to do it with *more strength* or *force*. We have chosen to use not just our rational appetite but also our sense appetites in accomplishing the act. It is like having two horses pull a coach rather than just one: the coach moves with greater ease and more power in the direction that it is going.

141.

Thus, for a man to rape a woman is a terribly evil act. For him to do this act "with passion" because he stimulated his sense appetites by viewing pornography is for him to make his act of rape *all the more* evil because of the manner in which he does it. This is an example of how a *circumstance* such as a person's manner can increase the evil of his act.

Emotion that is deliberately aroused, however, can also increase the goodness of an act. For example, in caring for cancer patients in a hospital, a nurse is able to do many good acts for them simply by using her will. If she deliberately tries to stimulate her emotion of love for her patients, especially when they are frustrated, angry or despairing, then her good acts are made *all the better* because of the manner in which she cares for them.

If the emotion is **not** deliberately aroused, then its presence cannot *increase* either the goodness or the evilness of an act because the person is not responsible for it. The emotion could, however, *decrease* the goodness or evilness of an act to the extent that the emotion makes the person doing the act *less free* and his act *less deliberate*.

Thus, a person who in the heat of anger -- an emotion that he did not deliberately cause -- kills a man will be held less responsible than if the killing had been premeditated. The fact that he was experiencing strong emotion at the time that he did an evil act makes him less free to act reasonably. The emotion makes him less able to think clearly and thus he acts less deliberately. It is as if one of the two horses pulling a coach "runs away with it." The driver will find it all the harder to move the coach in the right direction because of the run-away horse. (This does not, of course, make the evil act of murder a good act.)

In a similar way, emotion can make doing a good act less meritorious. If a person, moved *principally* by emotion, does a good act, he will receive less merit for the good he does than would a person who was moved *principally* by a deliberate choice of his will. It would be best, of course, for a person to be moved by *both* the emotions and a deliberate choice of the will when he does a good act. When both of these moving powers are at work in a person, he does the good act with "full force." That is, he uses all the powers at his disposal to accomplish the good act. This is why it is good to give generously to the poor as a deliberate act of your will. It is even better, however, if your emotions are involved and you take great *joy* in giving generously because you *feel* love for the poor. If both the will and the emotions are moving the

> "...[A] person is able to strive for the good with two motors -- those of desire and will. Such a person can be said to have real will power, because his will is supported by the desire for the good."
>
> Conrad Baars, p. 75

person, then he does the good act with greater ease and with more joy.

Conclusion

Of all creatures on earth, the human person has the unique privilege of being the only creature that can bear responsibility for his actions. He is the one who determines whether the end or goal for which he acts is in line with the Ultimate End he seeks. He is the one who judges for himself whether the objects of the acts that he consents to are in accord with the objective moral law. He is the one who assesses the goodness or badness of the circumstances of his acts. He bears responsibility for his human acts, then, because his intellect understands them and his will consents to them.

For this reason man is said to be the "master" of his human acts. He bears *ultimate* responsibility for whether or not these acts take him closer to *true* Happiness or further away from it.

Being the master of his human acts is so vitally important because it is through these acts that he makes or forms himself to be the kind of person that he becomes. Remember that Happiness is not simply a matter of possessing an external Supreme Good. Happiness is also a matter of my *inner transformation as a person* so that I can genuinely find joy in that Good once I find it. Our next chapter will investigate the nature of this inner transformation of the person that is so essential to human Happiness.

Study Guide Questions:

1. Is a movement of the sensitive appetites -- in itself -- a human act? Explain.

2. How is it possible for a movement of the sensitive appetites to be a human act?

3. Why is it impossible that the object of the act of experiencing an emotion be evil?

4. What effect does emotion have on the morality of an act if we have freely chosen to stimulate the emotion?

5. What effect does emotion have on the morality of an act if we have not freely chosen to stimulate the emotion?

6. Why might the presence of an emotion that a person has not caused decrease the goodness or evilness of his act?

7. Why is it good to have both the intellectual appetite as well as the sensitive appetites involved when a person does a good act?

"The emotions together with their accompanying physiological changes exist in order to be ennobled and integrated harmoniously by reason, and thereby move us under its guidance toward the happiness for which we are created."

Conrad Baars, p. 76

Called to Happiness ~ Guiding Ethical Principles

CASES IN POINT

#1 -- After watching an abortion film and being emotionally moved by what she saw, Ruth signs up to spend some time helping out at the crisis pregnancy center in her area. When the time comes to help out at the center, however, Ruth does not show up. She has forgotten about her commitment and is busy about other things.

- *What effect do her emotions play in making it the kind of act that it is?*
- *Does the fact that Ruth so easily forgot about her commitment tell us anything about the nature of that commitment?*
- *Is Ruth's act of signing up to help out at the crisis pregnancy center a morally good act?*

#2 -- Ben has gone out of his way to try to make Jose, the new kid from Chile, feel welcome at his school. He took extra time to explain his schedule of classes to him as well as to show him exactly where he needs to go in order to find his way around the large building. One day, about a month into the school year, Ben overhears a group of kids laughing at and making fun of Jose. Jose, too, is aware of their ridicule. In anger, Ben walks over to them and tells them to stop the ridicule. Instead of stopping, one of the boys makes an even more degrading comment about Jose. Ben grabs him and pushes him aside. With that, a fight begins.

- *Do Ben's emotions make him more or less responsible for the fight? Explain.*

#3 -- Seldom does it happen that Patti goes along with friends who are shopping and does not buy anything. Because she lacks the self discipline she needs to stop herself from buying the nice things she sees, Patti keeps guard over herself by controlling what she sees. She often will ask a friend to pick something up for her from the store rather than risking the temptation to spend more money for things she really doesn't need. This is why her behavior the other day was so out of character. After paging through a store catalog, Patti took the pay check she had just received, drove down to the mall, and spent it all in a matter of a few hours. She even spent the money she needed to pay her monthly bills. She later complained that her *desire* for the nice things she saw in the catalog caused her to act unreasonably.

- *How responsible is Patti for her irresponsible act of shopping?*
- *Does her emotion of desire increase or decrease her responsibility?*

Point to Consider:
> "It is not enough to do good works; they need to be done well.
> For our works to be good and perfect,
> they must be done for the sole purpose of pleasing God."
>
> St. Alphonsius Liguori,
> Patron saint of moral theologians and confessors

Chapter VII

Virtue

Human acts -- both good and evil -- can have powerful effects on the lives of people. Just a quick and shallow reading of American history or a current newspaper gives plenty of evidence of how evil human acts have brought about terrific suffering for people. Consider the acts of terrorism, murder, slavery, theft, fornication, and adultery -- to name just a few. These acts cause human lives to be ended prematurely. They cause marriages and families to be shattered. They cause poverty and disease to increase.

Good acts, on the other hand, have helped to shape our world into a better place, a place where all human persons are able truly to flourish and to experience the level of happiness that is possible here. Think of the loving acts of Blessed Mother Teresa of Calcutta in her care for the destitute and forgotten people of our world. Or consider the many honest and just acts of ordinary people in their dealings with others. Think of the good people you know in your own everyday life, and the difference that is made in the lives of those around them, just by the ordinary kindness and generosity they do each day. Good human acts such as these help to bring about what Pope John Paul II called a "civilization of love." Such actions, motivated by love and self-giving, make it possible for us to move closer toward experiencing the happiness we seek.

As we have seen in the previous chapter, however, not only do our human acts affect the world outside of us; they also bring about an effect within us when we do them. It is to this internal change brought about by the human act that we would like to direct our attention in this chapter.

Remember what we said in Chapter Two about happiness: The *transformation of the human person* is essential for his attaining

Called to Happiness ~ Guiding Ethical Principles

NOTES

human happiness. It is not enough to possess the Greatest Good. We must also become *good persons* -- persons who will be able to take great delight in the Good once we have attained it. This present chapter will focus in depth on what we ourselves can do to bring about this personal transformation that is so key to human happiness.

> **Vocabulary**
>
> virtue   habit   restitution   moral virtue
> vice   character   prudence   common good

I. What is a Habit?

The transformation of ourselves that we are capable of bringing about occurs when we develop certain *habits*. The word **habit** comes from the Latin *habere*, meaning "to have." Very generally speaking, a habit refers to anything a person has. The ancient Greek philosopher Aristotle, however, helped to narrow the meaning of the term when he categorized a habit as a *quality* which a person has as a lasting disposition.[1] Accepting Aristotle's understanding of habit, St. Thomas defines habit as ***a firm and stable disposition to act in a certain way***.[2]

Habit - from the Latin *habere* (to have); a firm and stable disposition to act in a certain way.

In ages past, philosophers distinguished between two general kinds of habits: *habits of being* and *habits of acting*. *Habits of being*, which they called **entitative habits**, [from the Latin *ens*, meaning ***being***], are qualities such as beauty, strength, or health. These qualities of a person are relatively lasting dispositions that he possesses due to his being. *Habits of acting*, which they called **operative habits**, [from the Latin *operans*, meaning ***working***] are the relatively permanent tendencies that we have within us which we have acquired through our repeated acts. It is only this latter kind of habit that we today commonly refer to as a habit.

Entitative habits - from Latin *ens* (related to being); habits of being; relatively lasting dispositions that a person possesses due to his being.

Operative habits - from Latin *operativus* (cretive, formative); habits of acting; relatively lasting dispositions that a person possesses due to his repeated acts.

> Good habits make doing good acts *easier*, more *pleasant*, and more *perfect*.

To say that a habit is a *disposition* is to say that it is something "added on" to our already existing human nature as an accidental form. The human nature that we receive at the moment of our conception is endowed with certain powers of acting. As we begin to exercise these powers, they begin to be better suited to action. This means that each time we do something we will find it easier to do the same thing again. This development in the *ease* or *readiness* for doing something is the for-

146.

---
[1] Aristotle, *Categories*, Ch. 8, 8b 27.
[2] St. Thomas, *Summa Theologiae,* I-II, 49, a. 1.

mation of a habit. The more disposed our natural powers become to acting in certain ways, the easier it is for them to act that way and the more efficient they are in acting. It is somewhat like acquiring a "second nature" -- one for which we ourselves are responsible.

Take for example the habit of cracking one's knuckles. Every human person who has hands has the potential for cracking his knuckles. Some people, however, because they have exercised this potential, have *disposed* themselves to doing the act because they have developed the habit of doing it. They can crack their knuckles with ease and without much thought. We could say that cracking their knuckles has become *second nature* to them.

A habit, then, is an actualization of a potency. It is not, however, a *complete* or *full* actualization. Rather, a habit places the power somewhere between *being in potency* and *being fully in act*. The fact that a habit actualizes *to some extent* a power of the soul makes that power *more ready* to act. It is more ready to act than is a power which has not received a habit, that is, a power whose potency has not in any way been actualized. A habit, then, is a midway stage between an undeveloped power and one which is fully developed and operating.

in potency — **Power** — habit ⟶ in act

The person who has developed the habit of writing with his right hand, even though he is not now actually writing, is *disposed* to write because he has already *to some extent* actualized the powers that he needs in order to write. This is what we mean when we say that a habit *disposes* the person who possesses it to act in a certain way. He is *closer* to doing the completed act than is someone who is not disposed to act.

The person with the habit of writing with his right hand will find it much easier to pick up a pen and begin writing with that hand. He will also be more efficient at writing with his right hand; that is, he will not make as many mistakes.

NOTES

A person without the habit could also pick up a pen and begin to write using his right hand, but he would find it a much more difficult task because his powers are *completely* in potency regarding the act. He would probably also be more prone to making mistakes in his writing. *(If you want to experiment to see if what we are saying is true, try to write your name on a piece of paper using the hand that you do not normally use.)*

Principles of Action

Habits are principles of action: Acts come from habits. Yes, it is also true to say that habits come from acts, but they do so in a different way. Repeated acts form habits. Once formed, habits show themselves in repeated acts.

As principles of action, habits bear a special relation to the soul itself and to the powers of the soul which are also *principles of action.* The soul is the *first* principle of all of our activities. There would be no act in the body if the soul were not present. Built into the soul by nature are its powers or faculties. These faculties are more *proximate* (closer to the act) principles of a person's acts than is the *remote* (removed, or far from the act) principle we call the soul. Even closer yet as principles of our acts are the habits we form which are added to the faculties. It is because of this relationship among the various *principles of action* that we can say that the soul helps the person, the faculties help the soul, and the habits help the faculties.[3]

"The soul is the remote principle or source of all our activities; faculties are the proximate sources built into the soul by nature; habits are still more immediate principles added to the faculties either by personal endeavor or by supernatural infusion from God. Consequently, the soul helps the man, faculties help the soul, and habits help the faculties."

John A. Hardon, S.J.

Principles of Action

Soul
Faculties of the soul
Habits
Acts

Take for example the act of communicating my ideas to other people. My soul is the first but most remote cause within me of my being able to do this act because I would not be able to do it if I were dead. So the soul makes it possible for my person to do the act. My fac-

148.

[3] John A. Hardon, S.J., "The Meaning of Virtue in St. Thomas Aquinas," p. 11.

ulties of intellect and will help my soul to accomplish the act because they enable me to know objective reality and to command the parts of my body to do what it takes to communicate to others. Finally, my habit of writing with my right hand helps my faculties to accomplish the act because they make me do the act with greater ease, joy and efficiency.

Because they bear a relation to the soul, habits are found *only* in human beings -- creatures that possess a rational soul whose powers are not determined to one thing. Our powers are activated as we freely choose to activate them. God has no habits. He has no soul. He has no potentiality whatsoever; He is Pure Act. He does everything He does with perfect ease and efficiency. Animals have souls, but their souls are not rational. They have no potentiality for acquiring new ways of acting. Their actions are completely determined for them by their instincts. Thus, animals cannot have habits. Yes, human beings can *train* animals to act in certain ways, but these quasi-habits are not developed by the animals themselves. They are imposed on them from without by man.

Only human nature is flexible enough to be shaped or molded in various ways. This shaping is done by means of a person's free will as well as by his environment. With each repeated act, a person forms himself for better or for worse into the *quality* of human being that he becomes. Austin Fagothey, S.J., explains:

> Man cannot spread his abilities over the whole field of action possible to him, but must channel them along definite lines. Habits are these channels, cut deeper with each repetition for better or for worse, until the person's native temperament is carved out into the thing we call character.[4]

As Fagothey notes, these relatively permanent "qualities" of a person for which he bears responsibility are the habits he has formed. These habits, along with his basic temperament and other aspects of his personality -- the products of his upbringing, environment, education, free choices, and grace -- make up what we call his **character**. Thus, the person who repeatedly keeps calm and acts reasonably when it is difficult to do so develops the habit of being patient, and he forms himself to be a patient and prudent person. On the other hand, the one who repeatedly chooses to act unreasonably when situations become difficult, who allows himself to lose his temper or acts rashly, forms himself to be an impatient and imprudent person.

---

[4] Austin Fagothey, S.J., *Right and Reason*, p. 226.

Chapter VII
Virtue

NOTES

"Habitual behavior is especially significant because it is revealing of character. It declares who we are in terms of what we do."
　　D. Q. McInerny, p. 143

"Virtue consists of the habitual perfecting and ordering of the principles, the building blocks, of a human act."
　　Conrad Baars, p. 76

Character - from Latin *character* (distinctive mark or nature); moral qualities which distinguish a person.

Called to Happiness ~ Guiding Ethical Principles

NOTES

Acquiring Habits[5]

Human beings are not born with fully formed habits; we must acquire them. Habits differ, however, in the amount of effort a person must exert in order to acquire them. Some habits -- such as musical, artistic or athletic skills, for example -- develop only with consistent and conscientious practice, and they require continued exercise to retain them at their peak of efficiency. This is why accomplished musicians continue to practice their instrument long after they have acquired the habit of playing well. It is also why football pros continue to practice regularly, and singers do vocal exercises daily, etc.

Other habits -- like the intellectual habit of understanding -- are present in the intellect from the very first instant a person begins to exercise that power. Bad habits can form as the result of failing to develop our abilities. For example, the bad habit of poor penmanship can develop simply because a person fails to develop the ability to write legibly. Some habits are formed because we have developed a tendency of repeating certain acts until we get to the point where we do the acts without thinking. Swearing is an example of such a bad habit. It does not represent the development of any power within us.

Still other habits -- such as smoking cigarettes, drinking coffee, or using drugs -- develop because we have built up within ourselves an organic craving for them.

Finally, we at times refer to certain routine acts that we do as habits. For example, we might speak of the habit of making our beds or brushing our teeth. These acts, however, would more properly be called customs than habits. Even though we repeat these acts often, they always require an act of the will each time we do them. Even the act of going to Mass on Sunday is not properly speaking a habit. It is a custom because the will needs to be involved each time.

"We are what we repeatedly do. Therefore, excellence is not an act but a habit."
— Aristotle

[5] Ibid.

Destroying Habits

Habits are destroyed in either of two ways: by lack of use or by contrary acts. Failure to act on a habit starves the habit of what it needs to sustain its life. Thus, no longer smoking a cigarette or drinking coffee for a few months can eliminate the organic craving one has for it. Similarly, repeatedly choosing not to swear for a few weeks can help to remove the tendency to swear without thinking.

Acting contrary to a habit replaces it with an opposite habit. Thus, the habit of writing legibly can replace the habit of writing illegibly. The habit of not biting one's fingernails can replace the habit of biting them. The habit of holding a door for a woman can replace the habit of going through the door first.

Because habits make it easier and more efficient for us to act, getting rid of them is not usually a simple process. In acquiring habits, we have disposed ourselves to act in certain ways to such an extent that acting in these certain ways has become second nature to us. To destroy these habits, then, we must undo the disposition we have acquired and change our nature, so to speak. Viewing the process in these terms might help us to see why destroying a habit is not a quick and easy matter. It usually requires long and consistent effort.

Study Guide Questions:

1. *How does St. Thomas define a habit?*
2. *What is the difference between entitative and operative habits? Give an example of each.*
3. *What does it mean to say that a habit is a disposition? What does a habit do to our human nature?*
4. *Explain in what sense it is true to say that a habit is a "midway stage."*
5. *What is the relationship between the three principles of human action?*
6. *Why is it impossible for God and for animals to acquire habits?*
7. *What is the relationship between the habits a person acquires and the character he develops?*
8. *Explain three different ways a person might acquire a habit.*
9. *Why would it be not quite accurate to call going to Mass on Sundays a "habit"?*
10. *How can a person get rid of a bad habit he has? Why is this not an easy process?*

Called to Happiness ~ Guiding Ethical Principles

NOTES

> ### CASE IN POINT
>
> "Our personality may begin with a basic temperament, but it is clearly and significantly affected by environment, education, and free choices. ...
>
> "Temperament may be viewed as the raw material that an artist uses to create his masterpiece; the stone used in the sculpture may be carved easily or with difficulty; it has a certain color and pattern; it is durable or malleable. Yet the artist uses inspiration, experience, and talent to create a unique sculpture; even if the artist always sculpts in marble, the end product will be unique every time.
>
> "So, too, an individual's total personality will be affected by his education, experiences, free choice ... and grace. The raw material is temperament, but the final creation requires the artist's education, talent, and inspiration."
>
> Art & Laraine Bennett, *The Temperament God Gave You*, New Hampshire: Sophia Press, 2005, p. 6.
>
> ◆ *How would habits fit into the above analogy of the artist carving a sculpture?*
>
> ◆ *Can you draw any other parallels between the analogy above and the human experience of forming one's character?*

"Not every habit is a virtue, but only one that so improves and perfects a rational faculty as to incline it towards good -- good for the faculty, for the will and for the whole man in terms of his ultimate destiny."

John A. Hardon, S.J.

Virtue - from Latin *virtus* (manliness; strength); a good habit which disposes a person to act in accord with right reason.

Vice - a bad habit, one which inclines a person away from what is truly good.

"Virtue is soul-health."
Peter Kreeft, *Back to Virtue*, p. 192

II. Virtue and Vice

Since some habits dispose our natural powers to act in certain ways, we name them according to the "direction" in which they dispose us. If the habit inclines a person towards good, then we call the habit a ***virtue***. If the habit inclines a person away from what is truly good, then we call it a ***vice***.

To have a strong and healthy soul, develop virtue!

The word "virtue" comes from the Latin *vir* (man) and *vis* (power), implying a certain *manliness* or *strength*. The ancient Greeks and Romans, and even learned people of the Middle Ages, ranked the word "virtue" among the most exalted in their language. To possess virtue, they thought, was to possess that which deserves the highest praise.

In its very general meaning, the "virtue" of anything, St. Thomas explains, is determined by the maximum that it is able to produce.[6] Thus, the athlete's "virtue" is determined on the basis of his best possible performance. If he performs below this highest mark, we could say that his performance is inferior to his

---
[6] St. Thomas Aquinas, *Summa Theologiae*, I-II, q. 55, a. 3.

"virtue." Servais Pinckaers explains:

> Virtue would seem to be the capacity of a power to act to accomplish the maximum of which it is capable. In the case of a runner, his peculiar virtue will be a constant disposition which has developed his natural aptitude for running, to the point of enabling him to make a perfect run in the shortest possible time. The virtue will make a good runner of him, one who is able to achieve a record at running.[7]

In the ethical realm, virtue implies moral goodness and human perfection. Virtue disposes a person to produce the best he can *morally speaking*, that is, it gives his intellect and will, his sense appetites and bodily powers the ability to accomplish together the most perfect moral acts. Virtue, as a good habit, then, inclines a person to act in accord with his nature, in accord with right thinking. It makes the person good *as a whole* in terms of achieving his ultimate happiness.

From what we have said so far, we can see that virtue is a habit insofar as it is *a firm and stable disposition to act in a good way*, that is, in a way that moves us closer to genuine happiness. However, we can also see that virtue must be *unlike a habit* as habits are commonly understood today, because virtue does not bring about *automatic* activity.

Because virtue necessarily entails the intelligent mastery over one's self which produces the morally perfect act, a virtuous act cannot be done automatically, that is, without the full involvement of a person's intellect and free will. Rather, virtue requires that the intellect think rightly and that the will choose freely so that the person's good act is fully his own and is thus morally good for him. That the person knowingly and freely does the good act is the means by which he perfects himself and moves himself closer to happiness.

The characteristics of virtue, then, as noted by St. Thomas, can be stated as follows:

- Virtue is a constant disposition of a person's soul whereby it bestows upon the person a mastery over his emotions and over external obstacles which nothing, except his free choice, can destroy.

NOTES

"The virtues make us morally beautiful; the vices make us morally gross."
Wadell, *The Primacy of Love*, p. 107

"In the moral life, the only guarantee of goodness is the virtues."
Wadell, *The Primacy of Love*, p. 107

"The acts of virtue might be varied, but the goal of virtue is one -- to foster and protect the human good."
Jarosznski, p. 45

"Virtue is an active quality which disposes a man to produce the maximum of what he is able to do on the moral plane, which gives to his reason and will conjoined the power to accomplish the most perfect moral actions, actions, that is, of the highest human value."
Servais Pinckaers, p. 70

---

[7] Servais Pinckaers, "Virtue is Not a Habit," *Nouvelle Revue Theologique*, April, 1960, p. 69.

- Virtue produces action with readiness and ease. This is due to the fact that there is within the soul the perfect order and unity among the various powers. The intellect and will direct and command. The sense appetites are obedient to them, while making their own contribution to the act. The various powers of the body bring about the desired action to perfection. All the powers of the soul act harmoniously.

- Virtue causes joy in the one who acts because joy is the overflow of a perfect act, one done in accord with the person's deepest inclinations.[8]

Because virtue is a disposition which inclines a person to produce the morally perfect act, it must be primarily an *interior* matter, even though it reveals itself exteriorly. The interior act of thinking rightly by the practical intellect and of exercising mastery by the will -- if repeated so as to acquire perfection -- leads to the development of virtue. The mere repetition of exterior acts, without the involvement of intellect and will, however, will not result in virtue. For example:

> The virtue of discretion inclines us to observe a just measure in the use of speech. Like fortitude, it is acquired through contrary exterior acts. It often imposes silence upon us. In order to make a real conquest of this virtue, however, it is not sufficient simply to multiply victories over the desire to speak. It is also necessary to learn to speak when the situation demands it, and to conquer the timidity and fear one experiences when he has frankly to speak his mind. Discretion is as much opposed to muteness as it is to garrulousness. It knows when to speak and when to remain silent. The virtue of discretion is not acquired by repetition of the same type of exterior acts, but by the interior acts of mastery over speech which proceed from reason and will.[9]

The repetition of interior acts which results in virtue does not bring about a certain boredom or routine. On the contrary, the repetition is actually a series of personal victories. Pinckaers explains:

> Repetition in this case no longer engenders monotony, but newness. Such is the paradoxical nature of the work of authentic virtue. It is no longer a question of indefinitely beginning over and over again the same material actions, but a question of a surprising series of victories of intelligence and good will, giving rise to a continual renewal.[10]

Acquiring virtue, then, is not about merely repeating exterior acts. It is about educating our intellects to make good practical judgments and training our appetites to be subject to our intellects' judg-

---

NOTES

"The repetition of a material action engenders a habit, a routine, a certain boredom, which destroy the spiritual value of an action. Virtue, on the contrary, far from being diminished by repetition of the same action, is actually nourished by it and makes of it an uninterrupted sequence of spiritual renewals."

Servais Pinckaers, p. 75

---

[8] Ibid., pp. 75-76.
[9] Ibid., pp. 73-74.
[10] Ibid., p. 75.

ments. Acquiring virtue thus involves a progression in the quality of our repeated acts, moving from imperfect acts which are not yet virtuous to the perfect acts produced by the soul endowed with virtue.

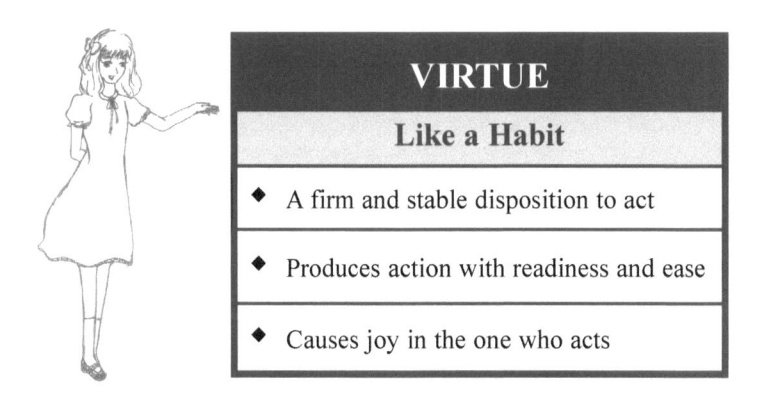

VIRTUE
Like a Habit
◆ A firm and stable disposition to act
◆ Produces action with readiness and ease
◆ Causes joy in the one who acts

VIRTUE
Unlike a Habit
◆ Does not bring *automatic* activity
◆ Requires the thoughtful and free involvement of the person
◆ Is *primarily* an interior matter
◆ Does *not* bring about a certain boredom or routine

A. Intellectual Virtue

Good habits which help to perfect a person's intellect are called **intellectual virtues**. They train the intellect to be more efficient in its act of thinking. Because good thinking does not always help to make a person *morally* good, the intellectual virtues are virtues only in the sense that they help to perfect a person *intellectually*. For example, a person can train his intellect to think well regarding mathematics or chemistry. A good mathematician or a good chemist, however, is not necessarily a good person.

A good mathematician is not necessarily a good person.

Every human person has only <u>one</u> intellect which seeks to know the truth about reality, but that one intellect can act for two different purposes. We speak of the intellect in terms of these two purposes:

Intellectual virtue - a habit which perfects the human intellect, disposing it to function well.

Called to Happiness ~ Guiding Ethical Principles

NOTES

Speculative intellect - from Latin *speculari* (to examine, observe); the intellect as it seeks to know reality simply for the sake of knowing it.

Practical intellect - the intellect as it seeks to know reality in order to do something with it.

Understanding - a virtue of the speculative intellect which enables the person to grasp basic self-evident truths.

Knowledge (Science) - a virtue of the speculative intellect which enables a person to draw correct conclusions from sound premises.

Wisdom - a virtue of the speculative intellect which enables a person to know all of reality in relation to its ultimate causes.

(a) The **speculative intellect** seeks to know the truth about reality just for the sake of knowing it. For example, when a person is interested in finding out about the order and nature of the planets in the solar system simply because he is curious, we would say that he is thinking *speculatively*.

(b) The **practical intellect**, on the other hand, seeks to know the truth about reality for the sake of human action. For example, when a person is interested in finding out the order and nature of the planets in the solar system because he wants to design a navigation system for a space ship, we would say that he is thinking *practically*.

Because the intellect needs to be perfected in both of its ways of thinking, there are virtues which correspond to each of them. The following virtues perfect the speculative intellect in its task of knowing reality for its own sake:

Speculative Intellect

i.) *Understanding:* the habit of being able to grasp basic self-evident truths that are fundamental to all knowledge. An example of this virtue would be the awareness a person has that a thing cannot both be and not be at the same time and under the same conditions.

ii.) *Knowledge (Science):* the habit of being able to draw correct conclusions from sound premises. This virtue makes it possible for us to reason correctly in applying principles to particular instances. For example, based on our understanding that a thing cannot both be and not be at the same time and under the same conditions, we are able to know that the lights in this room cannot be both on and off at the same time and under the same conditions.

iii.) *Wisdom:* the habit of being able to know all of reality in relation to its ultimate causes. This virtue, for example, enables a person to know that the planets are the way they are because God created them to be that way.

The practical intellect seeks knowledge for the sake of being able to *act* well. Human action takes two forms: making and doing. There is a virtue which corresponds to each of these forms of action:

156.

Practical Intellect

i.) *Art*: the habit of knowing how to make some external object. This virtue includes the mechanical, the liberal, and the fine arts.

ii.) *Prudence*: the habit of knowing what to do and how to do it in order to live well, that is, in order to achieve happiness. This virtue is concerned with perfecting the person, not with producing an external product.

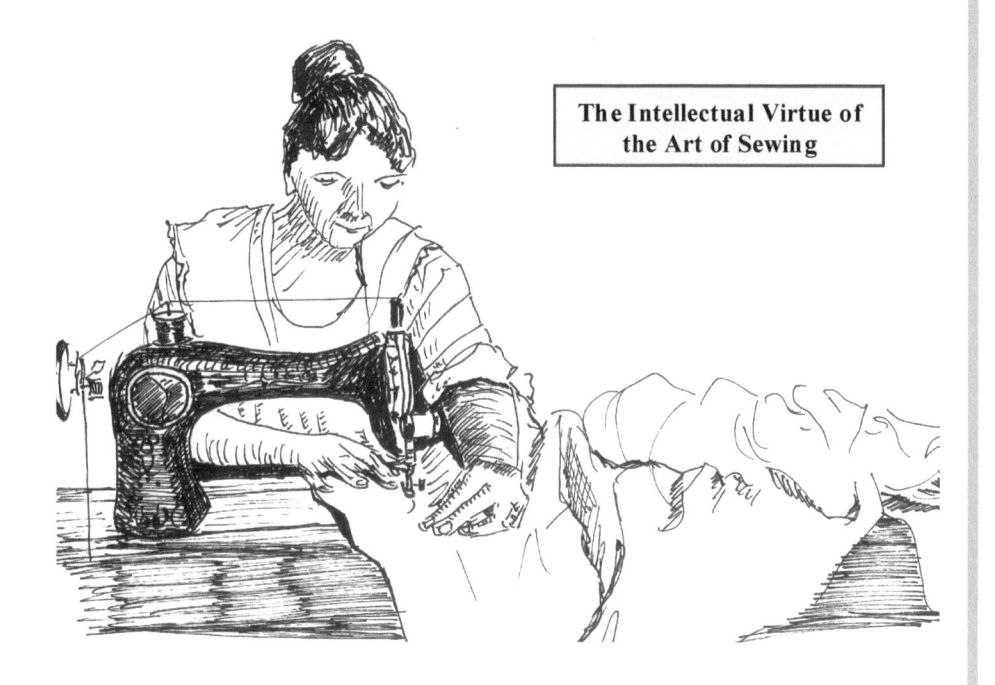

Chapter VII
Virtue

NOTES

Art - a virtue of the practical intellect which enables a person to make some external object.

Prudence - from Latin *prudentia* (foresight); a virtue of the pratical intellect which enables a person to know what to do and how to do it here and now in order to live well.

The Intellectual Virtue of the Art of Sewing

Study Guide Questions:

1. How do virtue and vice differ?

2. In what ways is virtue like a habit? In what ways is it not?

3. Why isn't the repetition of interior acts leading to virtue boring?

4. Why do we say that the intellectual virtues are virtues only "in a certain sense"? What limitation do they have?

5. How many intellects does a person have? What do we mean by the speculative and practical intellects?

6. List the virtues of the speculative intellect. What general purpose do these virtues serve?

7. List the virtues of the practical intellect. How do these virtues differ from each other?

B. Moral Virtue

Good habits which help to perfect the person *as a whole* in terms of reaching his Ultimate End are called **moral virtues**. They are virtues in the narrow and stricter sense of being habits which perfect the person *as a person*, thus making him to be *truly good*. ***Moral virtues are good habits of a person's appetites -- sensitive and rational -- disposing them to act in accord with the sound judgment of his intellect.*** If a person's appetites are inclined to follow the intellect's guidance, then the person will find it *easier*, *more pleasant*, and *more efficient* to do the good act. In other words, he will find it easier to become good himself.

> "The good of man consists in being in accord with reason."
> St. Thomas Aquinas,
> *Summa Theologiae*, I-II, 18, 5

Doing the morally good act is always a matter of "hitting the mean" (or "middle point") between too much and too little of whatever the act involves. This is why Aristotle spoke of moral virtue as a habit of choosing the mean between the extremes of excess and defect.[11] This is what we mean when we use the expression: "Virtue stands in the middle." For example, the virtue of courage is the mean between vice of rashness (too bold in the face of evil) and the vice of cowardice (too fearful in the face of evil).

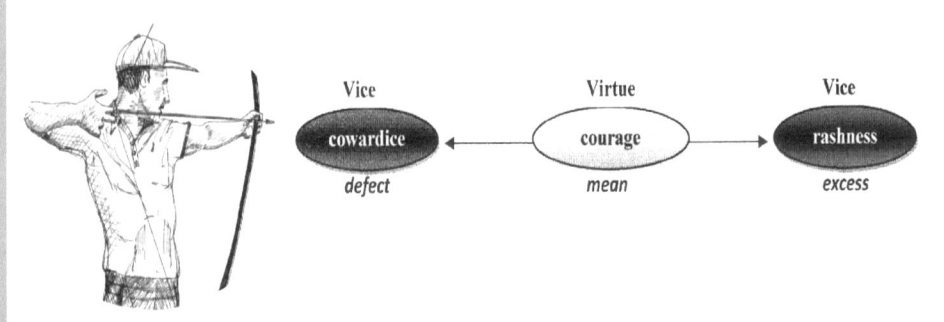

Vice	Virtue	Vice
cowardice	courage	rashness
defect	mean	excess

The virtue of generosity is the mean between stinginess (giving too little) and prodigality (giving too much).

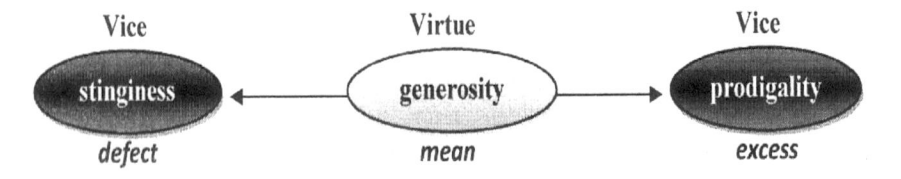

Vice	Virtue	Vice
stinginess	generosity	prodigality
defect	mean	excess

The virtue of friendliness is the mean between coldness (too little personal warmth) and flattery (too much personal warmth.

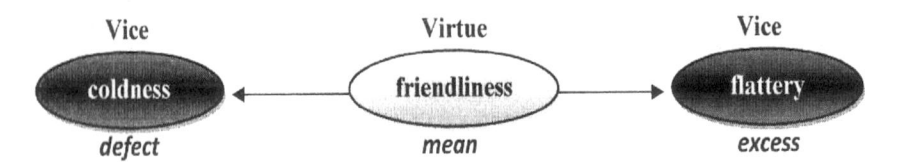

Vice	Virtue	Vice
coldness	friendliness	flattery
defect	mean	excess

The virtuous act directs us to our End. Overshooting or falling short of the mark keeps us from reaching our End. This is probably why

---
[11] Aristotle, *Nicomachean Ethics*, Book II, ch. 6, 1106b 36.

virtue is referred to as the <u>golden</u> *mean*: It is so vitally important to us. Virtue is our natural means to happiness!

Who or what determines the golden mean? ***A person's intellect, perfected by the virtue of prudence, determines the virtuous mean.*** This is why there can be no moral virtue without prudence.

For the virtues of fortitude and temperance, prudence determines what to do in a particular situation. What is the mean (the middle) action that should be done by *this* particular person in *his* particular situation? In other words, the golden mean is *relative* to the person performing the act. How much money should a person give? A generous gift of $100 from a poor person would be a stingy gift from a millionaire. Likewise, a policeman's courageous act of confronting an armed robber would probably be a foolish one for an unarmed woman. A moderate supper for a teenage athlete would be overindulgence for an elderly person. Because the golden mean of the virtues of fortitude and temperance is relative to each person and dependent upon his emotional responses, it is *subjective*.

The virtue of justice, however, is different. Because justice relates to *external objects* and not to *emotional responses*, the mean is an *objective* or quantitative mean. Any impartial third party would be able to judge it, for the just mean is completely dependent upon external objects. For example, how much do I owe for this bike? Or how much of the payment should we each receive?

Just as every physical thing is a composition of form and matter, so too is every virtue. The "matter" or raw material of virtue are the passions and actions of the human person. The "form" of virtue is provided by the intellect, which shapes and forms the matter in such a way as to make it in accord with right reason.

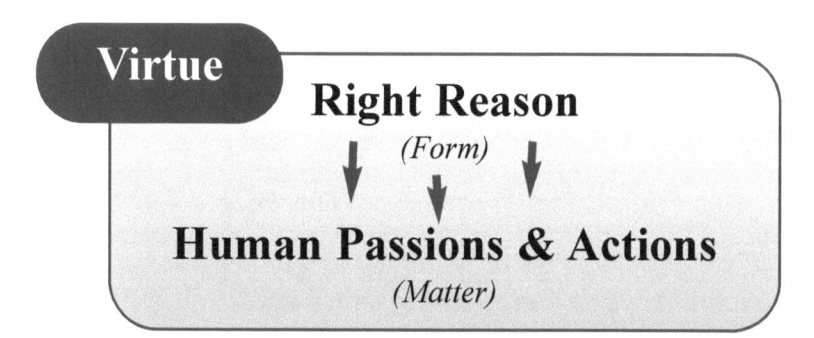

Virtue

Right Reason
(Form)
↓ ↓ ↓
Human Passions & Actions
(Matter)

An analogy might help to clarify: Virtue's matter is like the keys on a piano. Virtue's form is like the sheet music, which tells the pianist how much and when to play each note. With regard to its matter, virtue

NOTES

is a mean. It is possible to play too many or too few keys -- to have too much or too little passion or action. With regard to its form, however, virtue is not a mean. The sheet music is *the best* the author could do. Similarly, in terms of its form, virtue implies *the best* which a person's intellect can do.

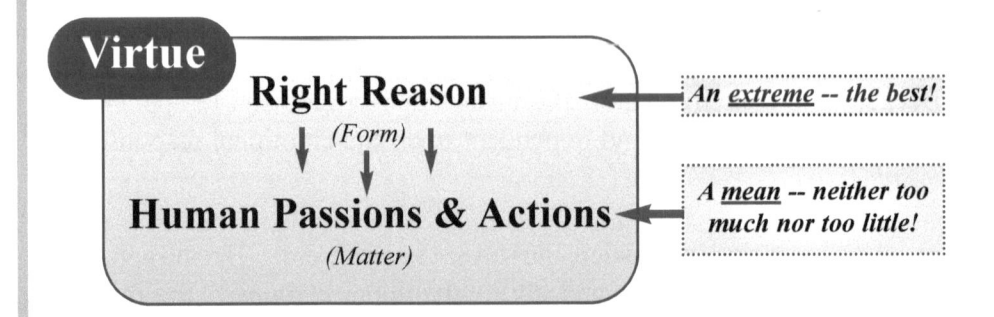

Virtue

Right Reason
(Form)
↓ ↓ ↓
Human Passions & Actions
(Matter)

An extreme -- the best!

A mean -- neither too much nor too little!

Study Guide Questions:

1. How does moral virtue differ from intellectual virtue?

2. What powers of the soul do the moral virtues perfect?

3. Why should a person want to acquire the moral virtues? What good are they?

4. "Virtue stands in the middle." Explain.

5. Why do we speak of the mean of virtue as a "golden mean"?

6. Who determines the mean of virtue?

7. How does the mean of fortitude and temperance differ from the mean of justice?

8. What are the form and matter of moral virtue?

9. "With regard to its matter, virtue is a mean." Explain.

Chapter VII
Virtue

CASES IN POINT

#1 -- "There is a difference between doing some particular just or temperate action and being a just or temperate man. Someone who is not a good tennis player may now and then make a good shot. What you mean by a good tennis player is the man whose eye and muscles and nerves have been so trained by making innumerable good shots that they can now be relied on. They have a certain tone or quality which is there even when he is not playing, just as a mathematician's mind has a certain habit and outlook which is there even when he is not doing mathematics. In the same way a man who perseveres in doing just actions gets in the end a certain quality of character. Now it is that quality rather than the particular actions which we mean when we talk of 'virtue.'"

C.S. Lewis, *Mere Christianity*, pp. 62-63.

- *Why is the distinction Lewis makes so important?*

- *Lewis later says that right actions done in the wrong way or for the wrong reason do not help to build the internal quality or character called a 'virtue,' and it is this quality or character that really matters. He explains: "If the bad tennis player hits very hard, not because he sees that a very hard stroke is required, but because he has lost his temper, his stroke might possibly, by luck, help him to win that particular game; but it will not be helping him to become a reliable player." Explain why this is so important. Can you give an example to illustrate his point?*

- *Later, Lewis notes that virtues are necessary not only for this present life but also for the next. Why would Lewis claim that we will need the virtues in Heaven? Will we need to be just and brave there?*

* * * * *

#2 -- C.S. Lewis, in *The Great Divorce*, presents the following dialogue between the main character and his Teacher as they travel through Heaven and Hell:

'I am troubled, Sir, because that unhappy creature doesn't seem to me to be the sort of soul that ought to be even in danger of damnation. She isn't wicked: she's only a silly, garrulous old woman who has got into a habit of grumbling, and feels that a little kindness, and rest, and change would due her all right.'

'That is what she once was. That is maybe what she still is. If so, she certainly will be cured. But the whole question is whether she is now a grumbler.'

'I should have thought there was no doubt about that!'

'Aye, but ye misunderstand me. The question is whether she is a grumbler, or only a grumble. If there is a real woman -- even the least trace of one -- still there inside the grumbling, it can be brought to life again. If there's one wee spark under all those ashes, we'll blow it till the whole pile is red and clear. But if there's nothing but ashes we'll not go on blowing them in our own eyes forever. They must be swept up.'

'But how can there be a grumble without a grumbler?'

'The whole difficulty of understanding Hell is that the thing to be understood is so nearly Nothing. But ye'll have had experiences ... it begins with a grumbling mood, and yourself still distinct from it: perhaps criticizing it. And yourself, in a dark hour, may will that mood, embrace it. Ye can repent and come out of it again. But there may come a day when you can do that no longer. Then there will be no you left to criticize the mood, nor even to enjoy it, but just the grumble itself going on forever like a machine.'

(pp. 76-77)

- *What point is C.S. Lewis trying to make in this dialogue?*

- *What is it about a habit that might explain its ability to turn a grumbler into a grumble?*

Called to Happiness ~ Guiding Ethical Principles

NOTES

C. Cardinal Virtues

The moral virtues are many in number. Traditionally, since at least the time of Plato and Aristotle, four of them have been singled out from among the group as being the most important in regard to ethical action. These four virtues are called the **cardinal virtues**, from the Latin *cardo*, meaning "a hinge," because they are the virtues on which the other moral virtues "swing." The other moral virtues -- all of which deal with perfecting the appetites -- can ultimately be reduced to these four.

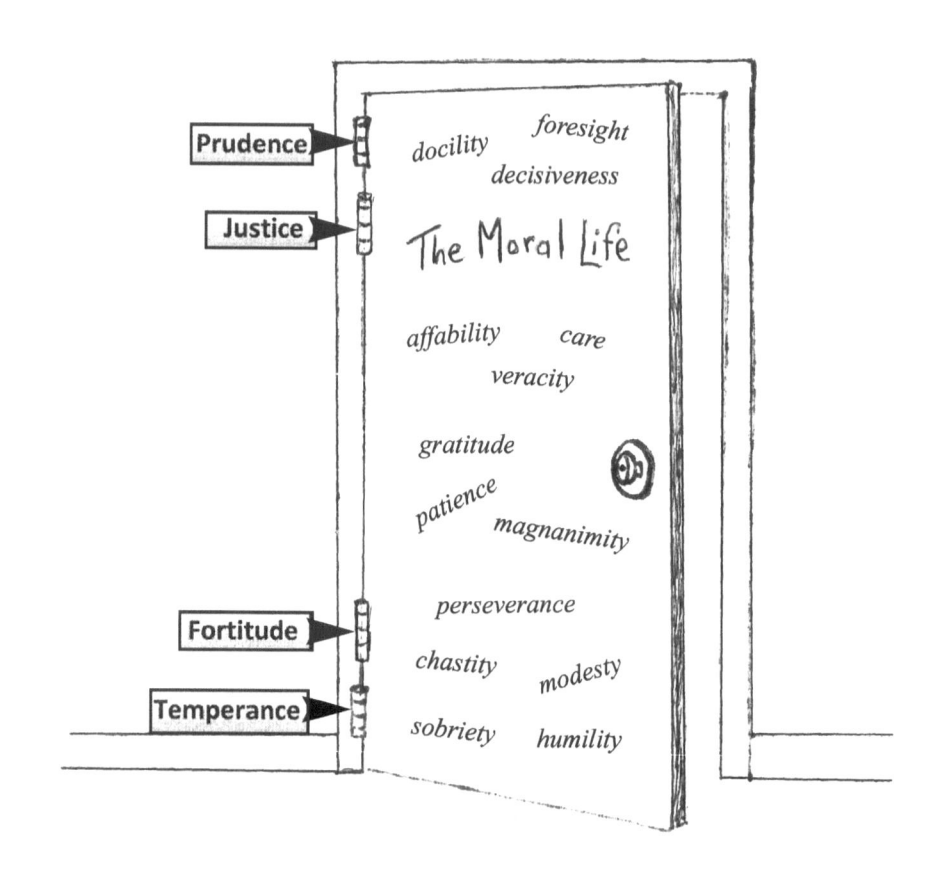

Cardinal virtue - from the Latin *cardo* (hinge); the four virtues to which all the other moral virtues can be reduced.

"The four cardinal virtues -- justice, wisdom, courage, and moderation -- are relevant to man in every age because they are relevant to man himself, not to the age. They fit our nature and our nature's needs."
Peter Kreeft,
Back to Virtue, p. 64

Prudence

Prudence *perfects the practical intellect, disposing it to make sound judgments about what ought to be done here and now.*

Prudence is first among the cardinal virtues because of its importance. Although it is essentially an intellectual virtue, prudence is also a moral virtue. It is a moral virtue because in order for the appetites of a person to move toward what is *truly* good, they need to be guided by the sound judgment of the intellect. Prudence provides this sound intellectual judgment by determining the best means in this situation here and now for doing what is good.

Notice that the virtue of prudence deals with the means, not the ends of our actions. Its purpose is to find the appropriate means for

Prudence - the cardinal virtue which perfects the practical intellect, disposing it to make sound judgments about what ought to be done here and now.

"Whatever is good must first have been prudent."
Josef Pieper, p. 7

162.

achieving the good end we seek. Without prudence there can be no other moral virtues because human acts are good only to the degree that they correspond to right reason.[12] Prudence applies right reason to human acts. This is why St. Thomas says that prudence is the form of all the moral virtues.[13] Thus, it is prudence that determines what the just, temperate, and brave act is here and now in this particular situation.

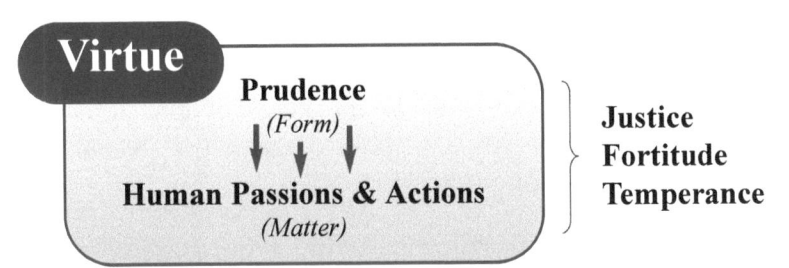

Virtue

Prudence *(Form)* ↓↓↓ Human Passions & Actions *(Matter)*

} Justice, Fortitude, Temperance

The flip side of the coin is also true, however: A person cannot be prudent without also being just, temperate, and brave. Prudence depends on the other cardinal virtues to keep the appetites in general right order, for without this order within the appetites, the intellect would be hindered in its ability to think clearly. Josef Pieper, a contemporary Thomistic philosopher, explains:

> Only one who previously and simultaneously loves and wants the good can be prudent; but only one who is previously prudent can do good.[14]

Perhaps this is why St. Thomas speaks of the "unity of virtue." The cardinal virtues come as a "packaged deal" -- all or none!

Acquiring the virtue of prudence is not an easy matter. It requires that a person *habitually* do the following:

♦ Be still in order to know objective reality. We need to quiet ourselves in order to get beyond our subjective view of things and "listen" to what objective reality is communicating to us. Being in touch with reality enables a person to choose appropriate ways and means.

♦ Cultivate open-mindedness (docility to good advice), clear-sighted objectivity in unexpected circumstances (avoid random action), and a memory which is true-to-being (honest in what it remembers). Each of these helps a person to be better in touch with objective reality, and thus better able to make appropriate decisions.

♦ Make decisions applying universal moral principles to particular acts.

♦ Execute decisions in a timely manner.[15]

---

[12] St. Thomas Aquinas, *De virtutibus cardinalibus*, 2.
[13] St. Thomas Aquinas, *De veritate* 27, 5 ad 5.
[14] Josef Pieper, *The Four Cardinal Virtues*, p. 34.
[15] Ibid., pp. 10-22.

NOTES

"All virtue is necessarily prudent."
Josef Pieper, p. 5.

"Courage is the sacrifice of self for the realization of prudent and just goals."
Alexander Havard, *Virtuous Leadership*, p. 71.

"'Conscience' is intimately related to and well-nigh interchangeable with the word 'prudence'."
Pieper, p. 11

Called to Happiness ~ Guiding Ethical Principles

NOTES

"Prudence is the ability to know means to the end, the means that will bring us to the end we have chosen."
Jarosznski, p. 55

"Prudence is the 'intelligent prow' of our nature which steers through the multiplicity of the finite world toward perfection."
Pieper, p. 22

"...the prudent man looks where he is going."
Proverbs 14:15

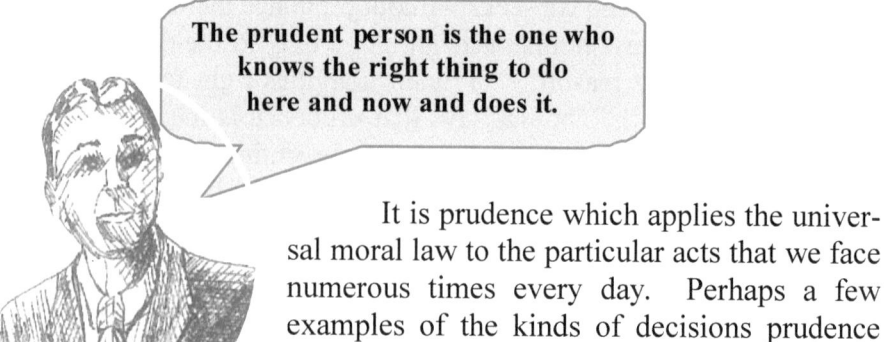

> The prudent person is the one who knows the right thing to do here and now and does it.

It is prudence which applies the universal moral law to the particular acts that we face numerous times every day. Perhaps a few examples of the kinds of decisions prudence helps a person to make will reveal just how important it is.

Prudence governs the following:

- who to pick as a companion and friend;
- when to speak to a teacher about problems in class and what to say;
- what time to go to bed and how long to sleep;
- how to dress and what to buy;
- how to relate to adults and peers;
- how much and what kind of food to pack for lunch;
- how to spend the extra time after school before going home;
- what is worth living and dying for.

As we said before, virtue reflects the mean between *excess* and *defect* with regard to its matter. The matter of prudence is human thinking about what to do here and now. The virtue of prudence, then, stands as a mean between the following two extremes:

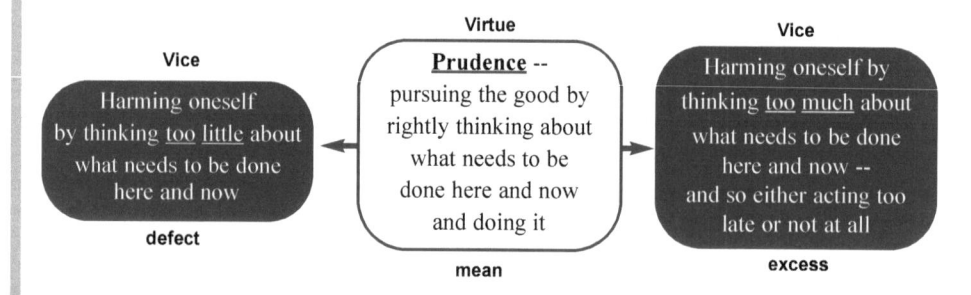

Vice (defect)	Virtue (mean)	Vice (excess)
Harming oneself by thinking <u>too little</u> about what needs to be done here and now	**Prudence** -- pursuing the good by rightly thinking about what needs to be done here and now and doing it	Harming oneself by thinking <u>too much</u> about what needs to be done here and now -- and so either acting too late or not at all

Study Guide Questions:

1. Why do we call four of the moral virtues "cardinal" virtues?

2. Which of the cardinal virtues is considered to be the most important one? Why?

3. What does it mean to speak of the "unity of virtue"?

4. What would be some common characteristics of people who have the virtue of prudence?

5. If we have a conscience, why do we need prudence?

Chapter VII
Virtue

> ### Prudence Complements Conscience
>
> Conscience is an act, not a habit; therefore, it cannot be a virtue. The judgment of conscience is purely *cognitive*. Thus, a judgment of conscience reveals our *intellectual ability* to know that we should or should not do a certain act. It enables a person to relate to the good cognitively, that is, to know it under the guise of *truth*.
>
> Moral virtue makes the person himself good and renders his action good. It enables a person to relate to the good *as good*, that is, to know it as the object of his appetite, as that which he seeks. In order to acquire the dispositions of appetite which we call justice, courage, and temperance -- dispositions whose ends are in line with the ultimate end, we need prudence. For prudence determines how we can, here and now, achieve the good that we seek.
>
> This explains why a person who knows what he ought to do because his conscience is alright might nevertheless choose to do evil: He is morally weak. His knowledge of the good is not complemented by his appetites' ordination to the good *as good*. His heart is elsewhere. St. Thomas explains:
>
>> That is why the **judgment of free will** is sometimes perverted whereas that of conscience is not; for example, when someone examines what is imminently to be done and judges ... that this is evil, for instance, to have sexual relations with this woman, yet, when he sets out to act in the light of this, other factors from a variety of sources come into play, like the promised delight of sexual activity, from desire of which reason is blinded and its assessment set aside. Thus one errs in choice and not in conscience, though he acts contrary to conscience and is said to act with a bad conscience insofar as his deed does not conform with his knowledge. (*On Truth*, q. 1, a. 1)

NOTES

Cognitive - of or pertaining to the act or process of knowing, perceiving, remembering, etc.

Justice

***Justice** perfects the will so that it is disposed to give to others what is their due.*

Justice ranks next to prudence in importance among the moral virtues. It is the cardinal virtue which perfects the will so that it is disposed to act in accord with the sound judgment of the intellect. When the will acts according to the order that prudence dictates, then it will give to the other person what he has a **right** to receive. Justice, then, presupposes rights. It presupposes that we owe somebody something. The virtue of justice, then, disposes a person habitually to look outward. The just person is the one who looks beyond himself to consider the rights of others.

Justice - from Latin *justitia* (uprightness; righteousness); the cardinal virtue which perfects the will, disposing it to give everyone his due.

Right - An appeal to the will of another through his intellect to act in accord with moral law. A right involves a claim to something, and respect for that claim is necessary for other people to attain their Ultimate End. Rights are founded on law: divine law (natural rights) and human law (positive rights). Only rational creatures have rights.

165.

Called to Happiness ~ Guiding Ethical Principles

NOTES

Common good - "the sum total of social conditions which allow people, either as groups or as individuals, to reach their fulfillment more fully and more easily."
Gaudium et spes 26, #1

"A thing is just not only because it is willed by God, but because it is a debt due to a created being by virtue of the relationship between creature and creature."
St. Thomas Aquinas, *Commentary on the Sentences*, Book 4, d. 26, 1, 2, 1

"To desire the common good and strive towards it is a requirement of justice and charity."
Benedict XVI, *Charity in Truth*, #7

"The more we strive to secure a common good corresponding to the real needs of our neighbours, the more effectively we love them."
Benedict XVI, *Charity in Truth*, #7

He understands that the good of every person and of society as a whole depends upon the fulfillment of the rights of each one. The just person is always ready to fulfill his "debt" to others. Justice, then, is the virtue that helps us to keep in mind the **common good**: the sum total of good which includes the good of each and every person involved.

This "debt" to which justice responds can vary greatly: It can be simply returning thanks for a favor granted, greeting a neighbor when I meet him on the street, paying the agreed-upon price for an article, or refusing to lie about another. All are acts of justice because of a "debt" that is owed, the obligation one has toward another.

The just response to the rights of other persons is an act of virtue because it perfects the one who is just. Those on the "receiving end" of the just act are not the only ones who benefit by it. As a good habit, justice disposes the person who acts justly to act that way habitually, and thus to move himself toward true happiness. This is why the one who does injustice is to be pitied more than the one who *suffers* it. Thus, the one who steals another's money *suffers more* from his evil act than does the one from whom he stole. The one who harms another's reputation actually hurts himself more than he does the other.

Josef Pieper expresses this same idea:

> The man who does not give a person what belongs to him, withholds it or deprives him of it, is really doing harm to himself; he is the one who actually loses something - indeed, in the most extreme case, he even destroys himself.[16]

Justice is usually divided into three kinds: *Commutative, Distributive,* and *Legal*. Josef Pieper's chart below might help us to see the relation between these three types of justice as we proceed to describe them:[17]

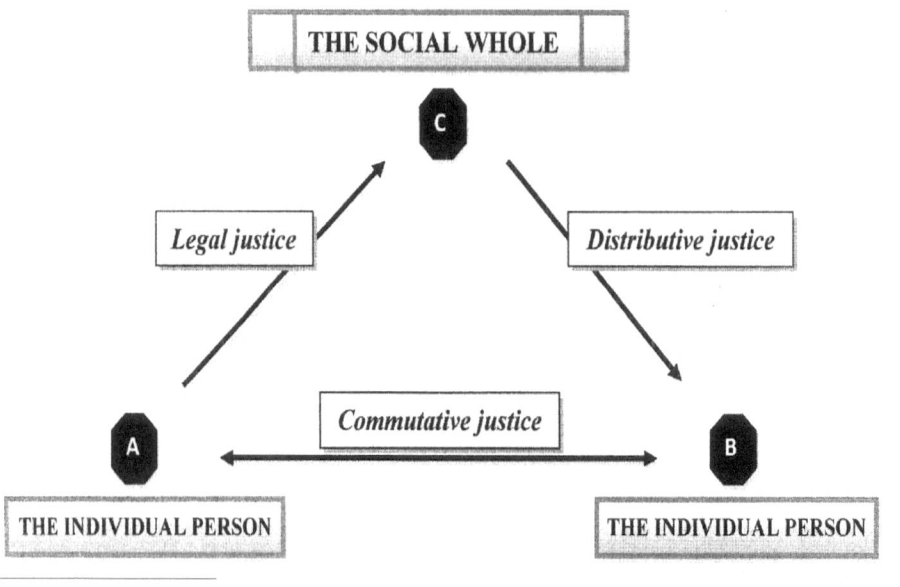

---

[16] Josef Pieper, *The Four Cardinal Virtues*, p. 47.
[17] Ibid., p. 113.

Commutative justice is between two equals. The equals could be either human persons or independent states. Commutative justice is the basis of contracts. For example, if two people agree that one will cut the grass for the payment of $10 dollars from the other, then it is justice which demands the payment once the grass is cut. The completion of one part of the agreement establishes an inequality between the two that needs to be eliminated by paying the amount owed.

Similarly, if one person harms the property of another, then justice demands that he compensate the person for the damage done. If one person takes what belongs to another, then a debt is owed which must be paid. Paying this debt or compensating a person for damage done to his property is what we refer to when we speak of making **restitution**. To make restitution is "to re-instate a person in the possession or dominion of his thing."[18] Thus restitution brings about a return to the balance which should exist between two persons who are equals.

Distributive justice concerns the relation between a superior and those subordinate to him, or between the community and its members. It is not between equals. It requires that the goods and burdens of a community be handed out to the members in a fair way. For example, if a ruler is just, then he will see to it that the resources available to his country are distributed to all of his citizens in a way that meets the needs of all. Such justice requires the one who distributes the goods to have an impartial respect for all.

On a smaller scale -- within a family the father acts with distributive justice when he demands more work from his eldest son for the upkeep of the home than he does from his youngest. It is also distributive justice that disposes the father to give a larger sum of money to his oldest son than he does to his youngest as a weekly allowance.

Legal justice is the reverse of distributive justice: it concerns the relation of the members to the community, or of those subordinate to their superior. Legal justice requires each person to make his contribution to the common good. Although it involves more than merely obeying the written law, legal justice is often manifested in law-abiding conduct. Because it involves *all* of the social virtues, legal justice is sometimes referred to as *general justice* and can be synonymous with virtue itself. Examples would be the following: not littering, following traffic

---

[18] St. Thomas Aquinas, *Summa Theologiae*, II-II, 62, 2.

NOTES

Restitution - from Latin *restitutuere* (to restore); to restore, hand back, refund.

"To do what is right and just is more acceptable to the Lord than sacrifice."
Proverbs 21:3.

"Holy Scripture speaks more than eight hundred times of 'justice' and 'the just man,' by which it means no less than 'the good, the holy man.'"
Pieper, p. 64.

NOTES

"Every external act belongs to the field of justice."
Pieper, p. 61.

"The good of reason shines more brightly in justice than in any of the other moral virtues."
St. Thomas Aquinas,
ST, I-II, 66, 4.

laws, doing your share of help at home, and being orderly and respectful of your parents, teachers, etc.

Precisely because legal justice is so general and involves all of the social virtues, it is not included as part of the cardinal virtue of justice. Only commutative and distributive justice -- sometimes referred to as *particular justice* -- make up justice as the cardinal virtue. They are referred to as *particular justice* because they deal not with *all* moral matters but only with what is owed by one person to another *about a particular good*, such as money, honor, or truthfulness.

The cardinal virtue of justice reflects the mean between *excess* and *defect* with regard to giving another person what is rightfully his. The virtue of justice stands as a mean between the following two extremes:

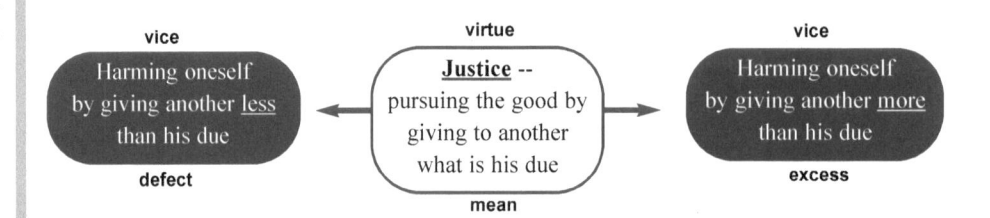

vice	virtue	vice
Harming oneself by giving another <u>less</u> than his due	**Justice** -- pursuing the good by giving to another what is his due	Harming oneself by giving another <u>more</u> than his due
defect	mean	excess

Study Guide Questions:

1. What power of the human soul does the virtue of justice perfect?

2. What is a right? Why does justice presuppose the existence of rights?

3. Why is the person who does an injustice to be pitied more than the one who suffers an injustice?

4. What does "making restitution" have to do with commutative justice?

5. What are the three kinds of justice?

6. Which of the three kinds of justice would be included under the cardinal virtue of justice?

Fortitude

Fortitude (courage) perfects the irascible appetite, disposing it to act in accord with the sound judgment of the intellect.

One is disposed for an act of fortitude when prudence dictates through justice what ought to be done here and now when an evil is threatening. In other words, prudence determines what is the right thing to do here and now. Justice makes this judgment a reality in a person's external act. It is the role of fortitude to dispose the person to "hold on to the good" no matter the evil he might suffer for doing so. For example, when one is afraid he might lose his friend by telling the truth, he has the courage to do so here and now, regardless of how his friend may respond.

Fortitude, then, presupposes that the person is vulnerable to suffering, even the suffering of death. Because of this vulnerability, his emotion of fear could respond in a way that would prevent him from doing what is good. Fortitude holds his fear in submission to right reason, so that he is free to do the good act. In holding fear in check, fortitude consequently frees the emotion of courage to respond.

Fortitude frees us from slavery to fear.

Thus, fortitude frees a person from slavery to fear. It enables him to do the good act when evil threatens to stop him. As a virtue, fortitude helps us develop the habit of self-mastery; it is the permanent disposition to let right reason govern our emotional response of fear.

From this we realize that there can be no fortitude without prudence and justice. To do the daring act or to risk death is virtuous only if it is reasonable to do so, that is, if it leads us to the happiness we seek.

> To rush into peril out of anger, ignorance, or stupidity is no sign of fortitude; the truly courageous man acts from a rational motive, whereby he appreciates the danger while counting it the lesser evil.... Fortitude enables us to overcome our abhorrence for death, and still more of lesser evils, when it is reasonable to do so.[19]

The virtue of fortitude reflects the golden mean determined by prudence. This mean between *excess* and *defect* concerns the emotions of the irascible appetite and the acts that can follow from them:

---

[19] Austin Fagothey, S.J., *Right and Reason*, p. 233.

NOTES

Fortitude - from Latin *fortitudo* (strong); cardinal virtue which perfects the irascible appetite, disposing it to follow the guidance of right reason.

"Man does not expose his life to mortal danger, except to maintain justice."
St. Thomas Aquinas
ST, II-II, 123, 12, ad. 3.

"The virtue of fortitude keeps man from so loving his life that he loses it."
Josef Pieper, p. 134.

"To suffer with the other and for others; to suffer for the sake of truth and justice; to suffer out of love and in order to become a person who truly loves -- these are fundamental elements of humanity, and to abandon them would destroy man himself."
Benedict XVI, *Spe Salvi*, #39

"He that feareth the Lord will tremble at nothing."
Sirach 34:14

"It is not injury that makes the martyr, but the fact that his action is in accordance with truth."
St. Augustine

"Only the prudent man can be brave."
Pieper, p. 123

"There is a big difference between the person who knows solely that something is evil and ought to be opposed, and the one who in addition also feels hate for that evil, is angry that it is corrupting or harming his fellow-men, and feels aroused to combat it courageously and vigorously."
Conrad Baars, p. 77

Called to Happiness ~ Guiding Ethical Principles

NOTES

"Man must be ready to let himself be killed rather than to deny Christ or to sin grievously."
St. Thomas Aquinas,
Questiones quodlibetales 4, 20.

Temperance - from Latin *temperantia* (moderation); cardinal virtue which perfects the concupiscible appetite, disposing it to act in accord with right reason.

```
   vice                    virtue                   vice
┌──────────────┐    ┌──────────────────┐    ┌──────────────┐
│Harming oneself│    │   Fortitude --   │    │Harming oneself│
│by having too  │◄──►│pursuing the good │◄──►│by having too  │
│little willing-│    │by reasonably     │    │much willingness│
│ness to stand  │    │standing against  │    │to stand       │
│against a      │    │a difficult evil  │    │against a      │
│difficult evil │    │                  │    │difficult evil │
└──────────────┘    └──────────────────┘    └──────────────┘
   defect                   mean                   excess
```

Temperance

***Temperance** perfects the concupiscible appetite in its response to a good that arouses our desires and gives us pleasure.*

The goods which seem to be the most inviting to us are the goods of taste and touch. Our desire for food, drink, and sexual pleasure can easily become excessive, causing a disturbance within us. This interior disturbance or disorder can actually bring about our self-destruction if we are not careful. The disorder arises because our emotions are rebelling against the right judgment of our intellect. The emotions are tending to move us in a direction that our intellect knows is harmful to us.

We have all probably experienced a desire for something that became so excessive that we found it hard to concentrate or to do the good act that we should have been doing -- like paying attention during the class just before lunch. When this happens, it is like a small battle being waged inside of us between the intellect and the emotions. The temperate person does not experience this "battle." Rather, the powers of his soul are all working together helping him to pursue the good.

Do you remember the analogy we made in the last chapter between a coach pulled by horses and a person moved by his appetites? We can use that same analogy to understand the problem that arises for the intemperate person. If the horses (the emotions) insist on going in a direction the driver (the intellect) does *not* want to go, then the driver could be in grave danger.

Emotions rebelling against intellect

Chapter VII
Virtue

When a person's emotions are disposed to follow the guidance of right reason, however, then his desires for sensed goods remain moderate. They do not disturb his inner peace and calm. Thus, the temperate person experiences an interior harmony because the powers within him are working as one unified and ordered whole. For example, I can easily decide to turn off the TV for the next two hours when I'm studying for exams, so that I can concentrate on my studies.

Temperance makes a person beautiful from within.

This order *within the human person* is the purpose of the virtue of temperance. Although temperance is the only cardinal virtue which focuses exclusively on the person himself, it does so in a *selfless* way. Temperance looks to the self only in order to discipline the powers of his soul so that they remain in right order, the intellect guiding them all. This *selfless* turning toward oneself which is temperance is necessary for the preservation of the person. This is so because the powers within us which are designed to sustain our existence can actually destroy us if they are not kept well ordered.

The self-destruction occurs when we "love ourselves" so much that we no longer seek a Good greater than ourselves. Temperance disciplines or purifies this self-love, thus making it a *true* love of self. Only the person who *truly* loves himself will seek a Good greater than himself and thus come to experience the happiness for which he longs. Josef Pieper explains:

> If he loves nothing so much as himself, man misses and perverts, with inner necessity, the purpose inherent in self-love as in all love: to preserve, to make real, to fulfill. This purpose is given only to selfless self-love, which seeks not itself blindly, but with open eyes endeavors to correspond to the true reality of God, the self, and the world.[20]

The virtue of temperance is all about happiness. It protects us from our own sinful inclinations to "love ourselves" in ways that will actually harm us. Temperance is therefore the virtue of true *manliness*, for it frees us to be the beings we were created to be: Human persons who are free to love God with our whole being.

The golden mean of temperance is the mean between *excess* and *defect* concerning the emotions of the concupiscible appetite and the acts that can follow from them:

---

[20] Josef Pieper, *The Four Cardinal Virtues*, p. 149.

NOTES

"Not only is temperance beautiful in itself, it also renders men beautiful."
St. Thomas Aquinas, *ST* II-II, 142, 4

"Temperance is selfless self-preservation. Intemperance is self-destruction through the selfish degradation of the powers which aim at self-preservation."
Josef Pieper, p. 148

"It is not the good my will preserves, but the evil my will disapproves, that I find myself doing."
Romans 7:19

"The virtue of temperance and moderation aims at preserving man uninjured and undefiled for God."
St. Augustine, *De moribus Ecclesiae* 15

"Temperance ... develops ... when the emotions are cultivated and given plenty of opportunity to run their natural course (i.e., to be accepted and respected and to be taken in hand and guided by reason). ...In this way the emotions, and also such bodily feelings as the desire for food, drinking, smoking, sex, etc., develop a habitual disposition to listen to their "master's voice," readily and effortlessly."
Conrad Baars, p. 78

NOTES

"Where do the wars and where do the conflicts among you come from? Is it not from your passions that make war within your members?"

James 4:1

"For the fourfold division of virtue I regard as taken from four forms of love. For these four virtues ... I should have no hesitation in defining them: that temperance is love giving itself entirely to that which is loved; fortitude is love readily bearing all things for the sake of the loved object; justice is love serving only the loved object, and therefore ruling rightly; prudence is love distinguishing with sagacity between what hinders it and what helps it."

St. Augustine,
De Moribus Ecclesiae Catholicae,
I, 15, 25

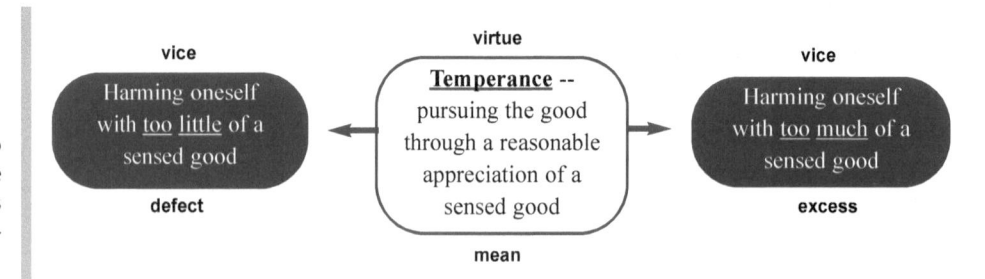

---

vice — Harming oneself with <u>too little</u> of a sensed good (defect) ← **virtue** — **Temperance** — pursuing the good through a reasonable appreciation of a sensed good (mean) → **vice** — Harming oneself with <u>too much</u> of a sensed good (excess)

Study Guide Questions:

1. What powers of the soul do the virtues of fortitude and temperance help to perfect?

2. The virtue of fortitude presupposes a vulnerability to suffering. Why?

3. What does controlling fear have to do with doing the good act?

4. Under what circumstances would controlling your fear be a reasonable thing to do?

5. Why is martyrdom considered to be "the essential and highest achievement" of fortitude?

6. Give a situation where a person displays too much willingness to stand against a difficult evil? Why is this unreasonable behavior?

7. What interior disturbance does the virtue of temperance help us to avoid?

8. How is it possible to harm oneself with too little of a sensed good?

9. "The virtue of temperance is all about happiness." Explain.

10. In what sense does the virtue of temperance make a person beautiful from within?

Chapter VII
Virtue

CASES IN POINT

#1 -- "Padre Pio had an unpleasant duty to perform. He was talking with a recently-widowed woman. Her husband had once left her and their two children to live with another woman for over three years. Unexpectedly cancer had claimed his life. Before his death, after urgent appeals, he had consented to receive the last Sacraments of the Church.

"The woman, short and plain, nervously adjusted the kerchief on her head and finally asked the inevitable: 'Where is his soul, Padre? I haven't slept, worrying.'

"Padre Pio watched her with troubled eyes. He could almost feel her grief filling his own heart. 'Your husband's soul is condemned forever,' he whispered.

"The woman shook her head and her eyes clouded with tears. 'Condemned?'

"Padre Pio nodded sadly. 'When receiving the last Sacraments he concealed many sins. He had neither repentance nor a good resolution. He was also a sinner against God's mercy, because he said he always wanted to have a share of the good things in life and then have time to be converted to God.'"

From *Prophet of the People: A Biography of Padre Pio*,
by Dorothy M. Gaudiose, Alba House Publishers, p. 158.

- Before he died, did the husband have a real *possibility* of being saved and going to Heaven?
  What would it have taken for this to have happened?
  What made this *possibility* less likely of being *actualized*?

- How significant for the husband was his *habit* of excluding God from his life?

* * * * *

#2 -- In Paris in 1954, Jacques Fesch, a young Frenchman with no prior criminal record assaulted a person in order to rob him. His attempt failed. He fled in panic and was eventually cornered. While attempting to escape, he shot and killed a policeman and seriously wounded another man. At his trial, he was condemned to death on the guillotine. After about three and a half years in jail, Jacques Fesch was executed for the crime of murder. He was twenty-seven.

During Jacques' long detention in isolation, a remarkable change took place in him. An atheist at the beginning of his time in prison, Jacques rediscovered his Catholic faith with the help of the prison chaplain, his lawyer, and a monk who had been a friend of his wife. The letters which he wrote from prison give us a picture of his spiritual journey from sinner to saint. They tell the tale of a man who became very open to God's grace and mercy, repented, and died very close to God.

In one of his letters, Jacques writes: "I am living through marvelous hours, and I feel as if I had never lived any other life than the one I've been experiencing now. Jesus draws me to Himself, and knowing the weakness of my soul He gives me much, while asking for so little. For each effort that I make I receive another grace, and, in view of the shortness of the time, this ascent toward God is being achieved far more quickly than it would be for someone who still had years ahead of him."

- To what do you attribute the fact that Jacques Fesch, a condemned murderer, became so totally changed that he could well be in Heaven today?

- What role do you think habit and the voluntary act played in his conversion?

Called to Happiness ~ Guiding Ethical Principles

D. Theological Virtue

***Theological Virtues** perfect a person's rational faculties disposing them to participate in the very nature of God Himself.*

In a number of ways, the theological virtues of **faith**, **hope**, and **charity** are unlike any of the virtues we have studied so far:

◆ <u>First</u>, these virtues are *directly* concerned with God, unlike all other virtues which are directly concerned with human activities. We could say that they have God as their *direct object*. For example, unlike the natural kind of hope we experience when we trust that other drivers on the road will stop at red lights, the theological virtue of hope entails trusting that union with God is truly possible. Similarly, it is not the theological virtue of charity which is responsible for a person's giving money to the poor unless the love of God is at least a part of the reason he does so.

◆ <u>Secondly</u>, these virtues are **infused** into our souls by God Himself, unlike the others which are acquired by human effort.[21] God does not force them upon us, nor does He override our free will. However, He does put them in our souls without any assistance from us. They are supernatural gifts from Him to us, won for us by the merits of Jesus Christ and given to us at baptism.

Infused at Baptism

◆ <u>Thirdly</u>, these virtues raise the activities of the powers of our souls to a divine level. In other words, they elevate our human nature, enabling us to do something that we could not naturally do: share in the nature and life of God Himself. For example, faith elevates the intellect to know God personally as our Ultimate End. Both hope and charity elevate the will. Hope makes us look forward to being one with God forever, and charity makes us love Him above every other good.

Charity: elevates the <u>will</u> to love God above everything else

Hope: elevates the <u>will</u> to look forward to being united with God forever

Faith: elevates the <u>intellect</u> to know God personally

Did you notice that infused virtues affect the powers of our soul differently than do the virtues we acquire through our own effort? An acquired virtue gives the power of the soul an *ability* or *capacity* to act with ease and efficiency. An infused virtue, however, does more. It gives not simply a *readiness* to act but *the very*

---

[21] There are also *infused* moral virtues which are "poured into" the rational soul at baptism along with the theological virtues. St. Thomas explains that these infused moral virtues are necessary because they aid the elevated human faculties in doing supernaturally good acts in the moral order.

NOTES

Theological virtue - Virtue which elevates the rational powers, disposing them to participate in the very nature of God Himself.

"Faith makes us know the God to whom we are going, hope makes us look forward to joining Him, and charity makes us love Him."
  John A. Hardon, S.J., p. 13

"Faith is a habit, that is, a stable disposition of the mind, through which eternal life takes root in us and reason is led to consent to what it does not see."
  St. Thomas Aquinas, *Summa Theologiae*, II-II, 4, 1

Infused - from Latin *infundere* (to pour in); the infused virtues are "poured into" the human soul at baptism.

"So remarkable are the divine graces that they elevate one from the lowest depths to the highest summit, and transform one to a greater holiness."
  Saint Lawrence Justinian, bishop. *Sermo 8, in festo Purificationis B.M.V.*

"If the habit is acquired, it gives the faculty power to act with ease and facility; if it is infused, it procures in supernatural activity not readiness, but the very activity itself."
  John A. Hardon, S.J., p. 11

activity itself. For instance, the theological virtue of faith is not the mere *ability* to know God. Rather, it is the gift of *actually* knowing Him.

◆ Fourthly, unlike the moral virtues, the theological virtues have nothing to do with the golden mean between extremes. We cannot possibly believe, trust, or love God too much. St. Thomas explains:

> God Himself is the rule and mode [mean] of virtue. Our faith is measured by divine truth, our hope by the greatness of His power and faithful affection, our charity by His goodness. His truth, power and goodness outreach any measure of reason. We can certainly never believe, trust or love God more than, or even as much as, we should. Extravagance is impossible. Here is no virtuous moderation, no measurable mean; the more extreme our activity, the better we are.[22]

◆ Fifthly, we know about the theological virtues because God has revealed their existence to us in both Scripture and Tradition; and He has made it possible for us to understand through the teaching of His Church how these virtues are at work in us. We would not know about them by using only our unaided human reason. All of the other virtues we have studied, on the other hand, can be known merely by using our unaided natural powers.

Relationship to Moral Virtue

Our interest in the theological virtues for our present study of ethics is limited. We will leave the important detailed study of them to a religion class. What we need to know about them for our purposes now is their essential relationship to moral virtue and thus to our achieving our Ultimate End.

The Ultimate End that we seek is infinitely beyond our nature. Left to our own natural powers we would not be able to approach Him who is Absolute Goodness. God takes care of this problem, however, by pouring into our souls gifts that elevate, or "raise," our natural faculties to His level, i.e., the supernatural level. That is what the theological virtues are: the means by which we can share in the very life of God Himself. Possessing these virtues is *essential* for our salvation. (The fact that God infuses these virtues into our souls at Baptism says something about *His* desires for us!)

Virtue: **CHARITY** → **Ultimate End**

---

[22] St. Thomas Aquinas, *Summa Theologiae*, I-II, 62, 3.

NOTES

"Faith begins the eternal life in us. The virtue of faith enables us to contact the living God. It orients us toward salvation."
— Rev. Wojciech Giertych, O.P.
Classnotes

"Faith is a tool given by God, infused in our reason and, in part,, the will, and which enables our mind to go beyond the limits of reason, towards the mystery."
— Rev. Wojciech Giertych, O.P.

"The virtue of faith can be cultivated through repeated acts of faith animated by love."
— Rev. Wojciech Giertych, O.P.
Class notes

"Charity is the 'greatest' gift, which gives value to all the others. ... In the end, when we find ourselves face to face with God, all other gifts will fail and all that will be left to last for eternity is love, because God is love and we will be like unto Him, in perfect communion with Him."
— Pope Benedict XVI,
Angelus, 1/31/10

Called to Happiness ~ Guiding Ethical Principles

NOTES

"The practice of all the virtues is animated and inspired by charity, which 'binds everything together in perfect harmnoy'; it is the *form of the virtues*; it articulates and orders them among themselves; it is the source and the goal of their Christian practice."
The Catechism of the Catholic Church, #1827

"'If I ... have not charity,' says the Apostle, 'I am nothing.' Whatever my privilege, service, or even virtue, 'if I ... have not charity, I gain nothing.' Charity is superior to all the virtues. It is the first of the theological virtues: 'So faith, hope, charity abide, these three. But *the greatest of these is charity.*'"
The Catechism of the Cathoic Church, #1826

"If we think of the saints, we recognise the variety of their spiritual gifts and their human characters. But the life of each one of them is a hymn to charity, a living canticle to the love of God."
Pope Benedict XVI, *Angelus*, 1/31/10

Faith makes us know the God we are seeking as our End. Hope makes us intent on being united with Him one day. Charity makes us one with God in love, even as we are still seeking Him. The virtue of charity, then, actually unites us with the End we seek.

Do you remember what we said about virtue being a good habit which perfects us *as a whole* in terms of reaching our Ultimate End? Perhaps now we are ready to see why St. Thomas says that **charity is the form of all virtue**, even the form of prudence itself.[23]

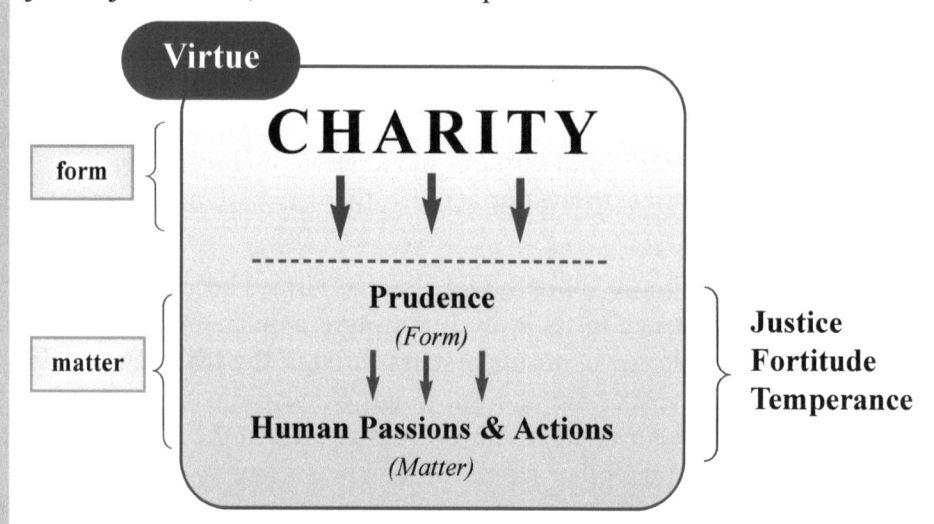

Virtue

form { **CHARITY** ↓ ↓ ↓

matter { **Prudence** *(Form)* ↓ ↓ ↓ **Human Passions & Actions** *(Matter)*

} **Justice Fortitude Temperance**

Without charity, there is no virtue, at least not in the fullest possible sense. This makes sense because virtue perfects us *as a whole in terms of reaching our Ultimate End*, and charity is our connection to that End. Without charity we are not connected to the End. With charity, even the smallest act we do is of tremendous value because in doing that act *for the love of God*, we move ourselves closer to the End we seek.

No doubt this is why St. Therese once said that picking up a pin off the floor *for the love of God* was a morally great act. St. John of the Cross echoes her point:

> The smallest act of perfect love of God is more effective, more meritorious than all other good works put together that one could perform.[24]

The flip side of the coin is also true, however: A good act done *without any love of God* as a motive does not in itself move the person any closer to his Ultimate End.

What this highlights for us is the importance of our intention: Why do we do the acts that we do? What are we seeking as our Ultimate End in each of our acts? With every act that we do we are forming ourselves to become either persons who love God above all else or persons who have made something else our god.

---
[23] St. Thomas Aquinas, *De Veritate* 14, 5 ad 11.
[24] St. John of the Cross, *The Spiritual Canticle*, 28.

In other words, by repeatedly acting *for the love of God*, we transform ourselves into *lovers of God*. It is this condition of being 'a lover of God' which is so essential for our eternal happiness. Only a lover of God will be able to take great delight in being in His presence for all eternity.

Conclusion

We began this chapter by pointing out the need for an interior transformation of the human person, so essential for attaining human happiness. Now after our study of the virtues, we can see more clearly precisely what that transformation will entail. It will, first of all, involve perfecting the intellect so that it can do its work of knowing objective reality well. Secondly, it will involve exercising the lower powers of the soul -- the appetites -- training them to act in accord with the sound guidance of the intellect. Finally, and most importantly, it will involve receiving supernatural gifts which will enable us to share in the very life of God.

Study Guide Questions:

1. *What are the theological virtues, and what powers of the human soul do they elevate?*

2. *What does it mean to say that the theological virtues have God as their object?*

3. *When and how do we get the theological virtues?*

4. *How do infused virtues differ from acquired virtues with regard to their effect on the soul?*

5. *Are there other infused virtues besides the theological?*

6. *Why doesn't theological virtue deal with a golden mean?*

7. *How do we know there are such things as theological virtues?*

8. *What problem of ours do the theological virtues solve?*

9. *Why are the theological virtues essential for salvation?*

10. *"Without charity there is no virtue." Explain.*

NOTES

"Love is God's very essence, it is the meaning of creation and history, it is the light that gives goodness and beauty to the existence of each man and woman. At the same time love is, so to say, the 'style' of God and of believers, it is the behavior of those who, responding to the love of God, order their lives as a gift of self to God and to neighbor."
Pope Benedict XVI,
Angelus, 1/31/10

"We who are wayfarers make our way back to God through the virtues. We return to God not by change of place, but by change of person, and that is what the virtues achieve. They work the transformation in us that enables our reunion with God."
Wadell,
The Primacy of Love, p. 108

"If a man has a great love within him, it's as if this love gives him wings, and he endures life's problems more easily, because he has in himself that light which is faith: to be loved by God and to let oneself be loved by God in Christ Jesus."
Pope Benedict XVI,
2/23/2011

Called to Happiness ~ Guiding Ethical Principles

CASES IN POINT

Identify the virtues being displayed in the following scenarios and explain the reasons for your choice. If no virtue is displayed, note that as well.

◆ Steve is a new player on the football team. After their first home game, the team arranges to have an initiation of its new members. The initiation involves running along a busy, poorly-lit street at night while wearing dark clothing. Steve is fearful of making the run, but he does it because he doesn't want to be considered a coward.

◆ At the age of 16, Danielle is the oldest of her five siblings. She is used to having to look after them all, but especially giving a careful eye to the younger two who are not yet four years old. She remembers clearly from past experience how easily and quickly they can harm themselves. On one occasion recently, while her parents were out of the house on an errand, Danielle was trying to 'supervise' lunch. She asked the older two to make their own sandwiches while she made sandwiches for the two younger ones. One of the older ones complained that Danielle was playing favorites because she is always with the younger ones and doesn't give them "equal time." Danielle explained to them that she loves them all and sees them as special gifts God has placed in her life, but the younger ones need her more.

◆ Tim is used to looking out for those who don't quite fit in for some reason. His younger brother, Roger, has a physical handicap, and Tim has grown up looking out for him. When a new kid walked into his algebra class last week, Tim took special notice because the boy was Vietnamese. Tim went out of his way to show him around and introduce him to his friends. Just yesterday, however, a few of the upperclassmen started calling Tim names and threatened him that there would be "trouble" if he didn't stay away from foreigners who didn't "belong in their school." Tim thought about their warning and realized that they could indeed cause him trouble, but he could not in good conscience suddenly "drop" his new friend. He asked God for the strength to do what he knew God wanted him to do, and then he went on as usual.

◆ The football team was celebrating the end of their winning season. They had gathered at a restaurant that served "all you can eat" Italian food for a price of $10. Ben had been looking forward to this celebration all week long because he loves Italian food, but he didn't want this celebration to be an occasion of sin for him. He knew from past experience that he can easily let his desire for food get carried away and lead him to the sin of gluttony. That's why for the past few months he has been deliberately working at controlling his appetite. He is training himself to be reasonable in the amounts of food that he eats because he wants to love God even more than he loves Italian food.

◆ As a senior, Colleen has a reputation as a good student, especially in mathematics. She has spent her past four high school years in honor level math classes, is currently president of the Math Club, and intends to specialize in math in her collegiate studies. Whenever her younger sister asks Colleen to help her with her math homework, however, Colleen never takes the time to help out. She always says that she has her own work to do and doesn't have time.

Chapter VII
Virtue

A Beauty in God's Sight:
The Story of Blessed Margaret of Castello

Beholding their newborn daughter, Parisio and Emilia, prominent Italian nobles of the 13th century, stood aghast. The tiny child -- hunch-backed, blind, and severely crippled -- was hardly the picture of perfection that her parents had envisioned of their first child. While initial surprise at the child's defects might have been natural to any parents, this particular couple allowed their first impressions to color their thoughts of their daughter from that moment forward. Rather than looking beyond physical deformity to their baby's God-given dignity, they determined to banish her from public view and to spread the lie that death had claimed her at birth. In her parents' estimation, the child was unworthy even of a name, and so she was hidden, nameless, in the castle, with a maid as her only friend.

This one friend was a servant of good faith who desired the baby to share in God's life through Christian Baptism. Under her supervision, the daughter of Parisio and Emilia became also a daughter of God, receiving the baptismal name of Margaret. As Margaret grew, she often hobbled to the castle's chapel to pray. A visitor to the castle saw the blind hunchback limping along and inquired who she was. In fear that rumors would begin, Parisio and Emilia banished Margaret to a cellar in the forest where her only human contact would be with those who brought her food and her precious Blessed Sacrament.

The priest who brought Margaret Holy Communion soon found that in spite of her physical handicaps, she has a brilliant mind and a heart ablaze with love for God. The priest found no resentment or self-pity in Margaret, but only gladness at the opportunity to associate herself with the sufferings of Jesus. Twenty years after their child's birth

NOTES

and nearly fifteen years after her solitary confinement, Parisio and Emilia had all but forgotten Margaret when word reached them of miraculous healings taking place in Castello at the tomb of a Franciscan Third Order member, Fra Giacomo. Considering this news an opportunity to remedy their burden, the couple fetched Margaret and took her to the miraculous spot, thrusting her among a host of lame and sick people, ordering her to pray for healing. Ever obedient to her parents, Margaret asked God to heal her -- if it be his will.

A day passed with no cure. Impatient and typically selfish, Parisio and Emilia abandoned their daughter at the tomb, reasoning that the poor creature was better suited to a life among cripples than she was to their own high society. It was nightfall by the time Margaret realized that her mother and father were not coming back for her. In the moment when utter despair and hateful resentment could have possessed Margaret's heart, she again proved her nobility of soul, embracing desertion as the Father's will for her.

Beggars in Castello befriended Margaret, and soon she was known and loved throughout the town. One group who welcomed Margaret was the monastery of cloistered Dominican nuns. Margaret loved the nuns' life of prayer and strict observance of religious discipline. When, however, the major superior of the monastery died and some of the nuns began to be lax in their way of life, the ever-ardent Margaret was renounced by the community who felt threatened by her self-discipline.

In the streets of Castello, gossip flew that Margaret was morally unfit for religious life. As the truth became known, however, her reputation for sanctity grew more than ever. Margaret, unaffected by praise, was busy admiring a group called the Mantellata, Third Order Dominicans, who lived lives of penance and prayer and devoted themselves to serving the sick and poor. After insisting that she was not too young to join the ranks of the Mantellata, Margaret donned the white and black habit of the Dominican Order and began her ministry to the outcasts of Castello. Hers was a mission of hope, drawing sinners to repentance and assuring those rejected by society that they were indeed accepted and loved by their heavenly Father.

Chapter VII
Virtue

In Margaret's thirty-third year, her crippled frame could no longer endure her active apostolate. The little sister of Castello was ill, with no hope of cure. On April 13, 1320, Margaret died peacefully, surrounded by Dominican friars and Mantellata. As her body rested on its bier, a crippled child was brought forward to touch Margaret's hand. In that moment, the little girl experienced an astonishing change and went away free of deformity. Since then, over 200 miracles have been recorded at her tomb. To this day, Margaret's body remains incorrupt in Castello, Italy, and is a testimony that the poor creature who was repulsive to her own father and mother was -- and is for all eternity -- a true beauty in God's sight.

Beatified in 1609 by Pope Paul V, Blessed Margaret is a patron for the current era in which countless children are rejected by their parents, often even before the parents see their little ones. Had Blessed Margaret been conceived in the age of technology and ultrasounds, there is little reason to think that she would have been allowed to be born at all. As we strive to see the dignity of the human person honored from conception to natural death, Blessed Margaret offers her mighty intercession that all 'unwanted' persons, young and old, will come to be loved on earth and to know their genuine beauty as beloved children of God.

Sister Maris Stella Vaughn, O.P.

Point to Consider:

"The book of Genesis teaches that God made man in his 'image and likeness.' The Fathers of the Church set great store by the biblical text's distinction between image and likeness. In their view, this distinction served to bring out what they saw as the dynamic and relational character of the imago Dei. For the Fathers, the word 'image' refers to the similarity between the human copy and the divine Original, a similarity that characterizes man from the first moment of his existence. 'Likeness' on the other hand, is the dynamic dimension of the imago Dei, which man is called to perfect by growing ever closer to God in love. As the great theologian Saint Maximus Confessor puts it: 'To the inherent goodness of the image is added the likeness acquired by the practice of virtue and the exercise of the will.'

"For the Fathers, then, man is born as God's image, but he has to complete the imago Dei through his free yes to God. John Paul II shares in this vision. The divine image is seen as both a gift and a task: 'This likeness is a quality of the personal being ... and is also a call and a task.' Insofar as it is a task, and not just a gift, the image of God takes

NOTES

time -- indeed, a whole lifetime -- to unfold its riches. The imago Dei is much more like a play that tells the story of our lives than it is like a snapshot that reflects only one moment in the story."

From *Called to Love*, by Carl Anderson and Jose Granados, New York: Doubleday, 2009, pp. 85-86.

Conclusion

We have come to the end of our study about human happiness and the ethical principles that will help guide us in attaining it. Happiness is not simply a matter of *subjectively* choosing *whatever I want to make me happy.* Rather, it involves *rightly* understanding my nature as a human person and determining what will *truly* fulfill that nature. In other words, human happiness is fundamentally an *objective* matter.

That is why the science of Ethics is such an important course of study: It helps a person know *objectively speaking* how to go about his pursuit of happiness. Beginning first to come to an understanding of what the Greatest Good is, and then continuing through a thorough investigation of the human act as a moral act, the student of Ethics comes to realize the tremendous significance of each and every human act. With each act, we move ourselves either closer to or farther away from the Happiness we seek.

Not only that, but with each act we also shape and form ourselves into people who have come either to love or to hate the Greatest Good. Those who have come to love the Good by desiring and choosing the *true* good, make themselves to be *good* people, the kind of people who will take great delight in the Good once they possess It. Those who have come to "hate" the Greatest Good are those who have settled for only *apparent* goods. They have not cultivated a "taste" for or a love of *true* goodness. Thus they would not delight in the Good even if they could possess It.

As St. Thomas teaches us, happiness is not a sure thing. Attaining it requires consistent, life-long effort at choosing *only what is truly good for us.* This is why developing good habits -- the virtues -- are a tremendous help. They constitute the "second nature" we give ourselves so that doing the good act becomes easier, more enjoyable, and more certain.

Realizing this now, in your youth, you can understand why Saint John Paul the Great spoke so often about your unique and unrepeatable potential as young adult human beings. The *"treasure of youth,"* as he referred to it, is both the treasure of discovering your life's goal as well as the treasure of taking the first steps in achieving it.

NOTES

How you choose to respond to *moral good* and *evil* will determine the success of your life; that is, it will determine whether or not you will be truly happy. If you choose to make decisions in light of the "interior truth" known by your conscience, then you will develop the character and personal integrity that will enable you to go beyond yourself "in the direction of eternity."[1]

If, on the other hand, you choose to ignore the "light" offered by the moral law, preferring to walk in darkness, then you will be stuck in yourself and in your own *subjective* and limited perception of the good. Possessing limited, finite goods will always leave you longing for more. Thus, you will not be really happy.

The choice is yours in every human act you do. The consequences of your choices are profound -- for yourself as well as for the people your life will touch. They involve not only your eternal happiness but also the well-being of human beings on this earth.

Let us conclude our study with a challenge from Saint John Paul:

"The aspiration that humanity nurtures,
amid countless injustices and sufferings,
is the hope of a new civilization marked by freedom and peace.
But for such an undertaking, a new generation of builders is needed.
Moved not by fear or violence but by the urgency of genuine love,
they must learn to build, brick by brick,
the city of God within the city of man.
Allow me, dear young people, to consign this hope of mine to you:
you must be those "builders"!
You are the men and women of tomorrow.
The future is in your hearts and in your hands.
God is entrusting to you the task, at once difficult and uplifting,
of working with him in the building of the civilization of love."[2]

---

[1] Saint John Paul, *Apostolic Letter to the Youth of the World*, 1985, #3.
[2] Saint John Paul, *Address at World Youth Day*, 2002, #4.

Appendix A:

The Virtue of Tolerance[1]

Tolerance is a misunderstood term. Many people today use the word to imply a kind of *moral neutrality* on controversial issues. The tolerant person -- *so it is believed* -- is the one who doesn't take sides, the one who doesn't make moral judgments.

Three mistaken ideas follow from this view of tolerance as a kind of moral neutrality:

- The meaning of tolerance is tolerating. The more a person tolerates, the more tolerant he must be. *(If this were really the case, then shouldn't we tolerate intolerance?)*

- The best help for being tolerant is to avoid having any strong ideas about right and wrong. The more unsure a person is about what is right and wrong, the more tolerant he will be. *(If this were really the case, then shouldn't we refrain from thinking strongly that intolerance is wrong?)*

- If a person is unable to avoid having strong ideas about what is right and wrong, then he should not express them or act on them if he wants to be tolerant. *(If this were really the case, then shouldn't we hold back from expressing or acting on our tolerance?)*

Contrary to the mistaken understanding, the real meaning of tolerance is ***tolerating what ought to be tolerated***. Tolerance has to do with putting up with something that is bad in some way. This is easy to see if we remember that virtue stands as a *mean* between excess and defect. The virtue of tolerance stands mid-way between over-indulgence *(putting up with too much)* on the one hand and repressiveness *(putting up with too little)* on the other.

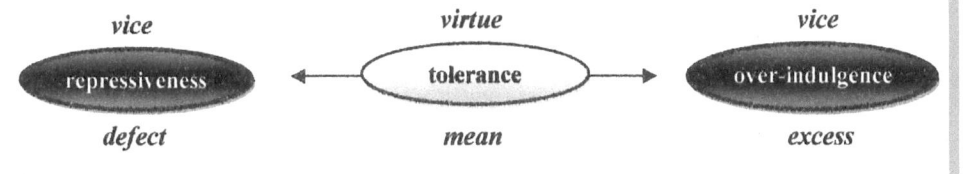

vice	*virtue*	*vice*
repressiveness	← tolerance →	over-indulgence
defect	*mean*	*excess*

The proper basis for the virtue of tolerance is not doubt about

NOTES

"The only thing necessary for the triumph of evil is for good men to do nothing."
— Edmund Burke,
British statesman

---

[1] See J. Budziszewski, "The Illusion of Moral Neutrality," in *First Things*, 35 (August/September, 1993).

NOTES

moral right and wrong. Rather, foundational to the virtue of tolerance is *being correct* about what is morally right and wrong. If we don't want to be repressive, then we need to put up with some bad things. The reason for putting up with them, however, is not because we are *unsure* whether they are good or evil. Rather, it is because we *are sure* that they are evils that are of such a kind that we ought to tolerate them so as to avoid bringing about a greater evil.

For example, parents might tolerate some of the messy ways of their teenage son for awhile because they are already struggling with him regarding his academic and social behavior. Of the three "bad" areas in their son's life, they choose to tolerate the one because they judge it to be the least important of the three. They also judge that they ought to tolerate this "evil" because if they repressed it, then a greater evil might easily result: their son's complete rebellion.

Another example: A teacher might tolerate certain behavior from her students in the classroom which she considers to be "less than ideal." If she does this because of the virtue of tolerance, then she is making a moral judgment that some "bad behavior" ought to be tolerated, and she's acting on that judgment. In her judgment, this bad behavior ought to be tolerated because if she acts against it, then she might cause her students to feel as if they are in a very rigid and formal environment. She would prefer to have a relaxed and "at home" feeling in her classroom. Thus, she will not tolerate students making comments that degrade others, but she chooses to tolerate on occasion their speaking "off topic" in class.

Yet another example of this would be the prohibition of alcohol in this country. In order to get rid of the evil of drunkenness, we prohibited the sale of liquor. This prohibition, however, caused more evil for our society than did the drunkenness itself. Because of this, we chose to tolerate the risk of the evil of drunkenness by allowing the sale of liquor.

Finally, the virtue of tolerance requires that we *act* on our strong ideas regarding right and wrong. We must **seek the good and avoid evil**. The ***virtue of tolerance*** helps us to do this by disposing us to judge correctly which evils ought to be tolerated and which ones not tolerated so that we protect greater goods.

Did you notice how similar the virtue of tolerance is to the virtue of prudence? Tolerance is actually a *sub-virtue of prudence*: Tolerance entails the use of right reason in judging what ought to be done here and now *with regard to putting up with evil*. Prudence is broader; it concerns making judgments about *all human action*, not just about putting up with evil.

Tolerance - moral virtue which disposes a person's practical intellect to judge correctly which evils ought to be tolerated and which ones not.

Study Guide Questions:

1. How is tolerance wrongly understood by many people today?

2. Explain how tolerance stands "in the middle" as a mean.

3. What is the relationship between the virtue of tolerance and moral judgment?

4. Why is doubt about moral right and wrong not helpful for making a person tolerant? What is helpful?

5. Using the correct meaning of tolerance, give an example of a person being tolerant.

6. To which of the cardinal virtues is tolerance most closely aligned? Explain.

Appendix B:

Ethical Principles Used in Medicine

A. *Principles of Integrity and Totality* -- The well-being of the whole person must be taken into account in deciding about any therapeutic intervention or use of technology. **Therapeutic** procedures that are likely to cause harm or undesirable side effects can be justified only by a proportionate benefit to the patient. St. Thomas Aquinas explains:

> "A member of the human body is to be disposed of according as it may profit the whole…. If a member is healthy and continuing in its natural state, it cannot be cut off to the detriment of the whole."[1]

This is why it is ethically good to cut into a person's body to remove a diseased organ, but it is ethically bad to **mutilate** a healthy human being.

1. **Integrity** -- refers to each person's duty to preserve a view of the human person in which "the values of intellect, will, conscience and fraternity are preeminent."[2] Medical interventions should not unreasonably compromise the functionality and order of the body and its systems.

    Application of the Principle of Integrity: Diagnostic tests, medical treatments, and surgeries *run the risk* of harming the person's integrity. That's why we look for *good* doctors and nurses who understand the dignity of the human person as a body-soul unity, so that the risk is lessened. Vasectomies and tubal ligations *always* violate the integrity of the person receiving them. Any time we treat a person *simply* as a physical body without regard for his spiritual soul, we violate his integrity.

2. **Totality** -- refers to the presumption of preserving intact the body of the person, whereby every part of the human body "exists for the sake of the whole as the imperfect for the sake of the perfect."[3]

    Application of the Principle of Totality: A woman who discovers that she has a cancerous breast which threatens her life may remove the breast in order to preserve her life. In doing so, she sacrifices a part of her body for the well-being of the whole.

NOTES

Therapeutic - from Latin *therapeuticus* (to minister to, treat medically); of or pertaining to the healing of disease.

Mutilate - from Latin *mutilare* (to cut or crop off); to cut off or otherwise destroy the use of.

Integrity - from Latin *integritas* (wholeness, completeness); condition of having no part or element lacking.

"There cannot be holistic development and universal common good unless people's spiritual and moral welfare is taken into account, considered in their totality as body and soul."

Benedict XVI,
Charity in Truth, #76

Totality - the state of being whole.

---

[1] St. Thomas Aquinas, *Summa Theologiae*, II-II, 65, 1.
[2] *Gaudium et Spes*, #61.
[3] St. Thomas Aquinas, *Summa Theologiae*, II-II, 65, 1.

Called to Happiness ~ Guiding Ethical Principles

NOTES

Inviolable - from Latin *inviolare* (not to do violence to); not to be violated or assaulted.

Steward - a person who manages another's property or affairs for him.

Common good - "the sum total of social conditions which allow people, either as groups or as individuals, to reach their fulfillment more fully and more easily."
CCC, #1906

Subsidiarity - from Latin *subsidiarius* (serving to help, assist, or supplement).

"Subsidiarity respects personal dignity by recognizing in the person a subject who is always capable of giving something to others."
Benedict XVI,
Charity in Truth, #57

Autonomy - from Greek for self-rule; the making of one's own laws, administering one's own affairs.

B. *Principle of the Inviolability of Human Life* -- The first and most fundamental *right* of a person is the right to his own life. This right places on all others a *duty* to respect it. Deliberately violating this most basic right of a person is always gravely wrong.

   Application: Direct abortion, euthanasia, and any direct assault on an innocent human being are gravely wrong.

C. *Principle of Stewardship over the Gift of Life* -- Requires that the gifts of human life and its natural environment be used with profound respect for their intrinsic ends (their natural purposes). The principle is grounded in God's absolute dominion over creation, and in our creation in His image and likeness, which are the basis for our limited dominion over creation and our responsibility for its care.

   Application: We are obligated to do what is reasonably necessary to sustain our lives. We do not have the authority to decide to put an end to our lives or the lives of others, or to harm them in any way.

D. *Principle of the Common Good* -- Requires the flourishing of the community as a whole. The good of each individual makes up the common good. We understand common good to mean "the sum total of social conditions which allow people, either as groups or as individuals, to reach their fulfillment more fully and more easily."[4]

   Application: We should be concerned about the well-being of every person with whom we deal.

E. *Principle of Subsidiarity* -- Requires that a community of a higher order not interfere with the life of a community of a lower order, taking over its functions. In case of need, the higher community should support the smaller community and help to coordinate its activity with the activities in the rest of society for the sake of the common good.

   Application: The state should not interfere with decisions about how families are to run their lives. The state can step in to help families out in providing them with services that the families themselves are unable to provide, like electricity, gas, and food supplies.

F. *Principle of Respect for Autonomy* -- Requires every person to respect every other person's self-determination to an appropriate extent within the context of the common good.

   1. Involves refraining from inappropriately interfering with others' choices.

   2. Entails providing them with the necessary conditions and oppor-

---

[4] *The Catechism of the Catholic Church*, #1906.

tunities to exercise autonomy. *(Informed consent)*

Application: I should not tell my friend what medical procedure she should have done, nor should I force her to make a particular decision. Rather, I should do all that I can to help her be fully informed regarding the decision she must make.

G. *<u>Principle of Informed Consent</u>* -- It is the right and responsibility of every competent individual to advance his or her own welfare, i.e., freely and voluntarily to consent or to refuse consent to recommended medical procedures, based on a sufficient knowledge of the benefits, burdens, and risks involved.

1. Adequate disclosure of information includes the diagnosis, the nature and purpose of treatment, the risks of treatment, and treatment alternatives.

2. Other forms

    a. **Presumed consent** -- When persons are unconscious or for some reason unable to make decisions for themselves, their consent can be presumed so long as the procedures performed are necessary and cannot be postponed until the person has regained consciousness or decision-making capacity.

    b. **Vicarious consent** -- When a person is incompetent or incapacitated, another person *(a surrogate)* may speak on his behalf in giving consent.

    Application: We should never expect a person to give consent without first adequately informing him of all the information he needs to make an intelligent decision.

Presumed - from Latin *pre-sumere* (to take for granted); to take upon oneself, undertake without adequate authority or permission.

Vicarious - from Latin *vicarius* (change, turn, stead); that takes or supplies the place of another thing or person.

H. *<u>Principle of Distributive Justice</u>* -- Refers to what society or a larger group owes its individual members in proportion to (1) the individual's needs, contribution and responsibility, (2) the resources available to the society or organization, and (3) the society's or organization's responsibility to the common good. In health care, distributive justice requires that everyone receive equitable access to the basic health care necessary for living a fully human life.

Application: Justice does not always mean that everyone receives or gives *the very same amount* of goods, services, etc. It is just for those who have a greater need to receive more and for those with greater resources to give more.

I. *<u>Principle of Toleration</u>* -- Those responsible for governing may at times tolerate the evil actions of others if two criteria are met: (1) if a greater good or set of goods would be lost if the evil action were not tol-

Toleration - from Latin *tolerabilis* (that may be borne, can bear or endure); the action of sustaining or enduring evil.

erated, and (2) if greater evils would occur were the original evil not tolerated.

> *Application:* Because parents want their children to enjoy being at home with each other, they do not usually tell them what they should be doing with all of their free time. Parents think that it is better to tolerate their children making some poor choices regarding their use of time than cause them not to enjoy being at home.

J. *Principle of Inseparability* -- Recognizes that God, as Creator, has ordered the sexual activity of spouses around the two ends of union and procreation.

> *Application:* Whenever husband and wife engage in the sexual act, they should allow the act to function the way it was designed to function. They should not disorder the act by separating the sexual union from the possibility of conceiving a child. Nor ought they seek to produce a child by any means that does not involve their union in the sexual act.

K. *Principle of Confidentiality* -- The following rights belong to patients who put their confidence in their caregivers:

1. A right to confidentiality, that is, that those to whom they have legitimately entrusted their secrets, treat them with respect.

2. A right to privacy, that is, that no secret will be unwillingly, unnecessarily, or unwittingly extracted from them.

3. A right to hear the truth, as it is known and as it pertains to their particular situation.

4. A right that information given about them be as accurate as possible.

> *Application:* In the exchange of communication between persons, we should be mindful that what we hear from them and what we say to them or to others about them entails a duty for us. As persons, they have rights that we are obligated to respect.

Confidence - from Latin *con-fidere* (to trust thoroughly); a reliance on another's discretion regarding what belongs to the one who places the trust.

Glossary

Absolute freedom - the ability to do as one pleases.

Antecedent passion - from Latin *antecedere* (to go before); an emotional response which precedes an act of the will.

Appetite - from the Latin *appetitus*, "natural desire;" an active tendency within a being towards a goal that is proper to it.

Art - a virtue of the practical intellect which enables a person to make some external object.

Autonomy - from Greek for self-rule; the making of one's own laws, administering one's own affairs.

Beatific Vision - from Latin *beatificus* (making blessed); imparting supreme happiness; the sight of the glories of Heaven.

Cardinal virtue - from the Latin *cardo* (hinge); the four virtues to which all the other moral virtues can be reduced.

Certain conscience - a moral judgment about which a person has no doubts.

Character - from Latin *character* (distinctive mark or nature); moral qualities which distinguish a person.

Choice - a selection between at least two options.

Circumstances - from Latin *circumstare* (to stand around); those conditions of an act which have no moral bearing whatsoever on the act or which merely increase or decrease the act's moral quality. Those conditions which enter into the moral object because they actually change the moral quality of the act would *strictly speaking* not be circumstances.

Common good - "the sum total of social conditions which allow people, either as groups or as individuals, to reach their fulfillment more fully and more easily."

Concupiscible appetite - sense appetite whose object is the easy good or evil which is sensed.

Confidence - from Latin *con-fidere* (to trust thoroughly); a reliance on another's discretion regarding what belongs to the one who places the trust.

Conscience - from Latin *conscientia* (knowing with); an intellectual judgment applying moral law to a particular act.

Consent - from Latin *consentire* (to feel with, agree); to agree or approve through an act of the will.

Consequent passion - from Latin *consequeri* (to follow closely); an emotional response which follows an act of the will.

Consequentialism - ethical system which determines the moral quality of an act based solely on the foreseeable consequences of the act.

Correlative - so related that each implies or complements the other.

Deliberation - the act of weighing a thing in the mind; careful consideration with a view to decision.

Descriptive science - a science which describes objects and phenomena but does not pass judgment on their subject matter.

Disordered - lack of the regular or proper arrangement.

Divine law - law of which God is the origin.

Doubtful conscience - a moral judgment about which a person has doubts.

Duty - a person's obligation to do or not to do something or that which a person is obligated to do or not do.

Emotion - from the Latin *ex-movere*, "to move out;" a movement of the sense appetites.

End - from the Latin *finis* (end), an intended result of an action; an aim, purpose.

Entitative habits - from Latin *ens* (related to being); habits of being; relatively lasting dispositions that a person possesses due to his being.

Erroneous conscience - from Latin *erroneous* (straying); a judgment of conscience which is in error, not true.

Essence - from the Latin *esse*, "to be;" what a thing is, the underlying identity or nature of a thing.

Eternal - infinite in past and future duration; without beginning or end.

Eternal law - the unchanging order of things as it exists in the mind of God.

Evil - the privation of good.

Exterior act - an act commanded by the will carrying out the command of reason but executed by the other powers of the soul and the bodily members.

Faculty - from the Latin *facere*, "to make;" a power of the soul that produces certain operations.

Finite - from the Latin *finere*, "to limit;" having a limit or end point.

First Principle - from Latin *principium* (origin, source); the ultimate basis upon which our reasoning depends; a self-evident truth that serves as a starting oint for our reasoning.

Form - the essence of a thing, the determining principle of a physical thing that makes it to be the kind of thing that it is. Form can be either substantial or accidental.

Formal - from Latin *formalis* (form); pertaining to the form of a thing; possessing a thing actually.

Formal cooperation - from Latin *cooperari* (to work together); working together with another while agreeing with the other in the act they are doing together.

Formal Object - the angle or point-of-view from which the subject matter of a science is studied.

Fortitude - from Latin *fortitudo* (strong); cardinal virtue which perfects the irascible appetite, disposing it to follow the guidance of right reason.

Genuine freedom - the ability to do the good act so as to achieve happiness.

Good - (relative) conducive to well-being, to happiness; (absolute) the reality of completeness according to the nature or design of a thing.

Habit - from Latin *habere* (to have); a firm and permanent disposition to act in a certain way.

Happiness - man's complete flourishing wherein there is nothing more he desires.

Hierarchy - a body of persons or things ranked in grades, orders, or classes, one above another.

Hierarchy of goods - a body of goods ranked in order one above another.

Human act - an act for which a person bears responsibility because he deliberately chose to do it.

Human law - law of which human persons are the origin.

Human Nature - from Latin *natura* (birth, constitution, character); the general inherent character or disposition of mankind.

Impute - from Latin *imputare* (to charge); to attribute or ascribe to a person; to charge with a fault.

Infinite - from the Latin *infinire*, "not to limit;" unlimited; inexhaustible; endless.

Infused - from Latin *infundere* (to pour in); the infused virtues are "poured into" the human soul at baptism.

Innate - from Latin *innatus* (inborn); existing in a person from birth.

Integrity - from Latin *integritas* (wholeness, completeness); condition of having no part or element lacking.

Intellect - from the Latin *intus*, "within" and *legere*, "to read;" the knowing power in human beings which is able to grasp the essences of physical beings.

Intellectual virtue - a habit which perfects the human intellect, disposing it to function well.

Intention - the action of directing the mind or attention to something.

Interior act - an act elicited from the will; an act of willing as such.

Intrinsic - from the Latin *intrinsecus*, "inward;" in and of itself, or essentially. It is the opposite of *extrinsic*, meaning external or unessential.

Intrinsically evil act - from Latin *intrinsecus* (inwards); an act considered to be evil in itself with the proximate end that is willed, apart from any further intentions of the will to which the act is ordered.

Invincible ignorance - from Latin *in-vincere* (not to overcome); ignorance of which a person is not aware and which he is unable to overcome by himself. A person bears no responsibility for this ignorance.

Inviolable - from Latin *inviolare* (not to do violence to); secure from violation or assault.

Irascible appetite - sense appetite whose object is the difficult good or evil which is sensed.

Justice - from Latin *justitia* (uprightness; righteousness); the cardinal virtue which perfects the will, disposing it to give everyone his due.

Knowledge (Science) - a virtue of the speculative intellect which enables a person to draw correct conclusions from sound premises.

Law - an ordinance of reason for the common good, promulgated by him who has the care of the community; a rule or measure of acts directing them to their proper ends.

Magisterium - from the Latin *magister*, "teacher;" the teaching authority of the Catholic Church regarding all matters pertaining to salvation. The Church's bishops in union with the Pope, as successors to the apostles, are charged with the sacred duty of passing on the truth and interpreting faithfully those teachings that come from Sacred Scripture and Sacred Tradition.

Matter - the receptive principle of a physical thing; that out of which a physical being is made. Matter can be either *secondary* or *primary*.

Material cooperation - from Latin *cooperari* (to work together); working together with another because of duress, although not agreeing with the other in the act they are doing together.

Material Object - the subject matter of a science; that which a science studies.

Means - an action or thing that is used to achieve something else.

Merit - from Latin *mereri* (to earn as pay; deserve); that which is deserved; due reward or punishment.

Glossary

Moral - having to do with human activities that are free and that are in conformity to God's will.

Moral evil - evil which does involve directly a free act of the will.

Moral Law - law which governs the voluntary acts of human persons.

Moral Object - all that is considered when determining whether, materially speaking, the act is morally good or evil: the exterior act, its object, and circumstances.

Motive - from Latin *movere* (to move); the goal of a person's actions.

Mutilate - from Latin *mutilare* (to cut or crop off); to cut off or otherwise destroy the use of.

Nature - from Latin *natura* (birth, constitution, character); the essential qualities or properties of a thing; the essence of a thing which it has from its beginning; what a thing is.

Natural law - moral law which is made known by man's very nature; the eternal law as it applies to and exists in human creatures.

Necessity - the quality of following inevitably from logical, physical, or moral laws.

Normative science - a science which deals with the norms or criteria by which the objects of its study are judged.

Object of the Act - the object of the exterior act; the *matter* of the act.

Objective - (related to object) whatever is determined by the object or based on the object. The term is often used in contrast to the *subjective*, i.e., to what is based on the subject.

Operative habits - from Latin *operativus* (cretive, formative); habits of acting; relatively lasting dispositions that a person possesses due to his repeated acts.

Passions - from the Latin *pati,* "to undergo." The passions are movements of the sensitive appetite.

Person - from the Latin *persona,* "a mask used by actors," a "role;" in theology: a being who is essentially relational; in philosophy: an individual substance of a rational nature.

Practical intellect - the intellect as it seeks to know reality for the purpose of doing or making something.

Precept - from Latin *praeceptum* (a rule, command); an authoritative command to do some particular act; an order.

Proximate end - the end which is the act itself.

Philosophy - the study of reality, focusing on its ultimate causes. This knowledge can be arrived at through natural reason. Philosophy is literally translated as "love of wisdom."

Physical evil - evil which does not involve directly a free act of the will.

Positive law - from Latin *ponere* (to place, put, lay down); law which has been formally laid down or imposed; law made known to us by an external sign.

Practical intellect - the intellect as it seeks to know reality in order to do something with it.

Premise - from Latin *praemittere* (to put before); a previous statement from which another is inferred or follows as a conclusion.

Presumed - from Latin *pre-sumere* (to take for granted); to take upon oneself, undertake without adequate authority or permission.

Principle - from the Latin *principium*, "beginning;" the source or origin of something; that from which a thing comes into being.

Proper object - the end or goal of a power of a soul; that in reality which the powers of the soul were designed to know.

Proportionalism - ethical system which determines the moral quality of an act based on the proportion between good and evil effects which come from the act.

Prudence - from Latin *prudentia* (foresight); a cardinal virtue which perfects the pratical intellect, disposing it to make sound judgments about what ought to be done here and now.

Rash judgment - forming a judgment of another person without sufficient evidence.

Rational - from the Latin *ratio*, "reason." It refers to the human way of thinking because our minds move in a step-by-step fashion from understanding one idea to understanding another one, to understanding a third. It is as if we come to knowledge in "piece-meal" fashion. Sometimes the word "rational" is used interchangeably with "intellectual," but strictly speaking they have different meanings.

Rational powers - the intellect and free will.

Reason - the power of reasoning; an activity of the intellect whereby it moves from knowing one truth to knowing another, and from the knowledge of these two, it comes to know a third truth.

Reasoning - an act of the intellect whereby it makes one judgment based on another; a step-by-step process of acquiring knowledge.

Remote End - the end which is removed from the act itself.

Restitution - from Latin *restitutuere* (to restore); to restore, hand back, refund.

Revelation - the manifestation of the hidden by God, as a result of the personal word and witness of God Himself (via the Prophets, Scripture and Tradition).

Right - An appeal to the will of another through his intellect; the moral power to do, hold, or exact something.

Science - from Latin *scientia* (knowledge); an organized body of knowledge.

Seat - the place in which something belongs, occurs, or is established.

Sense appetites - an active tendency within a being towards an object that the senses present to it. The two sense appetites are call the Concupiscible and the Irascible appetites. The various movements of the sense appetites are called emotions or passions.

Sin - the voluntary decision to act contrary to God's moral law.

Sin of omission - from Latin *omittere* (to law aside); a deliberate failure to do what one can and ought to do.

Soul - in Latin *anima*, "living;" the first principle of life; the substantial form of a body which has the potency to be alive; the form of a living physical being.

Speculative intellect - from Latin *speculari* (to examine, observe); the intellect as it seeks to know reality simply for the sake of knowing it.

Steward - a person who manages another's property or affairs for him.

Subsidiarity - from Latin *subsidiarius* (serving to help, assist, or supplement). Requires that a community of a higher order not interfere with the life of a community of a lower order, taking over its functions. In case of need, the higher community should support the smaller community and help to coordinate its activity with the activities in the rest of society for the sake of the common good.

Summa Theologiae - literally, "a summary of theology;" an exhaustive five-part work that is St. Thomas Aquinas' great gift to the Church and which is still widely studied and quoted.

Syllogism - an argument expressed in the form of two propositions containing a common or middle term, with a third proposition resulting necessarily from the other two.

Synderesis - from the Greek word meaning "guarding or preserving closely;" the natural or innate habit of the mind to know the first principles of the moral order without recourse to a reasoning process. Developed by Aristotle, the term was introduced to the West by St. Jerome who referred to it as the "spark of conscience." St. Thomas later accepted the term to explain the intellect's natural habit of knowing very basic moral truths.

Temporal - from Latin *temporale* (a point in time); lasting or existing only for a time; passing, temporary.

Temperance - from Latin *temperantia* (moderation); cardinal virtue which perfects the concupiscible appetite, disposing it to act in accord with right reason.

Theological virtue - Virtue which elevates the rational powers, disposing them to participate in the very nature of God Himself.

Theology - the study of God and things pertaining to the divine, using both faith and reason.

Therapeutic - from Latin *therapeuticus* (to minister to, treat medically); of or pertaining to the healing of disease.

Tolerance - the moral virtue which disposes a person's practical intellect to judge correctly which evils ought to be tolerated and which ones not.

Toleration - from Latin *tolerabilis* (that may be borne, can bear or endure); the action of sustaining or enduring evil.

Totality - the state of being whole.

Truth - conformity of the mind with reality: I know the truth when what I have in my mind matches objective reality. St. Thomas argues that truth is universal, immutable and can be known by human beings who diligently seek it.

Ultimate End - from Latin *ultimus* (last, final); the end that lies beyond all others.

Understanding - a virtue of the speculative intellect which enables the person to grasp basic self-evident truths.

Universal - from the Latin *unus*, "one," and *vertere*, "to turn;" the idea of the many "turned or combined into one." A universal concept is one which applies to many instances of it in reality.

Vicarious - from Latin *vicarius* (change, turn, stead); that takes or supplies the place of another thing or person.

Vice - a bad habit, one which inclines a person away from what is truly good.

Vincible ignorance - from Latin *vincere* (to overcome); ignorance which a person can and should overcome. A person bears responsibility for this ignorance.

Virtual - from Latin *virtus* (faculty); possessing the capacity or faculty for producing a thing, even though we do not yet have the thing itself.

Virtue - from Latin *virtus* (manliness; strength); a good habit which disposes a person to act in accord with right reason.

Voluntary - from Latin *voluntarius* (freely undertaken); performed or done knowingly and freely, with one's own free will.

Will - a free and active tendency within a being towards or away from an object that the intellect presents to it. It is also called the *intellectual* or *rational appetite*.

Wisdom - a virtue of the speculative intellect which enables a person to know all of reality in relation to its ultimate causes.

Resources Cited

Anderson, Carl and Jose Granados. *Called to Love.* N.Y.: Doubleday, 2009.

Aquinas, St. Thomas. *Commentary on the Sentences.*
    ----, *De Veritate.*
    ----, *Questiones quodlibetales.*
    ----, *Summa Theologiae.*

Aristotle, *Categories.*
    ----, *Nicomachean Ethics.*
    ----, *Politics.*

Augustine. *De Moribus Ecclesiæ Catholicæ et de Moribus Manichæorum.*
    ----, *The Confessions.*
    ----, *The City of God.*
    ----, *De Libero Arbitrio*

Ashley, Benedict M., O.P. and Kevin D. O'Rourke, O. P., *Health Care Ethics*, 4th edition. Georgetown University Press, 1997.

Baars, Conrad, M.D., Rev. ed. Suzanne M. Baars and Bonnie N. Shayne, *Feeling and Healing Your Emotions.* Gainsville, FL: Logos International, 1979; Plainfield, NJ: Bridge-Logos, 2003.

Bennett, Art & Laraine. *The Temperament God Gave You.* New Hampshire: Sophia Press, 2005.

Bonaventure (Saint). *In II Librum Sentent.*

Budziszewski, J. "Natural Law in Our Lives, in Our Courts," Part 2, *Zenit.org*, April 1, 2004.

The Catechism of the Catholic Church.

Compendium of the Social Doctrine of the Church. Vatican, 2005.

Derrick, Christopher. "Pursuing Happiness, Finding Despair," *Catholic Twin Circle*, 9/19/1990.

Fagothey, Austin, S.J. *Right and Reason.* 2nd Edition. Illinois: Tan Books, 1959.

Finnis, John. *Fundamentals of Ethics.* Washington, D.C.: Georgetown University Press, 1983.

Gaudiose, Dorothy M., *Prophet of the People: A Biography of Padre Pio.* N.Y.: Alba House Publishers, 1974.

Gaudium et Spes, Vatican, 1965.

Giertych, Wojciech, O.P,. "Human cloning a form of biological slavery: Reflection on 'Dignitas personae,' in *L'Osservatore Romano*, April 29, 2009..

Gregory of Nyssa (Saint). *On the Soul and the Resurrection.*

Hardon, John A. Hardon, S.J., "The Meaning of Virtue in St. Thomas Aquinas."

Havard, Alexandre, *Virtuous Leadership ~ An Agenda for Personal Excellence.* New York: Scepter Publishers, Inc., 2007.

Jarosznski, Piotr and Mathew Anderson. *Ethics: The Drama of the Moral Life.* N.Y.: Alba House Press, 2007.

John of the Cross (Saint), *The Spiritual Canticle.*

Kant, Immanuel. *Foundations of the Metaphysics of Morals.*

Keiser, Kevin F. "The Moral Act in St. Thomas: A Fresh Look," *The Thomist* 74 (2010): 237-82.

Kreeft, Peter. *Making Choices.* Ohio: Servant Books, 1990.
    ----, *Back to Virtue.* San Francisco: Ignatius Press, 1986.

Lewis, C.S. *Mere Christianity.* N.Y.: The Macmillan Company, 1971.
    ----, *The Great Divorce.* Michigan: Fountain Publishing, 2002.

McInerny, D. Q. *A Course in Thomistic Ethics.* Elmhurst, PA: The Priestly Fraternity of St. Peter, 1997.

Pieper, Josef. *The Four Cardinal Virtues.* Indiana: University of Notre Dame Press, 1966.

Pinckaers, Servais. "Virtue is Not a Habit," *Nouvelle Revue Theologique,* Aptil, 1960.

Plato, *Protagoras.*
    ----, *Republic.*

Philippe, Jacques. *Fire & Light: Eucharistic Love and the Search for Peace,* Neal Carter, Tr., New York: Scepter Publishers, Inc., 2016.

Pope Benedict XVI, "The Changing Identity of the Individual," an address to members of an interacademic conference in Paris, January 28, 2008.
    ----, *Address to Catholic Educators of the United States*, April 17, 2008
    ----, *Sermon,* September 4, 2004, translated by Martin Henry and published in *The Conscience of Our Age: A Theological Portrait* (San Francisco: Ignatius Press, 2007).
    ----, *Address to the Community of hte Roman Major Seminary*, 2/20/09.
    ----, *Spe Salvi.*
    ----, *Caritas in Veritate.*

Saint John Paul II, *Apostolic Letter to the Youth of the World on the Occasion of International Youth Year*, 1985, #3.
    ----, *Angelus Address*, July 7, 2002.
    ----, *Message for the VI World Youth Day*, 1990.
    ----, *Message for XI World Youth Day.*
    ----, *Message to the Youth of the World,* February, 2001.
    ----, *Veritatis Splendor*, August, 1993.
    ----, *Address to the Youth in Toronto*, July, 2002.
    ----, *Address to the International Congress of Moral Theology*, 4/10/1986.
    ----, *Message for the 14th World Youth Day.*
    ----, *Angelus Address, July 7, 2002.*

Pope Leo XIII, *Libertas Praestantissimum.*

Pope Paul VI, *General Audience,* March 28, 1973.

Ratzinger, Joseph Cardinal. (Pope Benedict XVI) "Truth and Freedom," *Communio,* 23 (Spring, 1996).
    ----, "Conscience & Truth,"Keynote Address.
    ----, *God and the World ~ A Conversation with Peter Seewald,* San Francisco: Ignatius Press, 2002.

Smith, Randall, "No Cooperation with Evil," *The Catholic Thing,* March 4, 2012.

Smith, Wesley J. "Nihilism as Compassion, *Catholic World Report,* April 2010, pp. 26-29.

Solomon, Robert, "In Defense of Freedom," *American Psychologist*, Jan., 2001.

Tarkorsky, Andrei, *Sculpting in Time,* Austin, TX: University of Texas Press, 1989.

Varga, Andrew C. *On Being Human.* N.Y.: Paulist Press, 1978.

Wadell, Paul. *Happiness and the Christian Moral Life: An Introduction to Christian Ethics.* Maryland: Rowman & Littlefield Publishers, Inc., 2008.

Wadell, Paul, C.P. *The Primacy of Love.* New York: Paulist Press, 1992.

Wojtyla, Karol. *Love and Responsibility.* N.Y.: Farrar, Straus and DGiroux, Inc., 1981.